WALKING CINCINNATI

Walking Cincinnati: 35 Tours Exploring Historic Neighborhoods, Stunning Riverfront Quarters, and Hidden Treasures in the Queen City

Second edition, third printing 2022

Distributed by Publishers Group West
Manufactured in China

Cover design: Scott McGrew
Book design: Lora Westberg
Maps: Steve Jones and Scott McGrew; map data: OpenStreetMap
Copy editor: Susan Roberts McWilliams
Proofreaders: Emily Beaumont, Amber Kaye Henderson, and Holly Cross
Indexer: Rich Carlson

Library of Congress Cataloging-in-Publication Data

Names: Korman, Danny, author. | Meyer, Katie, 1984- author.
Title: Walking Cincinnati : 35 tours exploring historic neighborhoods, stunning riverfront quarters, and hidden treasures in the Queen City / Danny Korman and Katie Meyer.
Description: 2nd edition. | Birmingham, Alabama : Wilderness Press, [2019]
Identifiers: LCCN 2018061562 | ISBN 9780899979038 (pbk.)
Subjects: LCSH: Cincinnati (Ohio)—Tours. | Walking—Ohio—Cincinnati—Guidebooks. | Neighborhoods—Ohio—Cincinnati—Guidebooks. | Historic sites—Ohio—Cincinnati—Guidebooks. | Architecture—Ohio—Cincinnati—Guidebooks. | Restaurants—Ohio—Cincinnati—Guidebooks. | Cincinnati (Ohio)—History—Miscellanea. | Cincinnati (Ohio)—Social life and customs—Miscellanea.
Classification: LCC F499.C53 K67 2019 | DDC 917.71/78—dc23
LC record available at https://lccn.loc.gov/2018061562

ISBN 978-0-89997-903-8 (pbk.); ISBN 978-0-89997-904-5 (ebook)

Published by 

An imprint of AdventureKEEN
2204 First Ave. S., Suite 102
Birmingham, AL 35233
800-678-7006, fax 877-374-9016

Visit wildernesspress.com for a complete list of our books and for ordering information. Contact us at our website, at facebook.com/wildernesspress1967, or at twitter.com/wilderness1967 with questions or comments. To find out more about who we are and what we're doing, visit blog.wildernesspress.com.

Cover photo: Roebling Suspension Bridge (see Walks 1, 27, and 28) © Jon Bilous/Shutterstock

SAFETY NOTICE: Although Wilderness Press and the authors have made every attempt to ensure that the information in this book is accurate at press time, they are not responsible for any loss, damage, injury, or inconvenience that may occur to anyone while using this book. You are responsible for your own safety and health while following the walking trips described here. Always check local conditions, know your own limitations, and consult a map.

WALKING CINCINNATI

35 Walking Tours Exploring Historic Neighborhoods, Stunning Riverfront Quarters, and Hidden Treasures in the Queen City

2nd Edition

by Danny Korman and Katie Meyer

Photos by Ken Stigler

 **WILDERNESS PRESS** . . . *on the trail since 1967*

Acknowledgments

When the authors wrote the first edition of *Walking Cincinnati,* they relied heavily on friends and family, as well as experts from local historical societies, historic preservation organizations, and chambers of commerce. With the second edition, they still relied on others while taking a fresh look at everything on their walks. One difference this time was for Danny, who relocated to Boulder, Colorado, in the fall of 2017 and therefore counted on a small band of friends to help with updates. Julie Carpenter, a local historian, provided detailed feedback on 16 of his 22 walks. Katie took the chance to re-explore the region's neighborhoods, recognizing the ebb and flow of small businesses, the evolution of public spaces, and the ways that change looks and feels in our walkable communities.

Daniel Becker provided much of the content you'll see in the new East Walnut Hills and Old Milford and Terrace Park walks. Christian Huelsman of Spring in Our Steps mapped out points of interest and background for the new Clifton Heights, University Heights, and Fairview walk.

Others vital to walking and proofreading: Kelly Adamson (Over-the-Rhine Chamber of Commerce), Caitlin Ayers, Carlton Farmer and Jackie Petit, Marie Finn (Western Wildlife Corridor), Michael Frazier, Henna Frazier, Mackenzie Farmer Low, Denise Hovey, Rebecca Johnson, Wade Johnston, Jen Lile, Jack Martin, Nikki Mayhew, Bonnie Meyer, Andrea Poling, Marissa Reed and Seth T. Walsh (College Hill Community Urban Redevelopment Corporation), Samantha and Shannon Renick, Jody Robinson, Mindy Rosen (Downtown Cincinnati, Inc.), Justin Rosenacker, Jim and Eileen Schenk (Enright Ridge Urban Eco-Village), Ann Senefeld, Betty Ann Smiddy, and Dann Woellert. And many thanks to Ken Stigler, who took all photos, and his wife, Susan Miller-Stigler, who helped keep him on task.

Lastly, a nod to some of the key reference materials that helped guide the development of this edition: John Clubbe's *Cincinnati Observed: Architecture and History* (1992), Greater Milford Area Historical Society's *Milford, Ohio* (2008), ArtWorks and Cincinnati Observatory websites, *Walnut Hills: A Walking Tour* (2010) by Cincinnati Preservation Association, Digging Cincinnati History blog posts on East Price Hill and Hyde Park, and City of Cincinnati local conservation guidelines for various historic districts.

Authors' Note

Cincinnati is a wonderful city for walking because its older areas were designed before the automobile arrived. We did not cover every walkable neighborhood in and around Cincinnati, although we added seven that highlight the diversity of our region. The walks in this book were chosen to allow you to explore neighborhoods in surprising ways. Some routes hug hillsides and the riverfront, while others follow quiet residential streets. Cincinnati is known for its urban forest. Streets covered in tree canopies are some of the prettiest and most desirable in the city. People who live on Epworth Avenue in Westwood and Grand Vista Avenue in Pleasant Ridge know this firsthand. The basin area, which includes downtown, Over-the-Rhine, and West End, is flat as a piece of paper. Once you reach its edges, the hillsides climb. Whether justified or not, many locals use these hills as an excuse not to take a walk or ride a bike. You are among the adventurous individuals who accept the challenge and know our city is the better for it.

Geier Esplanade is a small linear park in the center of Oakley's busy shopping and dining district (see Walk 14).

Table of Contents

Walking Cincinnati

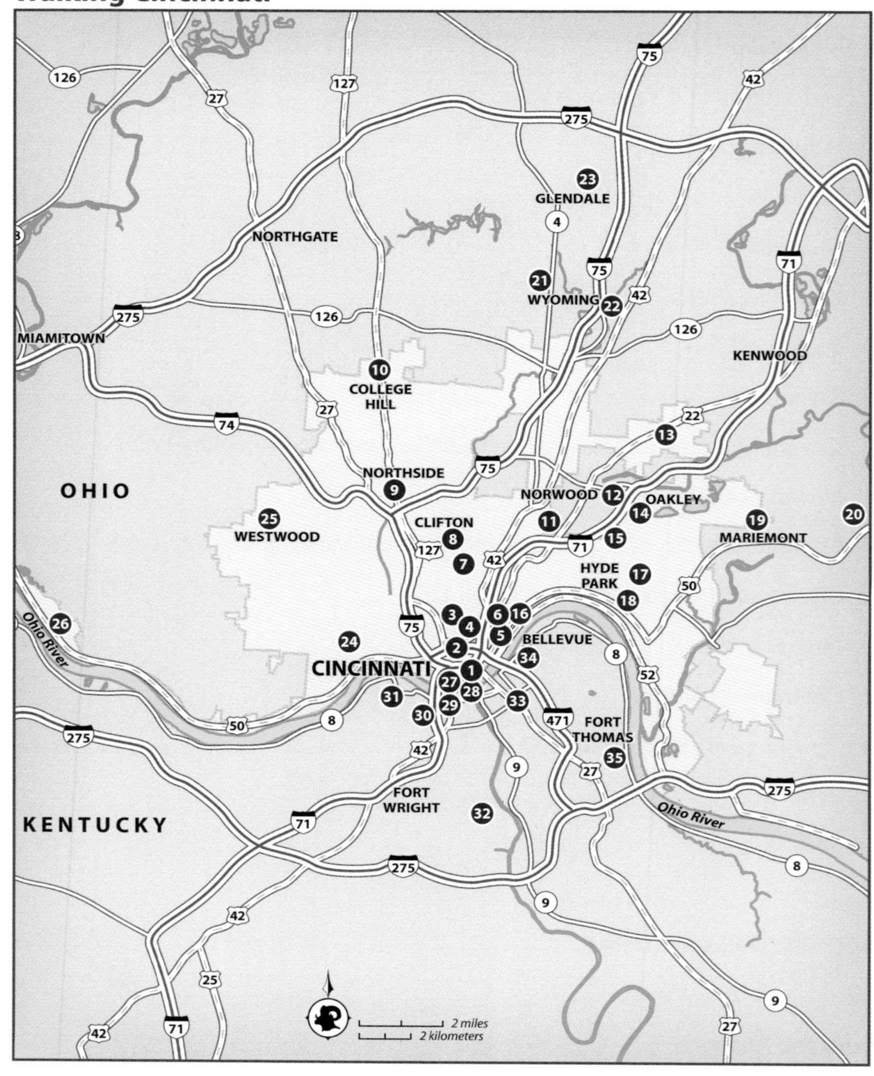

Introduction

Cincinnati and the places that surround it are best explored on foot. Your senses are sharpened. You are free and mostly anonymous. When walking Cincinnati's neighborhoods and historic suburbs, and Northern Kentucky's old towns, you realize you're in a special place. Cincinnati started as a small river town in the late 1700s and rapidly grew to become a thriving cultural and economic center in the mid-1800s. It earned the nickname "Paris of America" due to its impressive architecture, and it became a city of firsts: Cincinnati was home to the first professional baseball team (1869 Cincinnati Red Stockings) and the first women-run, large-scale manufacturing operation with Rookwood Pottery.

Cincinnati and its surroundings are in a constant state of change. Some of these changes feel good, while others are hard to swallow. It's all here for you to experience and make you feel something about your environment. Throughout this book, we will draw your attention to these places and what makes them special. This book's 35 walks span the Queen City, from the river towns of Northern Kentucky to the northern historic railroad suburbs of Glendale and Wyoming, and from Cincinnati's westernmost neighborhood of Sayler Park to the planned community of Mariemont 10 miles east of downtown.

With the second edition, we have dropped a few walks, updated the rest, and added seven new ones:

- Mount Auburn (Walk 4)
- Walnut Hills (Walk 6)
- Clifton Heights, University Heights, and Fairview (Walk 7)
- Old Milford and Terrace Park (Walk 20)
- Reading (Walk 22)
- Ludlow (Walk 31)
- Covington: Latonia (Walk 32)

While we recommend our own routes, feel free to take detours and just keep walking. Put away your phone and headphones. Walk with someone else or alone. Walk with intention. Maybe we'll bump into each other as we scout this intriguing part of the country.

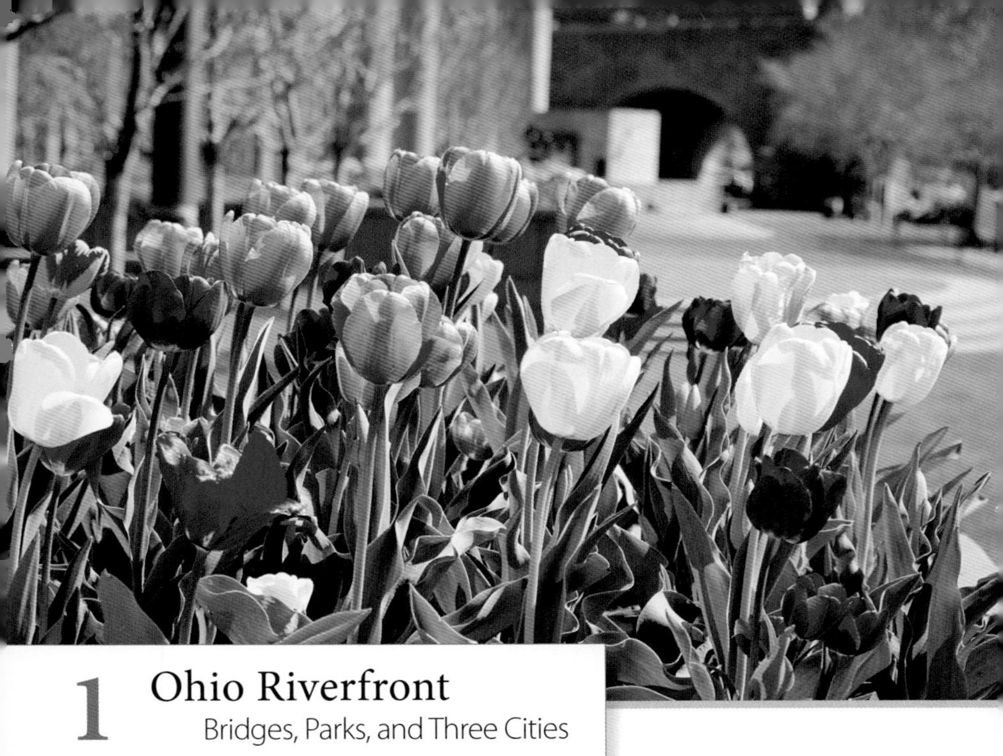

1 Ohio Riverfront

Bridges, Parks, and Three Cities

Above: Tulips bloom near the Purple People Bridge along the Cincinnati riverfront.

BOUNDARIES: Smale Riverfront Park, Theodore M. Berry International Friendship Park, Third St. in Newport, Fourth St. in Covington, Greenup St. in Covington
DISTANCE: 4.2 miles
DIFFICULTY: Easy
PARKING: Metered parking on streets; or inside Central Riverfront Garage, 99 E. Second St., underneath Moerlein Lager House
PUBLIC TRANSIT: Metro (go-metro.com) and TANK (tankbus.org) buses serve downtown Cincinnati and Northern Kentucky, respectively. Southbank Shuttle Trolley (tankbus.org/routes/ss) connects the riverfront cities of Newport, Covington, and downtown Cincinnati, with signs marking each stop. Cincinnati Bell Connector streetcar (cincinnatibellconnector.com) connects the Cincinnati riverfront, downtown Cincinnati, and Over-the-Rhine with 18 stations. Cincinnati Red Bike (cincyredbike.org) has bicycle rental stations at 122 E. Second St. (Great American Ball Park), 97 E. Freedom Way (Freedom Center), 5 W. Merhring Way (Smale Riverfront Park), and elsewhere.

Cincinnati Riverfront Park is the place where locals and visitors alike go for recreation and relaxation, mostly during warmer months, although hardy outdoorsy city lovers visit year-round. The action happens in four separate and connecting parks along the Ohio River, with Theodore M. Berry International Friendship Park to the east, Sawyer Point Park and Yeatman's Cove in the middle, and John G. and Phyllis W. Smale Riverfront Park tucked between Paul Brown Stadium and Great American Ball Park.

The activities along here run the gamut, from sitting on a swing overlooking the river and having a picnic under a grove of trees, to walking through interactive fountains and a meditative labyrinth, or simply biking along the Ohio River Trail. Just north of the river and between both sports stadia are ❶ **National Underground Railroad Freedom Center** and ❷ **The Banks**, a mixed-use development designed to complement the massive public improvements along the riverfront. The initial phase, which opened in summer 2011, included Current at The Banks apartments atop 96,000 square feet of street-level retail, which includes mostly bars and restaurants.

Walk Description

Start your walk at the top of the Walnut Street Steps at Theodore M. Berry Way, which serves as the entrance to **Smale Riverfront Park**. Opened in 2012, Smale Riverfront Park was designed to be the new front yard for the region. The park is situated on 45 acres along the riverfront. It flanks the city's beloved **John A. Roebling Suspension Bridge**, which allows pedestrians to get between the sports venues in Cincinnati and attractions in Northern Kentucky. When the first pedestrians crossed on January 1, 1867, its 1,057-foot span made it the longest suspension bridge in the world, a record it retained until 1883 when Roebling's most famous project—the Brooklyn Bridge—opened. It's designated a National Historic Civil Engineering Landmark.

Next to the steps is Schmidlapp Event Lawn & Stage, a venue for concerts, small community festivals, and picnicking. Proceed down the steps past the interactive fountains and bike runnel, which helps facilitate walking a bicycle up and down the stairway. Once at the bottom of the steps, cross the Ohio River Scenic Byway to enter the park.

Walk through the Women's Committee Garden, which honors women who made the park possible. Turn left at the first walking path and pass through the meditative labyrinth on your left. Opposite the labyrinth and down the sloping lawn is Race Street Promenade, which follows the Ohio River. Walk past the Black Brigade Monument, the first piece of public art to be commissioned in Smale Riverfront Park and a monument to Cincinnati's little-known Black Brigade, an African American military unit that served during the Civil War.

Keep walking toward Main Street Fountain on the left. Across the Ohio River Scenic Byway at Joe Nuxhall Way is the ❸ **Moerlein Lager House.** This popular microbrewery and restaurant houses the Beer Barons Hall of Fame. Continue walking east past the swings—after you sit down and swing back and forth a little—and eventually back to the Ohio River Scenic Byway. Across the street is the ❹ **Great American Ball Park,** home field of the Cincinnati Reds, established in 1881. The Cincinnati Reds Hall of Fame and Museum is located on the west side of the ballpark, which has panoramic views of downtown, Mount Adams, the Ohio River, and Northern Kentucky.

Turn right on the Ohio River Scenic Byway and walk east past the U.S. Bank Arena on the left. Just past the Taylor-Southgate Bridge overhead is **Yeatman's Cove.** Opened in 1976 and the first big effort to reconnect downtown with the city's riverfront, the park features Serpentine Wall, a contoured concrete wall of steps used for special events and lounging. Along the northern edge of the park and in the shadow of One Lytle Place Apartments is Lytle Place Fountain, a respite on a hot summer day.

Continue eastward through the brick archways underneath the Purple People Bridge. Greeting you on the other side is a 12-foot statue of Cincinnatus, the Roman soldier and farmer after whom Cincinnati is named. **Sawyer Point Park** opened in June 1988, in celebration of Cincinnati's 200th birthday. Initially designed to educate natives and visitors with a riverwalk filled with late-1980s environmental sculpture, Sawyer Point has evolved into a lush park with maturing trees and gardens, concessions, tennis and volleyball courts, and a playground.

Veer left along the north edge of the central lawn past P&G Pavilion, host to concerts and other events during warmer months. North of the pavilion is the main entrance to Bicentennial Commons, which includes a whimsical flying pig sculpture and a model of the Ohio River and accompanying locks. ***Gateway Sculpture*** honors the Ohio River with a spectacular environmental

The National Steamboat Monument sits across from the Great American Ball Park.

Backstory: CROWN

This section of the Ohio River Trail bears significance on a local, regional, and national scale. A plan has emerged in recent years to link this riverfront haven for pedestrians and bicyclists to several other multi-use trail corridors in development in Cincinnati. CROWN (Cincinnati Riding Or Walking Network) is a vision for a 104-mile active transportation network connected by a 30-mile trail loop traversing many Cincinnati neighborhoods. Led by local advocacy organization Tri-State Trails, CROWN plans to connect the Ohio River Trail, Mill Creek Greenway Trail, Wasson Way, Lunken Airport Trail, and Little Miami Scenic Trail to other local trails and on-road bicycling infrastructure. CROWN will improve bike and pedestrian connectivity between residential neighborhoods and destinations like employment centers, schools, parks, retail establishments, recreation areas, and entertainment hubs. Benefits include expanding active transportation options, encouraging economic development, improving public health, increasing transportation equity, and promoting environmental sustainability. Information: tristatetrails.org.

installation by Andrew Leicester. This 250-foot-long by 50-foot-wide sculpture depicts Cincinnati's history in 18 sections and offers a child's-eye view of the city.

Continue east under the Daniel Carter Beard Bridge, past the fitness area, playground, volleyball courts, tennis complex, and all-weather skating rink. To the right are limestone foundation ruins of the old Front Street Pumping Station, which supplied the Mount Adams reservoirs and is used today as a performance venue. Running parallel to this path is a walkway with jutting overlooks offering relaxing views of the river and Northern Kentucky's hillsides. Continue walking east past The Boathouse, which houses veteran barbecue chain ❺ **Montgomery Inn–The Boathouse** and gives diners impressive views. Look east from the railroad tracks in front of Montgomery Inn–Boathouse to see where the Oasis Trail will connect Lunken Airport to Sawyer Point.

Past the long parking lot is the **Theodore M. Berry International Friendship Park,** featuring an impressive display of sculpture and flora representing five continents. It has two intertwining walkways guiding park visitors through gardens of the continents in a celebration of international peace and friendship. Named for Cincinnati's first African American mayor, the park draws inspiration in part from a child's friendship bracelet. One of Cincinnati Parks' premier rental facilities is the pavilion toward the middle of the park. You can choose to walk the winding path past the pavilion to the end of the park for a longer walk, or turn around at any point to return to the Purple People Bridge, just beyond the statue of Cincinnatus.

Climb the stairs of the **Purple People Bridge** (purplepeoplebridge.com) and begin your interstate walk into Newport, Kentucky. Formerly the L&N Railroad Bridge, this is the only bridge in the region that is designated exclusively for pedestrians. Rails-to-Trails Conservancy named the Purple People Bridge one of the nation's top five pedestrian bridges in 2015. Follow the bridge to Third Street and turn right to walk in front of ❻ **Newport on the Levee.** The Levee is a hub of activity, with people seeking out bars and restaurants and first-run films at ❼ **AMC Newport on The Levee 20.**

Continue west along Third Street, past Newport on the Levee, and cross York Street before turning right on Columbia Street. Climb the steps to the top of the levee. Completed for the city's 1995 bicentennial, Newport's Riverwalk is a pleasant stroll through the town's 200-year history, with views of the Ohio River and Cincinnati skyline. Newport's history is depicted on seven weather vanes individually mounted on 30-foot poles. At the end of the levee sidewalk, you'll come to the Fourth Street Bridge, officially known as Veterans' Memorial Bridge. Turn right and cross the Licking River into Covington. Continue until you reach Greenup Street.

Turn right on Greenup Street and enter the tiny Roebling Point business district, home to multiple restaurants and bars and an independent bookstore. On the left across the large parking lot along Fourth Street is ❽ **Molly Malone's Irish Pub & Restaurant,** a three-story eatery with a good beer selection. Continue north on Greenup Street past Park Place for more dining options. ❾ **Blinkers Tavern** specializes in steak and seafood, while ❿ **Keystone Bar & Grill** is known for its macaroni and cheese menu. At the corner of Third and Greenup Streets is ⓫ **Roebling Point Books & Coffee,** a compact coffee shop and bookstore that is also home to Wilderness Press's Ohio office. Continue north on Greenup Street past E. Third Street. On the left at E. Second Street is ⓬ **The Gruff,** a spacious outpost serving Neapolitan-style pizza, sandwiches, and craft brews steps from the Roebling Suspension Bridge. Cross E. Second Street and follow the elevated sidewalk around the small brick building to the bridge expanse. Cross the Roebling and return to the start.

Ohio Riverfront

Points of Interest

1. **National Underground Railroad Freedom Center** 50 E. Freedom Way, 513-333-7739, freedomcenter.org
2. **The Banks** Freedom Way, thebankscincy.com
3. **Moerlein Lager House** 115 Joe Nuxhall Way, 513-421-2337, moerleinlagerhouse.com
4. **Great American Ball Park** 100 Joe Nuxhall Way, 513-765-7000, cincinnati.reds.mlb.com/cin/ballpark
5. **Montgomery Inn–The Boathouse** 925 Riverside Dr., 513-721-7427, montgomeryinn.com
6. **Newport on the Levee** 1 Levee Way, Newport, 859-291-0550, newportonthelevee.com
7. **AMC Newport on The Levee 20** 1 Levee Way, Newport, 859-291-0550, amctheatres.com
8. **Molly Malone's Irish Pub & Restaurant** 112 E. Fourth St., Covington, 859-491-6659, covington.mollymalonesirishpub.com
9. **Blinkers Tavern** 318 Greenup St., Covington, 859-360-0840, blinkerstavern.com
10. **Keystone Bar & Grill** 313 Greenup St., Covington, 859-261-6777, keystonebar.com
11. **Roebling Point Books & Coffee** 306 Greenup St., Covington, 859-815-7204, roeblingpointbooks.com
12. **The Gruff** 129 E. Second St., Covington, 859-581-0040, atthegruff.com

2 Downtown Cincinnati

Historic Architecture, Corporate Headquarters, and Transit

Above: The Taft Museum of Art features paintings by American and European masters.

BOUNDARIES: Plum St., Court St., Pike St., Fourth St.
DISTANCE: 3 miles
DIFFICULTY: Easy
PARKING: Metered parking on streets; $1 parking for up to 59 minutes at 2 garages, including Fountain Square
PUBLIC TRANSIT: Metro (go-metro.com) and TANK (tankbus.org) buses serve downtown with routes radiating from Government Square. Cincinnati Bell Connector streetcar (cincinnatibellconnector .com) connects The Banks, downtown, and Over-the-Rhine with 18 stations. Cincinnati Red Bike (cincyredbike.org) has bicycle rental stations at Fountain Square, Duke Energy Convention Center, Main Library, and elsewhere.

As Ohio's third-largest city, Cincinnati benefits from a downtown that is walkable and easy to navigate, mostly because it was built before the invention of the automobile. Although most streets are one-way and connect with a freeway ramp or other major thoroughfare, downtown has retained its human scale. It has a growing mix of entertainment options, green spaces that encourage both interaction and relaxation, and diverse architecture. Eateries boast a range of flavors and ethnicities, while Broadway tour productions and museums offer people multiple ways to spend their days. In all, downtown Cincinnati is a good place to experience city life.

Walk Description

Start your tour with a cup of coffee at ❶ **Booksellers on Fountain Square** inside Fountain Place. Maybe you bought this book there! Across the street is **Fountain Square,** Cincinnati's primary public space and its heart since 1871. Enlarged and remodeled most recently in 2005, Fountain Square serves as the site of free concerts, festivals, demonstrations, and relaxation year-round. At its center is the Tyler Davidson Fountain, possibly Cincinnati's most recognizable landmark, dedicated in 1871 and named in honor of hardware magnate Henry Probasco's brother-in-law and business partner. Aside from the fountain, Probasco is known for his historic Oakwood mansion in Clifton.

Walk south on Vine Street and turn right on Fifth Street. On the left is ❷ **Carew Tower,** Cincinnati's second-tallest building. Built in 1930 and rising 49 stories, it offers spectacular views of the city for $4 from its observation deck. Carew Tower and the adjoining **Hilton Cincinnati Netherland Plaza** together create one of the nation's finest French Art Deco ensembles. The hotel is a member of Historic Hotels of America, a program of the National Trust for Historic Places. Its famed shopping arcade is the final point of this tour.

Turn right on Race Street. On the left, between Fifth and Sixth Streets, is the headquarters for ❸ **84.51°.** This nine-story, charcoal-gray, concrete tower features an asymmetrical zipper design with first-floor restaurant space. Past Fountain Place on the right is the former **Terrace Plaza Hotel.** Designed by Skidmore, Owings, & Merrill and built in 1948, the hotel was the first major building to rise in downtown after World War II and the first International Style hotel building constructed in the United States. Architectural historians claim it as one of America's Modern Movement buildings. *Cincinnati's Terrace Plaza Hotel: An Icon of American Modernism,* by Shawn Patrick Tubb, is a good source of additional reading on this often-misunderstood building. As this book was going to press, development offers continued to be presented and considered. Across from Terrace Plaza Hotel on Sixth Street is ❹ **The Cincinnatian Hotel,** the city's finest surviving French Second Empire building from 1882.

Cross Sixth Street and enter the **Race Street Historic District,** a group of 24 contributing buildings listed on the National Register of Historic Places. The Streamline Moderne building at

Backstory: Betts-Longworth Historic District

The Betts-Longworth Historic District on the eastern edge of the West End is named for its early landowners: William Betts and Nicholas Longworth. Betts owned 111 acres in the West End where he and his family farmed and ran a brickyard. His house, the oldest brick house in Ohio still on its original site, stands at 416 Clark Street and is now a museum. The family slowly began subdividing their property in the early 1800s, around the same time Longworth acquired 33 acres adjacent to the Betts parcel. Longworth immediately divided his entire property for development, including selling a small lot on Chestnut Street to a Jewish congregation for a cemetery, now the oldest Jewish cemetery west of the Allegheny mountains. The neighborhood was home to well-to-do businessmen, including architects Henry and William Walter, department store owners Frederick Alms and William Doepke, jeweler Frank Herschede, and James Gamble, cofounder of P&G.

604 Race St. was originally a two-story J.J. Newberry department store and is now Newberry Lofts on Sixth. For a quick alley tour, turn right on Morand Alley and then left on College Street. To the right is the rear of the former Cincinnati Enquirer Building, at 617 Vine St. Designed by the firm of Lockwood Greene and Company and completed in 1926, it is now a Hampton Inn and Homewood Suites. To the left is the gleaming back side of the Macy's Inc. Building, at 7 W. Seventh St. Turn left on Seventh Street and walk to Race Street, one of downtown's most impressive corners. The four buildings contributing to this epicenter of urban architecture include (clockwise from the southwest corner) Shillito Place, Pearl Market Bank Building (1910), The Groton (1895), and Jewelers Exchange (1915). The most notable building is the massive John Shillito & Co. department store. Designed by James McLaughlin and built in 1878 (and modernized in 1937), it originally featured five elevators and is considered a precursor to Marshall Field's State Street flagship store in Chicago. The landmark building is now Lofts at Shillito Place apartments. It served as a set for the movie *Carol,* starring Cate Blanchett and Rooney Mara and filmed almost entirely in Cincinnati in early 2014.

Turn right on Race Street and walk to Garfield Place and then **Piatt Park,** the city's oldest park. Donated to the city in 1817, the park stretches between Vine and Elm Streets. A bronze statue of President James Garfield stands at the east end of the park. On the south side of the park is the Doctor's Building (19 Garfield Pl.), a stunning Late Gothic Revival building from 1923 that serves as headquarters for LPK, an international design agency. North of the park is Cuvier Press Club Building (22 Garfield Pl.), a rare surviving Italian Renaissance residence designed by Samuel Hannaford and built in 1861.

Turn left on Garfield Place and walk past Gramercy on Garfield and Greenwich apartment buildings to the statue of William Henry Harrison on horseback at Elm Street. Cross Elm Street to ❺ **Covenant First Presbyterian Church,** which nicely terminates this end of Piatt Park with its elegant Gothic-style 1875 facade. Cross Eighth Street and turn left at Waldo apartments, 801 Elm St. Built in 1891, it's one of four surviving late 19th-century apartment houses that brothers Thomas J. and John J. Emery built downtown.

Turn right on Goshen Alley and then left on Weaver Alley. An overlooked part of Cincinnati's downtown, alleys serve as a safe space for bicyclists and pedestrians to navigate clear of motorized vehicles. Cross through the parking lot on the left and return to Eighth Street and walk west to Plum Street, another one of downtown's great corners where politics and religion are represented. On the southeast corner is the ❻ **Isaac M. Wise Temple,** built in 1866 and a majestic example of Moorish Revival architecture. Under the leadership of Rabbi Isaac M. Wise, it was the site of the first ordination of rabbis in America and is one of Cincinnati's most important buildings. On the southwest corner is ❼ **St. Peter in Chains,** completed in 1845 with a 200-foot steeple visible throughout much of downtown. ❽ **Cincinnati City Hall** takes the northwest corner with its massive facade of red granite stone and nine-story clock tower. Designed by Samuel Hannaford in Romanesque Revival style, it was completed in 1893. On the northeast corner, at 802 Plum St., is a modest Streamline Moderne building. It would likely be more at home on a more subdued street corner.

Walk north on Plum Street and turn right into the **Ninth Street Historic District,** three blocks of more than 40 buildings from the mid-19th century to the early 20th century. Walk to Elm Street and go to the northeast corner. **Crosley Square** (140 W. Ninth St.), was designed by Harry Hake and built in 1922. Originally home to the WLW radio station, this impressive Classical Revival–style building currently houses the Cincinnati Hills Christian Academy.

Continue walking east toward Race Street. While there's an empty lot on the northeast corner, the other three compensate for the void with solid historic buildings listed individually on the National Register of Historic Places. On the southeast corner is **The Phoenix,** built in 1893 to accommodate Cincinnati's first professional Jewish men's club. On the southwest and northwest corners, respectively, are **Saxony** and **Brittany** apartment buildings, designed by Samuel Hannaford & Sons.

Turn left on Race Street and walk to Court Street. On the left is ❾ **Cappel's,** one of four locations for the local retailer of party supplies and costumes, founded in 1945. Turn right and walk to Vine Street. On the left is the headquarters for Kroger (1104 Vine St.), a Cincinnati-based company founded in 1883. To the right is ❿ **Scotti's Italian Restaurant.** Complete with red-checkered tablecloths and wax-covered wine bottles, Scotti's menu hasn't changed much since 1953.

Cross Vine Street and stay on the south side of Court Street. This block retains its 19th-century scale and is almost completely intact, with just one missing building. According to Ann Senefeld of Digging Cincinnati History, all of Court Street, from Central Avenue to Main Street, was once lined with market booths, while the market building stood between Vine and Walnut Streets. By 1912 the city declared the market building a health hazard, and it was torn down in 1915. Perhaps as a partial nod to Court Street's market past, Kroger built a 45,000-square-foot supermarket below a parking garage and 139 apartments that opened in summer 2019 at the northeast corner of Court and Walnut Streets. Ahead is the ⓫ **Hamilton County Courthouse.** This neoclassical megalith from 1919 is the easternmost terminus of Court Street.

Turn right on Walnut Street and look to the left at *Homecoming (Blue Birds)* ArtWorks mural on the side of Courtland Flats, at 119 E. Court St. It is based on a painting in Charlie Harper's geometric style and depicts two bluebirds returning home. The ⓬ **Public Library of Cincinnati and Hamilton County** fills the blocks on the right from Prior to Eighth Streets. The main library opened in the southwest building in 1955 and underwent expansions in 1982 and 1997. Established in 1853, the library system includes 40 regional and branch locations and is the 12th largest in the United States. Across from the library, on the southwest corner of Eighth and Walnut Streets, is ⓭ **St. Louis Catholic Church,** headquarters for Cincinnati's Roman Catholic archdiocese. The church parsonage is attached. Cross Walnut Street and walk east on Eighth Street. At 110 E. Eighth St. is a restored firehouse. Built in 1889, it now functions as an office building. Next door, at 114 E. Eighth St., is the Citadel, designed by the Hannaford firm and built in 1905 for the Salvation Army.

Proceed to Main Street. In the ground along Main Street is track for the reborn Cincinnati Streetcar, which opened in September 2016. Across Main Street (on the left behind the fabric awning with a large "A") is ⓮ **Arnold's Bar and Grill,** the city's oldest tavern. Turn right on Main Street and cross Seventh Street. On the right is the smallest of three theaters found inside ⓯ **Aronoff Center,** a performing arts center designed by Argentine American architect Cesar Pelli that opened in 1995. The rest of the west side of the 600 block of Main Street is an intact row of late 19th-century commercial buildings, which date from when this was the city's main commercial thoroughfare. The businesses here are a time capsule: Hathaway Stamp (1901), Bay Horse Cafe (1817, reopened 2015), Spitzfaden Office Supplies (1951), and Richter & Phillips Co. (1896). Famed architect Ernest Flagg designed the 12-story **Gwynne Building** (1904), Cincinnati's most ornamental early skyscraper, on the northeast corner of Main and Sixth Streets.

Turn right on Sixth Street and enter Cincinnati's reemerging restaurant row. Most notable are **Sotto, Boca,** and **Nada**—all three the product of the Boca Restaurant Group. At Sixth and Walnut

Streets is the Zaha Hadid–designed ⓰ **Contemporary Arts Center,** one of the oldest contemporary arts centers in the United States. Next door is ⓱ **21c Museum Hotel,** which opened inside the restored Hotel Metropole in 2012.

Turn left on Walnut Street and left again on Fifth Street. Walk through Government Square, Metro's downtown transit hub. Dominating the left side of the square is Potter Stewart U.S. Courthouse (100 E. Fifth St.), built in 1939. The next three blocks east of Main Street are where corporate Cincinnati functions. It's a quiet place after office hours, with the exception of the ⓲ **Taft Theatre** and ⓳ **Cincinnati Masonic Center complex.** Walk these remaining blocks of Fifth Street past the Procter & Gamble towers on the left and turn right on Pike Street.

Around the corner is **Lytle Park Historic District,** one of the oldest areas in the city. The 2.31-acre park, updated in 2018, is known for its seasonal floral displays and an 11-foot-tall bronze statue of Abraham Lincoln. East of the park is the ⓴ **Taft Museum of Art.** Built in 1820, the house was home to several prominent Cincinnatians, including Charles P. Taft, half-brother of President William Howard Taft. Charles Taft donated the house in 1917 and the park's statue of President Abraham Lincoln in 1932 to the city. On the north edge of the park is the Literary Club, at 500 E. Fourth St., an excellent example of Georgian-style architecture from 1820. On the southwest edge is Guilford School, 421 E. Fourth St., the original site of Fort Washington.

Turn right on Fourth Street, which is Cincinnati's version of Chicago's North Michigan Avenue and New York's Fifth Avenue. One mile long, it starts with the ease of Lytle Park behind you and then gradually becomes the city's main financial thoroughfare before terminating at its increasingly residential western edge. Cross Broadway Street and continue west on Fourth Street. Christ Church Cathedral, 318 E. Fourth St., was completed in 1835 and rebuilt in 1957; it remains the street's only church. Cross Sycamore Street and continue west past Atrium I and II office buildings. Garber & Woodward designed the Classical Revival–style Duke Energy building, completed in 1929, at the southwest corner of Fourth and Main Streets. Next door on Fourth Street is a tiny row of three buildings dating to 1870.

Walk to Walnut Street for a view of downtown's most towering historic corner. Significant buildings include (from the southeast corner, clockwise) Fourth & Walnut Centre, designed by Daniel H. Burnham (1903); Dixie Terminal (1921), with a grandiose barrel-vaulted lobby offering a view of Roebling Suspension Bridge; Bartlett Building, also designed by Daniel H. Burnham (1901) and reborn as a Renaissance Hotel in 2014; Formica Building (1971); and Mercantile Library Building (1905). North of the library at the southeast corner of Fifth and Walnut Streets is Tri-State Building (1902), another Burnham building. Cross Fourth Street and walk to Fourth National Bank

Building (1905), on the north side of the street. It was the last one built of four early 20th-century downtown skyscrapers designed by the Chicago firm headed by Burnham.

On the northeast corner of Fourth and Vine Streets is the 15-story Ingalls Building, the world's first reinforced concrete skyscraper, built in 1903. On the southwest corner is the 34-story PNC Tower, designed by the same architect (Cass Gilbert) behind Manhattan's Woolworth Building. Finished in 1913, it was once the tallest building west of the Hudson River. Cross Vine Street and walk to Race Street. This block was historically department store territory and a hive of activity up through the late 1990s. Today, it's a mix of other commercial and residential uses. Continuing west is West Fourth Street Historic District, the finest intact remnant of Cincinnati's turn-of-the-19th-century downtown streetscape. Turn right on Race Street and walk to the entrance of ㉑ **Carew Tower Arcade.** Inside are about two dozen shops and restaurants, including two Cincinnati classic restaurants in the midst of Art Deco colors and floral motifs: **Hathaway's Diner** (since 1956) and **Frisch's.** Exit the arcade at Vine Street and return to Fountain Square.

Points of Interest

1. **Booksellers on Fountain Square** 505 Vine St., 513-258-2038
2. **Carew Tower/Hilton Cincinnati Netherland Plaza** 441 Vine St., 513-579-9735
3. **84.51°** 100 W. Fifth St., 513-632-1020, 8451.com
4. **The Cincinnatian Hotel, Curio Collection by Hilton** 601 Vine St., 513-381-3000, cincinnatianhotel.com
5. **Covenant First Presbyterian Church** 717 Elm St., covfirstchurch.org
6. **Isaac M. Wise Temple** 720 Plum St., 513-793-2556, wisetemple.org
7. **St. Peter in Chains** 325 W. Eighth St., 513-421-5354, stpeterinchainscathedral.org
8. **Cincinnati City Hall** 801 Plum St., 513-591-6000, cincinnati-oh.gov
9. **Cappel's** 917 Race St., 513-621-9499, cappelsinc.com
10. **Scotti's Italian Restaurant** 919 Vine St., 513-721-9484
11. **Hamilton County Courthouse** 1000 Main St., courtclerk.org
12. **Public Library of Cincinnati and Hamilton County** 800 Vine St., 513-369-6900, cincinnatilibrary.org/main
13. **St. Louis Catholic Church** 29 E. Eighth St., 513-263-6621
14. **Arnold's Bar and Grill** 210 E. Eighth St., 513-421-6234, arnoldsbarandgrill.com

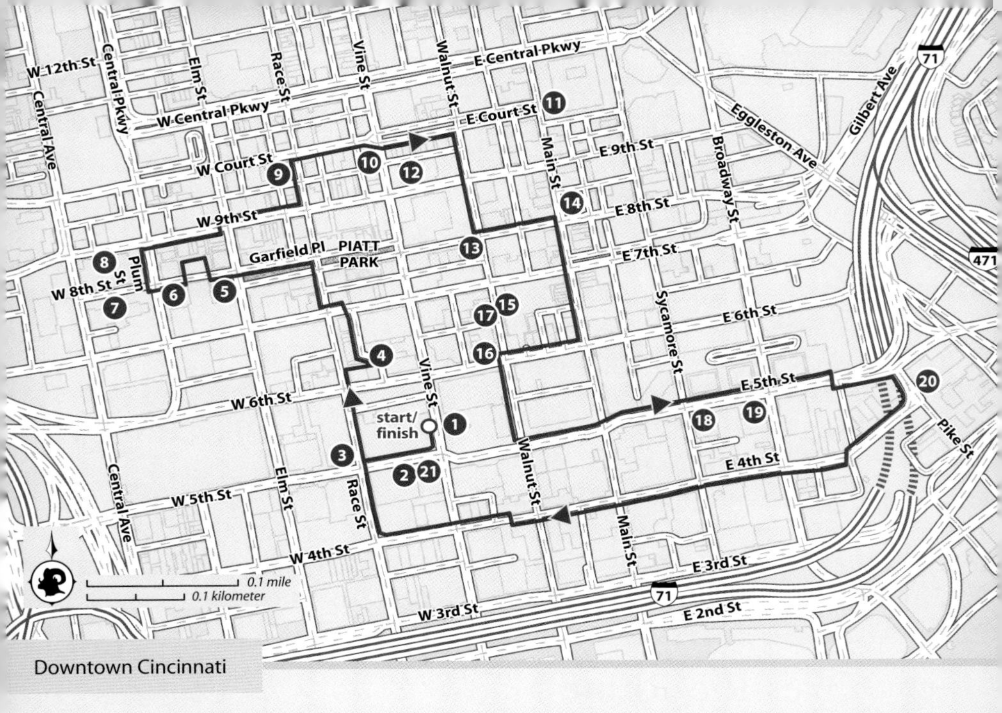

Downtown Cincinnati

- **15** Aronoff Center 650 Walnut St., 513-621-2787, cincinnatiarts.org/aronoff-center
- **16** Contemporary Arts Center 44 E. Sixth St., 513-345-8400, contemporaryartscenter.org
- **17** 21c Museum Hotel 609 Walnut St., 513-578-6600, 21cmuseumhotels.com/cincinnati
- **18** Taft Theatre 317 E. Fifth St., 513-232-6220, tafttheatre.org
- **19** Cincinnati Masonic Center 317 E. Fifth St., 513-421-3579, cincinnatimasoniccenter.com
- **20** Taft Museum of Art 316 Pike St., 513-241-0343, taftmuseum.org
- **21** Carew Tower Arcade 441 Vine St.

Connecting the Walks

To connect with Walk 1: Ohio Riverfront, walk south on Walnut Street from Fountain Square to the top of the Walnut Street Steps, which lead to the riverfront.

To connect with Walk 3: Over-the-Rhine, from Scotti's, walk north 1 mile on Vine Street, then turn left on Findlay Street. Turn right on Elm Street to reach Rhinegeist.

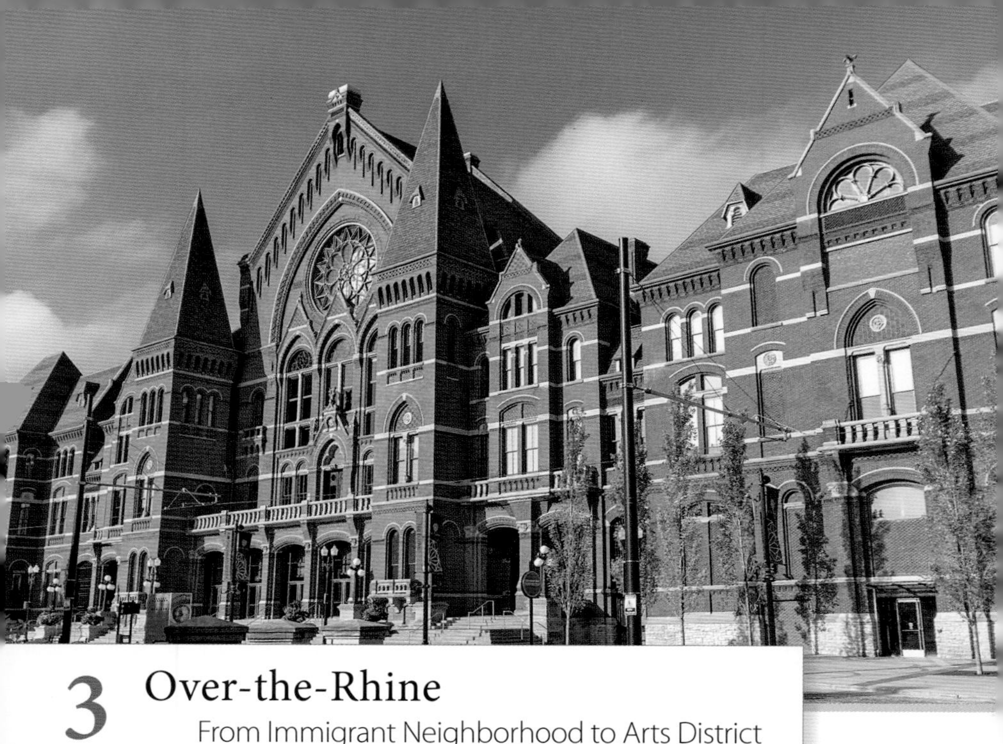

3 Over-the-Rhine

From Immigrant Neighborhood to Arts District

Above: The Cincinnati Music Hall is one of the city's most recognizable historic buildings.

BOUNDARIES: Eton Pl., Race St., 12th St., Young St.
DISTANCE: 1.9 miles
DIFFICULTY: Easy
PARKING: Start at Findlay Market (118 W. Elder St.), 3 blocks north of Liberty St. between Elm St. and Race St. There are parking lots north and south of the market and on Elder St. west of Elm St. Better yet, ride your bike and park at one of the racks on either end of the market house.
PUBLIC TRANSIT: Take Metro (go-metro.com) routes 46, 64, or 78 to Elder St. and Race St., or routes 6 and 17 to Elder St. and Vine St. or Elder St. and Central Pkwy. Cincinnati Bell Connector streetcar (cincinnatibellconnector.com) connects The Banks, downtown, and Over-the-Rhine with 18 stations. Cincinnati Red Bike (cincyredbike.org) has bicycle rental stations at 1723 Pleasant St. (Findlay Market), 1384 Elm St. (Washington Park), 1425 Main St., and elsewhere.

Over-the-Rhine is Cincinnati's chief claim to a walking city. The neighborhood is unlike anything else in Cincinnati or the Midwest. The whole area (about 365 acres) is listed on the National

Register of Historic Places and is the city's largest local historic district. Believed to have the single largest grouping of Italianate architecture in the nation and the largest collection of tenement buildings outside New York City, its significance is comparable to other well-known national historic districts around the country.

The neighborhood's distinctive name comes from its early residents and builders: German immigrants of the mid-19th century. The Miami and Erie Canal separated the area from downtown and was nicknamed The Rhine in reference to the Rhine River in Germany, and the neighborhood north of the canal was dubbed Over-the-Rhine. The 20th-century transition to Appalachian and African American migrants, as well as immigrants arriving after each World War from eastern Europe, influenced the area's social and political mix even more. The residential styles are varied because the neighborhood was economically diverse for so many decades. Two of Cincinnati's biggest industries—brewing and ironwork—are still evident throughout.

Over-the-Rhine is an urban survivor after suffering decades of neglect and indifference, and it retains an incredible 19th-century sense of place in its compact blocks, brick buildings, and human scale that usually maxes out at five stories. Just like the Germans who first settled here, people today take great pride in their neighborhood. You can see it in the well-kept houses on Orchard Street, the swept sidewalks in front of Main Street storefronts, and the well-traveled aisles at Findlay Market.

In addition to being a living neighborhood, Over-the-Rhine is a regional attraction. Most visitors come to the neighborhood to experience activities related to the arts, which has led to a surge in bars and dining options, especially along Race, Vine, and Main Streets. A handful of long-time merchants, including Silverglades (since 1922), Suder's Art Store (since 1924), and Tucker's Restaurant (since 1946), hold their own in a neighborhood experiencing dynamic change. This walk passes numerous monuments to Over-the-Rhine's Germanic cultural traditions, while calling out newer additions that give the neighborhood its appeal.

Walk Description

Start your walk at ❶ **Rhinegeist,** at the corner of Elm Street and Eton Place in a resurgent area of Over-the-Rhine. Rhinegeist, a sprawling brewery, opened in 2013 in the former Christian Moerlein Brewery bottling facility. Walk one block east along Eton Place to the venerable ❷ **Rookwood Pottery Company.** Founded by Maria Longworth Storer in 1880, it thrived until the Great Depression and has rebounded under new ownership since 2006. (There's a company retail store at 1209 Vine St.)

Backstory: Pendleton

While points of interest on Sycamore Street are highlighted in the Over-the-Rhine walk, the neighborhood east of Main Street is called Pendleton; it is mostly residential with pockets of commerce. Here is a quick tour of some neighborhood highlights. Walk east along 12th Street to Broadway, where a cluster of restaurants, bars, and a brewery have emerged on 13th Street in recent years. At Pendleton Street is the headquarters for the Verdin Bell Company (444 Reading Rd.), inside St. Paul Catholic Church from 1850. The large Romanesque Revival church is the centerpiece of a group of church-related buildings constructed after 1850. The Verdin Company led the restoration of all these buildings in the mid-1980s to create spaces for local designers. Turn left on Pendleton Street and walk to 13th Street. Ahead is the Pendleton Arts Center (1310 Pendleton St.). Built in 1909 for Krohn-Fecheimer Shoe Co.—the company that later became U.S. Shoe—the eight-story building houses studios for more than 200 artists and is headquarters for Final Friday and Second Look Saturday art walks. Turn left on 13th Street. On the right is St. Mary Baptist Church, housed inside one of the city's former bathhouses. Spring Street (on the right) dead-ends at Liberty Street and features town houses, gardens, and carriage houses that serve houses on Broadway. Turn right on Broadway. On the east side is an impressive row of houses that defy urban life with their front lawns, large trees, and gardens. The Renaissance Revival limestone-fronted house at 1324 Broadway was built in 1852 and home to Christian Boss, owner of Gambrinus Stock Co. Brewery at 12th and Sycamore Streets. Follow the cast-iron railings to 1342 Broadway, a rare Federal house from 1834 and one of the city's oldest. Seven houses on Broadway's west side north of 14th Street are mostly Italianate.

Turn right on Race Street, and go two blocks south to W. Elder Street. On your right is ❸ **Findlay Market,** the oldest continuously operated public market in Ohio. Findlay is the last remaining public market of the nine that once served Cincinnati. It's Cincinnati's closest thing to a European shopping experience, especially on a Saturday when the market is teeming with people buying, hugging, laughing, looking around, chatting, and just being. Nineteenth-century architecture surrounds the market, with Renaissance Revival, Greek Revival, Queen Anne, and Italianate all in full view.

After exploring the market, continue south on Race Street. Over-the-Rhine Recreation Center, hidden behind 1708 Race St., is a mix of refurbished historic buildings and infill from 1971. [Detour: Head east two blocks on Green Street to Vine Street for Tucker's Restaurant (1637 Vine St.), the neighborhood's oldest diner (since 1946) serving comfort food classics for breakfast and lunch.]

Continue south on Race Street, and cross Liberty Street. Race Street is a street of churches. On the left is the Gothic facade of ❹ **Prince of Peace Lutheran Church** (1871). Just down the street on the right is St. Paul's Church (1850). Empty and neglected for decades, it now houses 5 **Taft's Ale House,** with tongue-in-cheek references to William Howard Taft, the 27th president of the United States and Cincinnati resident. There are more up ahead, as you will see. On the right is the **Race Street Garden.** While it looks like a private yard, it is indeed a community garden that holds its own in a rapidly changing neighborhood. In 1989 Pleasant Street gardeners created the little oasis with infrastructure support from the Civic Garden Center Community in Avondale.

A cluster of culinary businesses has emerged in these blocks: Poke Hut (1509 Race St.), Anchor OTR (1401 Race St.), Zula Restaurant & Wine Bar (1400 Race St.), Salazar (1401 Republic St.), and more in a neighborhood with a regular stream of new business openings. Anchor OTR benefits from a restored wooden veranda, an important part of the area's architectural heritage, facing Washington Park.

Washington Park, on the right between 14th and 12th Streets, is older than most buildings that surround it. Cincinnati's second-oldest park was the site of four separate cemeteries for several churches before the city acquired the land between 1855 and 1863. The 6-acre park is a popular destination year-round and features concerts in the bandstand, a water park, mature trees, and a playground.

Enter the park at 14th and Race Streets, follow the right walkway past the open-air stage and great lawn, and head toward Elm Street. Several magnificent buildings dominate this stretch of Over-the-Rhine. Here you see 6 **Music Hall** and 7 **Memorial Hall** (both designed by Samuel Hannaford & Sons) up close. Music Hall provides a massive High Victorian Gothic western wall for the park. Inside, it hosts the opera, symphony, pops orchestra, and May Festival (the oldest choral festival in the United States). To the left of it is the Beaux Arts–style Memorial Hall, a concert venue inside a building erected in 1908 as a memorial to pioneers and soldiers. As you head south along Elm Street, six houses create a stunning late 19th-century streetscape: 1209 Elm Street is the most unrestrained with its French Renaissance facade. 8 **Vestry at the Transept** is located inside St. John's Church. Once the home of Cincinnati's oldest German Protestant congregation, the Gothic church was finished in 1868. Across the street and in stark contrast to the last two blocks, see the 9 **Cincinnati Shakespeare Company,** modeled after the Royal National Theatre in London and Shakespeare's Globe.

South of Cincy Shakes, as the theater calls itself, is the towering **Central Parkway YMCA** (1918). The Italian Renaissance building with two-story arched windows is home to offices for the YMCA of Greater Cincinnati, along with 65 affordable apartments for seniors. Walk along 12th Street toward Race Street and take in the block-long rear facade of the **School for Creative and Performing Arts** (SCPA). Key to the revitalization of Washington Park, this was the first K–12 arts school in the United States. Founded in 1973 as one of the first magnet schools in the city, it relocated here from the old Woodward High School building on Sycamore Street. SCPA is a model of excellence in school integration.

Return to Race Street for two more historic churches. ⓾ **First English Lutheran Church** (behind the Washington Park streetcar station at 12th and Race Streets) presents a handsome red sandstone Romanesque-style facade from 1894. Go one block north on Race Street, where just north of 13th Street, ⓫ **Over-the-Rhine Community Church** (inside Nast Trinity Methodist Church) features a rock-faced masonry facade with terra-cotta detailing and an "1880" inscription above the right door dating the building, another project of Samuel Hannaford & Sons.

Remain standing at 13th Street for a closeup view of two ArtWorks murals. Each is part of more than 50 elaborate murals painted on the sides of buildings in Over-the-Rhine and downtown. You'll notice them almost everywhere you go. (For even closer inspection, ArtWorks student apprentices provide guided walking tours.) The ***Vision of Samuel Hannaford*** shows a portrait of Samuel Hannaford resting on blueprints, symbolizing his architectural legacy in Cincinnati. The ***Golden Muse*** features a larger-than-life figurine from an 18th-century mantel clock in the Taft Museum of Art's collection.

Return to 12th Street and turn left. **Tender Mercies** is a longtime Over-the-Rhine institution and a model for retaining diversity and inclusiveness through housing service in a rapidly changing neighborhood. Continue east toward Vine Street, the spine of Over-the-Rhine. In the late 1800s, Vine Street once contained 136 saloons, taverns, and beer gardens. Today, the street is a thriving commercial district with a mix of restaurants, bars, and retail stores. There are far too many to list here. (For a listing of Over-the-Rhine businesses, visit otrchamber.com.) A few doors south is ⓬ **Ensemble Theatre of Cincinnati.** For a long time, it was one of the only businesses, and the only theater, in the neighborhood.

Continue walking east along 12th Street, crossing Vine. Walk one block to Jackson Street. On the left is the ⓭ **Art Academy of Cincinnati.** On the right is ⓮ **Know Theatre of Cincinnati.** Formed in 1997, this theater group started in the basement of Gabriel's Corner Church on Sycamore Street. Both the Art Academy and Know Theatre have played pivotal roles in stabilizing and energizing this section of Over-the-Rhine.

Walk one block east to Walnut Street and turn right. Opposite are two popular local bars (Halfcut at 1126 Walnut St. and Below Zero Lounge at 1120 Walnut St.) and Gomez (107 E. 12th St.), a walk-up burrito-and-taco window. The first building on the right is Germania Building (1151–1199 Walnut St.), one of Over-the-Rhine's architectural treasures from 1877. Johann Bast designed this delightful stone Italian Renaissance facade. Its second-floor nave holds the statue of *Germania,* symbolizing the German spirit.

Proceed south down Walnut Street and notice the *Crazy Cat, Crazy Quilt* (1107 Walnut St.) mural on the back of the American Building (30 E. Central Pkwy.), one of the city's first Art Deco office buildings from 1927, later converted into condos. The colorfully depicted mural honors the accomplished life and career of Cincinnati Master artist Edie Harper, who later met fellow artist Charley Harper. He remained her partner in life and love until his death in 2007. Turn left at Central Parkway and cross Walnut Street to get an expansive view of **Emery Center Apartments.** Formerly the Ohio Mechanics Institute Building, Emery is another pivotal building in Over-the-Rhine's rebirth. Built in 1909 in Tudor Revival style, it contains 59 converted apartments upstairs, Coffee Emporium at ground level, and one of the city's abandoned gems: Emery Theater. An acoustically exceptional concert hall, it was built specifically for the symphony and was the first theater in the United States to have no obstructed seats.

After refueling at Coffee Emporium, walk east to Clay Street and turn left. At 12th Street are two more drinking spots: rhinehaus sports bar (119 E. 12th St.) and Revel OTR Urban Winery (111 E. 12th St.). Cross 12th Street and walk to ⓯ **Old St. Mary's Church.** Built in 1842, it is Cincinnati's largest and oldest remaining Catholic church. Masses are performed in English, German, and Latin. Tucked away next door are the Greek Revival parish house from 1845 and adjoining church school from 1843. Across the street are Brown Bear Bakery (116 E. 13th St.), specializing in sweet and savory pastries, and Longfellow (1233 Clay St.), a small corner neighborhood bar with great cocktails and creative snacks.

Turn right on 13th Street and walk east to Main Street, one of the finest and most intact late 19th-century streetscapes in the city. Many cite Main Street as their favorite street in the neighborhood for its independent and artistic spirit. Cross Main Street, turn right before popping into a shop or two, and then go left on 12th Street. Much of Over-the-Rhine's early revitalization efforts in the 1980s started here. At the end of this block on the left is the former Queen City Diner (1203 Sycamore St.). Built in 1955 and brought here in 1984 from Massillon, Ohio, it contrasts with its 19th-century neighbors and dazzles the eye compared to the vast parking lots across the street. Turn left on Sycamore Street past Olde Sycamore Square across the street. The five narrow Italianate buildings were beautifully restored in the mid-1980s, a decade before changes started on Main Street and two decades before Vine Street. Cross 13th Street. On the right is the massive Renaissance Revival structure built in 1910, the former Woodward High School and SCPA, recently converted into 142 apartments known as **Alumni Lofts.**

On the left is ⓰ **Ziegler Park,** a 4.5-acre green space with a pool and rock wall, water features, basketball courts, and a running track. Immediately north of Ziegler Park is ⓱ **Peaslee Neighborhood Center,** which has acted as an early learning center and welcoming place since 1974. Cross 14th Street. Go one block to ⓲ **Nicola's** (another neighborhood pioneer after more than two decades) in a former incline car barn. At the northwest corner of Orchard Street is the towering ⓳ **Salem United Church of Christ,** which dates from 1867. Immediately to the north at 1427 Sycamore is a fine midcentury cube that stands out from its 19th-century neighbors. Turn left on Orchard Street, one of the loveliest residential blocks downtown. It features simple Greek Revival and early Italianate town houses, as well as a spectacular tree canopy. On the north side, the former Fourth Presbyterian Church from 1859 has a turreted tower.

Proceed to Main Street, the ideal place to end this walk. Looking to your right just across Liberty Street is neo-Tudor **Rothenberg Preparatory Academy,** from 1913. The restored school features terra-cotta figures of children and elves. Most late 19th-century buildings south of Liberty Street are occupied upstairs with residents. At ground level are unaltered cast-iron storefronts where small businesses congregate. A significant Main Street player is ⓴ **Woodward Theater,** a music venue from the owners of MOTR Pub in a restored 1913 theater.

To return to the start of this walk, head west along 14th Street from Main Street to Race Street and turn right, returning to Findlay Market.

Points of Interest

❶ **Rhinegeist** 1910 Elm St., 513-381-1367, rhinegeist.com

❷ **Rookwood Pottery Company** 1920 Race St., 513-381-2510, rookwood.com

❸ **Findlay Market** 1801 Race St., findlaymarket.org

❹ **Prince of Peace Lutheran Church** 1528 Race St., 513-621-7265, poplcmscinci.org

❺ **Taft's Ale House** 1429 Race St., 513-334-1393, taftsalehouse.com

❻ **Music Hall** 1241 Elm St., 513-621-2787, cincinnatiarts.org

❼ **Memorial Hall** 1225 Elm St., 513-381-0348, memorialhallotr.com

❽ **Vestry at the Transept** 1205 Elm St., 513-841-9999, vestryotr.com

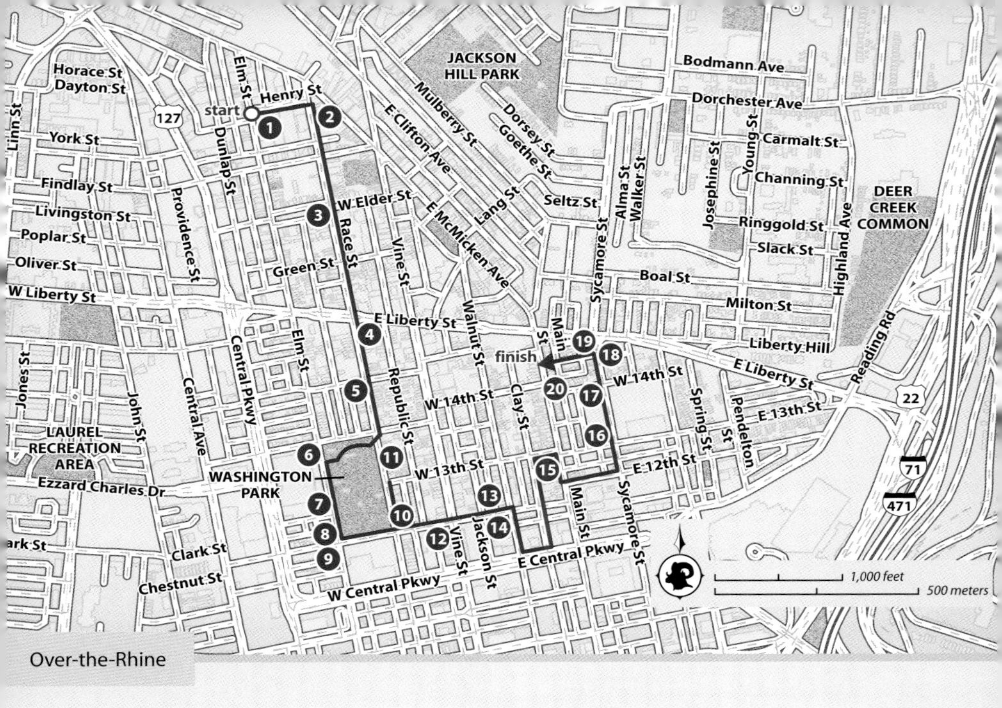

Over-the-Rhine

9. **Cincinnati Shakespeare Company** 1195 Elm St., 513-381-2273, cincyshakes.com
10. **First English Lutheran Church** 1208 Race St., 513-421-0065, firstlutherancincy.org
11. **Over-the-Rhine Community Church (Nast Trinity Methodist Church)** 1310 Race St., 513-871-1345, otrcc.org
12. **Ensemble Theatre of Cincinnati** 1127 Vine St., 513-421-3555, ensemblecincinnati.org
13. **Art Academy of Cincinnati** 1212 Jackson St., 513-562-6262, artacademy.edu
14. **Know Theatre of Cincinnati** 1120 Jackson St., 513-300-5669, knowtheatre.com
15. **Old St. Mary's Church** 123 E. 13th St., 513-721-2988, oldstmarys.org
16. **Ziegler Park** 1322 Sycamore St., 513-621-4400, zieglerpark.org
17. **Peaslee Neighborhood Center** 215 E. 14th St., 513-621-5514, peasleecenter.org
18. **Nicola's Restaurant** 1420 Sycamore St., 513-721-6200, nicolasotr.com
19. **Salem United Church of Christ** 1425 Sycamore St., 513-241-1796
20. **Woodward Theater** 1404 Main St., 513-345-7981, woodwardtheater.com

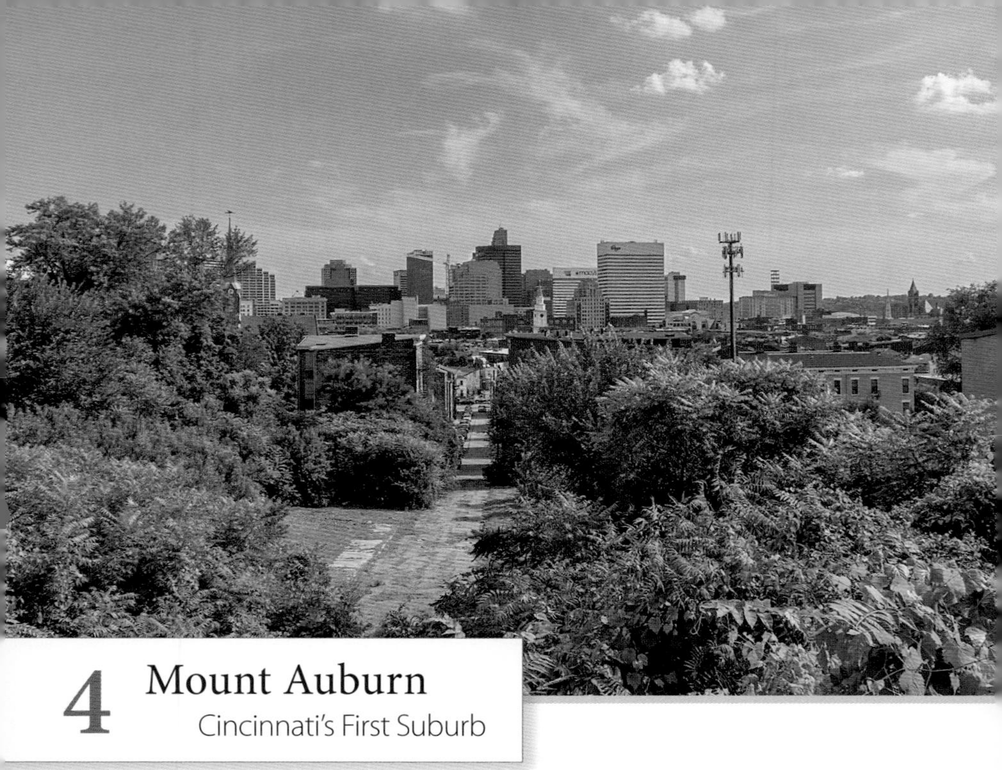

4 Mount Auburn

Cincinnati's First Suburb

Above: Mount Auburn offers multiple sweeping views of the city below.

BOUNDARIES: Sycamore St., Loth St., Wellington Pl., Highland Ave., Liberty Hill
DISTANCE: 3.2 miles
DIFFICULTY: Strenuous
PARKING: On-street parking is available on Milton and Sycamore Streets.
PUBLIC TRANSIT: Cincinnati Red Bike (cincyredbike.org) has nearby bicycle rental stations at 1422 Main St., 500 E. Liberty St. in Prospect Hill, and elsewhere. Metro buses (go-metro.com) serve this area.

After watching Over-the-Rhine undergo a major transformation over the past decade, Cincinnati's first hilltop neighborhood is poised for its moment on the revitalization stage. Mount Auburn, which saw virtually no new housing for decades, is now experiencing a rush of building rehabs and new construction. Thoughtful community leaders are making sure the neighborhood is home to people of all incomes, races, and ages. Mount Auburn, tucked between the still-booming Over-the-Rhine and growing Uptown neighborhoods, is made up of multiple parts. To the south is Prospect Hill, geographically more a part of Over-the-Rhine. To the east are streets with houses dating from 1870 to 1910. To the west is lower Mount Auburn, a somewhat forgotten area with an earlier building stock more closely related to Over-the-Rhine. In the middle is Auburn Avenue, the most visible symbol of the neighborhood's efforts to sustain itself. Despite some architectural losses in recent years, Mount Auburn retains much of its 19th-century housing stock. While the area lacks an official business district, the Auburn Avenue Corridor Strategic Development Plan calls for Auburn Avenue to become the commercial center of the neighborhood.

Walk Description

Our walk starts at ❶ **Milton's Prospect Hill Tavern,** which clings to the steep corner of Sycamore and Milton Streets. Stop in if the climb up Sycamore Street and subsequent hillside streets proves too much. Walk up Sycamore past Boal Street, and cross at Mulberry Street. Take Mulberry to Main Street. On the right is the base of the Main Street Steps, which intersect with three streets above and eventually summit at **Jackson Hill Park,** which offers a sweeping panorama. Climb the steps here to see for yourself, and then descend the steps to return to Mulberry Street. This was originally the site of the Mount Auburn incline, opened in 1872.

Continue along Mulberry Street. Rehabs, gutted buildings, and new town houses stand close together. Incredible views open up over the city. Mulberry narrows as it nears Rice and Loth Streets on the right. Before beer baron Christian Moerlein moved to his final home on Ohio Avenue in Clifton Heights (Walk 7), he lived in the mansion at the northeast corner of Mulberry and Loth Streets from 1870 to 1882. The once fine ❷ **Christian Moerlein House** is currently a shell. The Greater Cincinnati Redevelopment Authority got involved with the house around 2012 when it faced demolition, funding the purchase and stabilization of the historic structure. Hopes remain high that the former mansion will find a new purpose.

Turn right on Loth Street and walk two blocks north to Thill Street. Ascend the steps across the street into **Inwood Park.** The 20-acre scenic and rolling park, a former stone quarry, was the source for the foundation stones of many of the earliest buildings in Clifton Heights to the west of Vine Street. A granite monument (lacking its bronze plaque) commemorates Friedrich Ludwig Jahn, who founded in Germany what later became the Turner Society, a gymnastic club that doubled as a nationalist political group. The park's most noted feature is the lake. The pavilion is one of the earliest buildings still standing in Cincinnati's parks. Follow the footpath that veers to the right and proceed up the hill to the roundabout at Wellington Place. The top of the hill offers a great view of St. George's Catholic Church (looking north).

Follow Wellington Place to Auburn Avenue. On the right is One41 Wellington (2309 Auburn Ave.), a $45 million housing project that includes 60 renovated apartment units and a massive new complex that includes more than 250 units. It replaced a rare (at least in Mount Auburn) Tudor Revival building that was a commission of Samuel Hannaford & Sons in 1930. The original cast- and wrought-iron fence still surrounds the property.

The **Mount Auburn Historic District,** which extends along both sides of Auburn Avenue roughly between Ringgold Street and William Howard Taft Road, intersects here. It is significant for its collection of Federal, Greek Revival, Italian Villa, Romanesque Revival, and Georgian Revival styles. The houses date from 1819 to the turn of the 20th century and are associated with the prominent Cincinnatians who built them. The district suffered a big loss in 2014 when the former Mount Auburn Methodist Church at the southwest corner of Auburn Avenue and E. McMillan Street was demolished, despite community opposition and several months of hearings with the city's Historic Conservation Board. The site of the Gothic Revival structure remains a vacant lot. Across the street, the Elmore W. Cunningham House (2448 Auburn Ave.) faces a similar fate. Cunningham, a 19th-century meat-packer, hired Anderson & Hannaford (Samuel Hannaford) to design his home. The 1860 mansion is currently for sale as a redevelopment (demolition) site.

On the northwest corner of Auburn Avenue and Wellington Place is ❸ **Graveson House,** a massive asymmetrical composition with a neo-Baroque entrance. Turn right on Auburn Avenue, then turn left on McGregor Avenue, and left again on Auburncrest Avenue for a brief detour to ❹ **Gorham A. Worth House,** one of Cincinnati's most important historic homes. The central section of the Federal house was built in 1819, with the wings added in about 1860. Worth was a cashier at the Cincinnati branch of the Second Bank of the United States and a poet.

Retrace your steps to Auburn Avenue and turn left. Both 2210 and 2212 Auburn Ave., with their mansard roofs and elaborate dormers, are Second Empire in style. Cross Albion Place and Gilman Avenue. On the left is the former ❺ **Mount Auburn Firehouse,** now the property of ❻ **Christ Hospital** across the street. Cincinnati architect Harry Hake designed the Georgian Revival main hospital building (1930). The glow of light from the tower is a local landmark.

Cross Earnshaw Avenue; 2112 Auburn Ave. is an excellent example of Richardsonian Romanesque. Cross Southern Avenue to reach the ❼ **William Howard Taft National Historic Site,** the most noteworthy of the Mount Auburn houses. A National Historic Landmark and Cincinnati's only National Park Service site, the Greek Revival house (built around 1840) is notable for being the birthplace of William Howard Taft, born in 1857. Taft was the 27th president of the United States (1909–1913) and subsequently chief justice of the Supreme Court (1921–1930).

Cross Bodmann Avenue. Across the street is the ❽ **Adam Riddle House,** set on what may be Mount Auburn's highest point. Attorney and state legislator Adam N. Riddle built the house in 1857. The current owners have lovingly maintained and improved the condition of the Italian Villa–style house. Walk to Dorchester Avenue and carefully cross this tricky intersection where Auburn Avenue and Sycamore Street meet. Part of the race sequence in the 1993 in-line skating movie *Airborne* was filmed on the curve.

Across the street, the ❾ **Flatiron Building** takes full advantage of its location. The building has faced an uncertain future in recent years, though community leaders have helped to stabilize the structure. Built in 1857, it housed the Flat Iron Cafe in the 1950s. The Italianate ❿ **Henry Martin House** was built in 1870. In 1888 Henry Martin built the Mount Auburn Cable Railway, which ran from downtown up Sycamore Street, along Dorchester Avenue past the impressive cable house at 2001 Highland Ave., and then down Highland.

Follow Sycamore Street east, and turn left at Walker Street, which offers more stunning views of the valley below from a row of rehabbed homes. Walk to 1810 Walker St. and turn left on the footpath to Ringgold Street. Walk through Filson Park to Young Street. On the northeast corner is ⓫ **God's Bible School & College.** A mix of Italianate, Queen Anne, and Colonial Revival styles are found in the buildings that comprise the campus.

Surviving buildings in the Mount Auburn Historic District date from 1819 to the turn of the 20th century.

Turn right on Young Street toward the **Young Street Steps** at Pueblo Street. Descend the steps past Boal Street to Milton Street, and turn left. Milton Street is a steady climb from Sycamore Street to the west, and ground zero for the **Prospect Hill Historic District,** which is generally bounded by Liberty, Sycamore, Boal, and Channing Streets and Highland Avenue. It includes more than 200 buildings, which together comprise a community of architectural significance. The buildings are mostly tall brick structures with long, narrow floor plans. Among the architectural styles are Italianate, Queen Anne, Federal, and Greek Revival.

Proceed on Milton Street. Four identical Greek Revival two-story row houses (533–539) have setbacks in front for gardens and to provide some breathing room. From here, turn right and descend Hiram Steps. Turn left on Corporation Alley (more of a secluded street than an alley) to see a variety of 19th-century cottages, Italianate and Greek Revival houses, and carriage houses. Follow Corporation Alley to Highland Avenue and turn right. Ahead is the ⓬ **George Hunt Pendleton House,** a National Historic Landmark built in 1870. French Second Empire in style, the building is beautifully situated at the summit of Liberty Hill. The house is notable for being the home of Senator George Hunt Pendleton. He and his committee met here in 1882 to draft the Pendleton Act, the start of the Civil Service Commission.

Walk down Liberty Hill (north side) past one beautifully maintained house after another to Young Street. Just past the Liberty Hill split are two small frame houses (442 and 440), believed to date back to the 1830s. Walk past Cumber Street and Caitlin Alley to 412 Liberty Hill. Built in 1867, the First District Public School was converted into condominiums in the 1970s, an early adaptive reuse project. Walk to Broadway and turn right, uphill to Milton Street. Ahead is the Vogeler (334–336 Milton St.), a festively decorated apartment building with etched glass in the doorway. Turn left on Milton Street, and walk to admire 322–326 Milton Street, three Second Empire town houses with mansard roofs.

Turn left on Mansfield Street, returning to Liberty Hill. Turn right and walk to Sycamore Street. On the northeast corner is the John Walker House (1600 Sycamore St.), a splendid Greek Revival town house built in 1847. Head uphill one last time and look for the geometrical wrought iron fence in front of ⓭ **Sycamore Street Studio.** Inside is the sculpture studio of Ted Gantz; outside is his secret garden.

This walk ends where it began, at Milton's Prospect Hill Tavern. The neighborhood bar opened Halloween 1992 and welcomes all kinds, including people who walk in the door with this book.

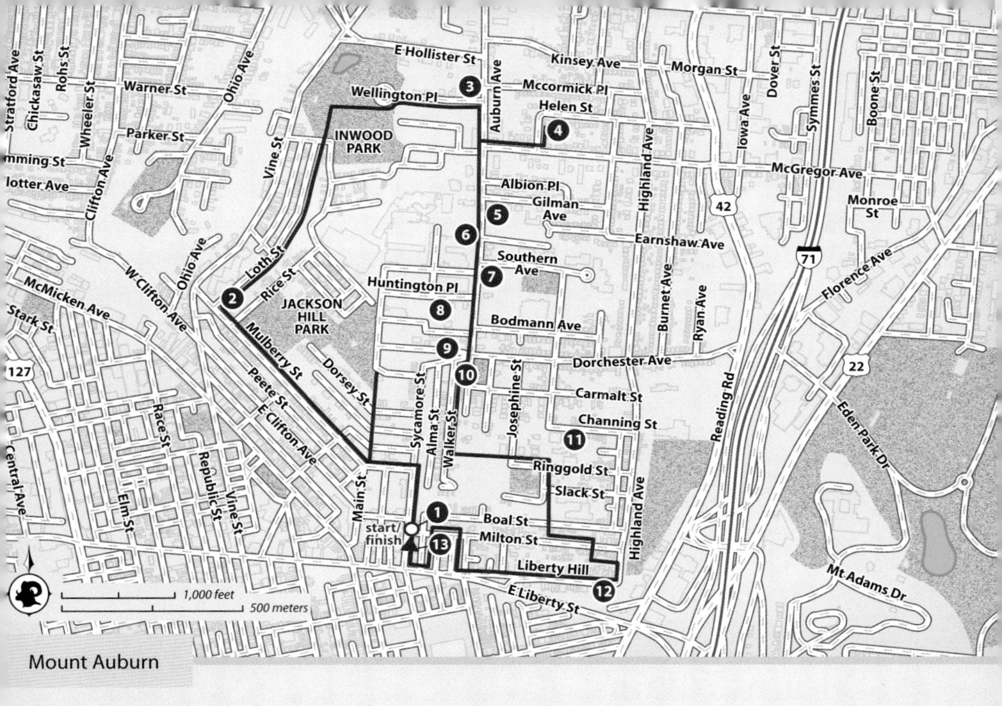

Points of Interest

1. **Milton's Prospect Hill Tavern** 301 Milton St., 513-784-9938
2. **Christian Moerlein House** 18 Mulberry St.
3. **Graveson House** 2343 Auburn Ave., 513-421-3900, schooltheatre.org
4. **Gorham A. Worth House** 2316 Auburncrest Ave.
5. **Mount Auburn Firehouse** 2142 Auburn Ave.
6. **Christ Hospital** 2139 Auburn Ave., 513-585-2000, thechristhospital.com
7. **William Howard Taft National Historic Site** 2038 Auburn Ave., 513-684-3262, nps.gov
8. **Adam Riddle House** 2021 Auburn Ave., 513-205-9520
9. **Flatiron Building** 1833 Sycamore St.
10. **Henry Martin House** 1947 Auburn Ave.
11. **God's Bible School & College** 1810 Young St., gbs.edu
12. **George Hunt Pendleton House** 559 Liberty Hill
13. **Sycamore Street Studio** 1604 Sycamore St., 513-381-0272

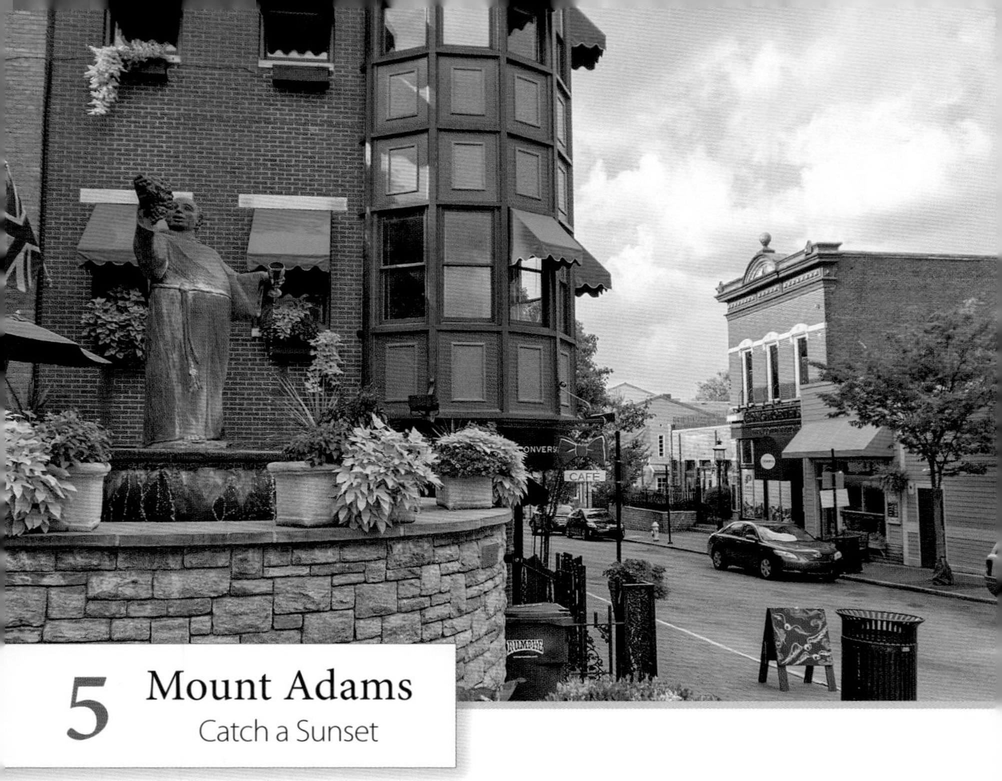

5 Mount Adams

Catch a Sunset

Above: Statue of Father Quinn, one of the neighborhood's mythic figures

BOUNDARIES: Celestial St., Martin Dr., Eden Park Dr., Ida St.
DISTANCE: 1.7 miles
DIFFICULTY: Moderate to strenuous
PARKING: Free street parking on St. Gregory St., Hill St., Jerome St., and other nearby streets
PUBLIC TRANSIT: The 1 bus line has stops along Parkside Dr., as well as Paradrome St. between Louden St. and Wareham Dr., both of which are points in the middle of this walk.

Mount Adams is a small tangle of streets lined with narrow, pristine old houses, all perched on a hill that offers some of the best views of the city. Surrounded by highways on three sides and Eden Park on the other, its isolation has always been part of its character—most days, Mount Adams offers its charms inside a blanket of pleasant quiet. Historically home to German and Irish Catholics, since 1950 Mount Adams has witnessed an influx of hippies, yuppies, empty nesters, and young families. Now, its views and proximity to downtown make homes there some of the most sought-after (and expensive) real estate in the city.

Eden Park contains some of the city's most visited attractions: the Cincinnati Art Museum, Playhouse in the Park, and the Krohn Conservatory. Mount Adams itself is probably most known to outsiders for its active nightlife, drawing young professionals from all over the city each weekend to its bars and restaurants.

This walk is best done on a sunny day so you can fully enjoy the various lovely views and sights. Spring and fall are especially wonderful times to see the park and the well-groomed gardens of the neighborhood. Mount Adams is one of the hilliest parts of the city—one of the reasons Cincinnati has earned the nickname San Francisco of the Midwest—so make sure you wear some comfortable shoes and are prepared for a few steep areas. If you come in the late afternoon, don't miss the chance to finish your walk with a bite to eat at one of the famous Mount Adams pubs.

Walk Description

Begin on St. Gregory Street between Jerome and Hill Streets. On the east side of St. Gregory, take the stone stairs (Mt. Adams Steps) up. There are about 90 steps; this should be the steepest portion of the entire walk, so take your time and, on the landings, feel free to turn around and note the incredible view emerging behind you.

Look above you: you're approaching the ❶ **Holy Cross Immaculata Church.** About 150 years ago, shortly after this church was first completed in 1860 (then the Church of the Immaculate Conception, home to the hill's German Catholics), a tradition known as "praying the steps" was begun. On Good Friday, pilgrims begin on Adams Crossing, cross Columbia Parkway, and slowly ascend the hill, ending with the steps you're climbing now, silently praying the rosary (one prayer on each step). This tradition is unique in Cincinnati and rare throughout the world.

At the top of the stairs, admire the view of downtown Cincinnati over the rooftops—you're at one of the highest points in the city. From here, go left around the church and begin to follow Guido Street. You'll pass the former rectory and school on your right.

When you reach Pavilion Street, glance to your left to see some of the main business strip; we'll return to that later. Instead, turn right on Pavilion. Ahead, as you continue forward, Pavilion will curve to the left and become Carney Street; walk on the left side to stay on the sidewalk and continue. For the next few blocks, headed mostly downhill, observe the colorful siding of the homes and the range of architectural styles. This is residential Mount Adams today: wealthy, private, filled with neat gardens and creeping ivy, settled closely together, intrinsically urban. Between the buildings to your right, you'll catch more glimpses of wonderful river views.

Turn right on Parkside Place. You are now walking along the borders of **Eden Park.**

Just before reaching Martin Drive, turn left on the small service road that is roped off to cars. Continue up the service road as you pass ❷ **Mirror Lake** to your right. Initially built as a reservoir, some of the remnants can be seen on the south side of the park. If you want to add a little distance to the walk, this is a great spot to loop around the lake and enjoy Eden Park, named after Nicholas Longworth's estate, which he called the Garden of Eden.

Continue along the road through two brick constructions and toward the back side of ❸ **Seasongood Pavilion,** built in 1959 and named after Cincinnati Mayor Murray Seasongood, who served 1926–1930. Walk around either side of the pavilion and continue up the path that goes through the middle of the grassy natural amphitheater. Many live music and theater events happen here, especially in the summer.

At the top of the bowl, you'll reach Art Museum Drive. If you look to your right, you'll see the ❹ **Cincinnati Art Museum.** The original building, which can't be seen from this view but which you can admire if you follow the driveway that leads off to the left around the new additions, was the first purpose-built art museum west of the Alleghenies. The museum's collections include some 60,000 works, and admission is free. Stop and peruse a few galleries if you have time, or continue your walk by turning left at the top of the amphitheater.

Follow Art Museum Drive away from the museum as the road curves around the hill. Continue right at the fork; do not turn left on Mt. Adams Drive.

Turn left on Ida Street. You're reentering the Mount Adams neighborhood, and to your right you will again see the beautiful narrow houses hanging off the side of the hill.

Turn left on Paradrome Street. On the corner here you'll see a staircase leading to your left up the hill; a short distance down Paradrome Street, you'll be able to look up and see a fine view of the beautiful ❺ **Playhouse in the Park,** which is at the top. Not quite visible from here are the Mount Adams playground and pool, which are hidden off to the right of the Playhouse.

Turn right on Wareham Drive, and then immediately turn left to continue on Paradrome Street.

Turn right on Louden Street. As you walk slightly uphill, you're nearing the main area for businesses and nightlife.

Turn right on Hatch Street. Here on the corner you'll find the ❻ **Mt. Adams Bar & Grill,** a former speakeasy that was the first establishment in Ohio to obtain a liquor license after Prohibition was repealed in 1933. If you step inside, you'll appreciate the elaborate old bar and gorgeous wooden paneling. Just next door to the bar, you can creep down some steps and through a low-ceilinged alleyway to enter the peculiar garden and live music of 7 **The Blind Lemon;** first, stop to see the plaque on the wall near the entrance that lists famous historical guests.

Outside the Blind Lemon, cross Hatch Street and begin to walk up St. Gregory Street. To your right you'll see the impressive 8 **Academy at St. Gregory** building. Designed by H. E. Siter and built as a public school in 1894, it was converted to host the Cincinnati Art Academy in the 1980s (which had previously occupied a building adjacent to the Art Museum in Eden Park). In 2005 the Art Academy moved to its current location in Over-the-Rhine, and this building has most recently been converted into 14 upscale condominiums.

Up St. Gregory Street a little, on the left, is a former firehouse that now houses 9 **Longworth's,** a large and popular bar, restaurant, and nightclub.

As you turn right on Pavilion Street, on the corner you'll find the 10 **Bow Tie Café,** a charming coffee shop and café that was opened by former NFL player Dhani Jones in 2010. After his friend Kunta Littlejohn was diagnosed with lymphoma, Jones started rocking Littlejohn-style bow ties to show his support, and now his Bow Tie Cause line of ties supports various charities like the Leukemia and Lymphoma Society.

As you head up the stair-stepped brick sidewalk, take a look at the statue of the wine-sloshing monk on the patio. He's called Father Quinn by the locals and is a tribute to one of Mount Adams's mythic figures: Father Quinn is said to have brought provisions to the needy during the brutal winter of 1888.

Turn right on St. Paul Place. In front of you is the 11 **Holy Cross Monastery** building, on a site that has been important in Mount Adams's history.

Originally called Mount Ida, after a washerwoman who was said to have lived there in the base of a sycamore tree, the entire area of Mount Adams was purchased by Longworth in 1831. He turned the barren, deforested land into a vineyard, on his way to becoming the first commercially successful winemaker in the United States. Later, he donated 4 acres at the top of the hillside to be made into an observatory (supposedly with a mind to increase his property's value). John Quincy Adams, in one of his last public speeches, presided over the dedication of the Cincinnati Observatory in 1843, and this is why the hill was redubbed Mount Adams.

The original observatory building was moved to Mount Lookout in 1873 to escape the air pollution from downtown, and the site in Mount Adams became home to the Holy Cross Monastery and Church. The building you're looking at was completed in 1901 and served as a monastery until 1977. The Holy Cross Church served the Irish immigrants of the hill, and later the parish combined with the German parish of the Immaculate Conception to become the Holy Cross Immaculata that you saw at the beginning of this tour, on the other end of Pavilion Street.

The monastery building is one of several Mount Adams buildings listed on the National Register of Historic Places, and today it houses commercial office space and an event center.

Turn left on Monastery Street and head down the hill. As you bear left on Celestial Street, you'll see wide views opening ahead of you again. Continue to bear left and carefully cross Celestial Street to the right side—only when you are safely past the intersection; traffic can approach quickly here.

On your right is ⓬ **The Rookwood,** an upscale bar and restaurant. It is located in the former studio and factory of the famous Rookwood Pottery Company, started in 1880 by Maria Longworth Nichols Storer, granddaughter of Nicholas Longworth, mentioned earlier. Rookwood Pottery was an important American brand, designed to be both decorative and useful, and some of its original tiles and pieces are still found in houses and institutions throughout Cincinnati. Although Rookwood Pottery went through some rough patches, it has returned to Cincinnati and now operates in Over-the-Rhine (see Walk 3).

Just past The Rookwood, continue straight into the parking lot of Highland Towers and walk to the end of the lot. Here you'll see an unrivaled view of downtown and the river. You're standing on the site that used to be the top of the Mount Adams Incline, the fourth of five inclines that connected Cincinnati to the surrounding hillside neighborhoods. Built in the 1870s and open until 1948, the incline carried passengers, cars, and buggies to the top of the hill, and it brought great growth to Mount Adams. The Incline remained a popular tourist attraction, as folks from the city rode up to eat, drink, and dance at the legendary Highland House.

By midcentury, Mount Adams was mostly home to blue-collar workers, and the neighborhood had fallen into disrepair; redevelopment and renovation began in the 1960s and started the upturn that the area is still experiencing today. ⓭ **Highland Towers,** the high-rise apartment building to your left, was built on the site of the old Highland House in 1963.

Walk back across the parking lot to Celestial Street, turn right, and continue. Turn left on Jerome Street, still paved with brick, and head slightly uphill once more. When Jerome Street ends, turn right on St. Gregory Street to return to your starting point.

Mount Adams

Points of Interest

1. Holy Cross Immaculata Church 30 Guido St., 513-721-6544, 2011.hciparish.org
2. Mirror Lake Eden Park, cincinnatiparks.com/eden-park
3. Seasongood Pavilion Eden Park, cincinnatiparks.com/eden-park
4. Cincinnati Art Museum 953 Eden Park Dr., 513-721-2787, cincinnatiartmuseum.org
5. Playhouse in the Park 962 Mt. Adams Cir., 513-421-3888, cincyplay.com
6. Mt. Adams Bar & Grill 938 Hatch St., 513-621-3666, mtadamsbarandgrill.com
7. The Blind Lemon 938 Hatch St., 513-241-3885, theblindlemon.com
8. Academy at St. Gregory 1125 St. Gregory St., condokey.com/academy
9. Longworth's 1108 St. Gregory St., 513-873-3850
10. Bow Tie Café 1101 St. Gregory St., 513-621-2233, bowtiecafe.com
11. Holy Cross Monastery 1055 St. Paul Pl.
12. The Rookwood 1077 Celestial St., 513-721-5088, rookwood.com
13. Highland Towers 1071 Celestial St., 513-241-2121, highlandtowersmtadams.com

6 Walnut Hills

From Prominent Suburb to Urban Neighborhood

Above: Be sure to visit Twin Lakes Overlook for a spectacular view of the city.

BOUNDARIES: Gilbert Ave., William Howard Taft Rd., Victory Pkwy., Eden Park Dr.
DISTANCE: 2.75 miles
DIFFICULTY: Moderate
PARKING: On-street or at the Walnut Hills Branch Library
PUBLIC TRANSIT: Metro bus to Taft Rd. and Gilbert Ave.

Walnuts Hills is a unique Cincinnati neighborhood that is in the process of redefining its identity through deep introspection and a genuine celebration of its history of diversity, walkability, and proximity to great amenities such as Eden Park. This walk traverses some of Cincinnati's most beautiful parkland, as well as some historic and commercial districts of Walnut Hills.

Reverend James Kemper purchased 150 acres for his homestead from John Cleves Symmes in 1791 and called it Walnut Hill. Kemper's legacy stretches far beyond naming Walnut Hills, however, as he and his family helped to establish the First Presbyterian Church of Walnut Hills and supported the development of the neighborhood as a racially and spiritually diverse community. During the 1830s, Kemper sold land to the Lane brothers, who opened the Lane Theological Seminary. The seminary was home to famous abolitionists Calvin and Harriet Beecher Stowe during those early years, and soon after Harriet moved out of Cincinnati, she published *Uncle Tom's Cabin*, one of the most influential books in the history of the United States.

Walk Description

Begin at the southeast intersection of Gilbert Avenue and William Howard Taft Road in front of the Alexandra Apartments. Before you set off, look to the northwest corner of the intersection, where you can see the lone remaining tower of the ❶ **Walnut Hills Presbyterian Church,** once a centerpiece of Walnut Hills life. This Gothic Revival church is another influential architectural gem designed by famous Cincinnati architect Samuel Hannaford. The church itself was founded in 1819 by Reverend James Kemper. This structure was erected in the late 19th century but underwent a variety of expansions through the 1930s. By the 21st century, much of the church had deteriorated beyond repair and was torn down and replaced with a parking lot. Preservation activists worked hard to successfully save the remaining tower.

Walk away from the tower and along William Howard Taft Road beside the Alexandra Apartments. This expansive property holds an important place in the development of Cincinnati's hillside neighborhoods, the original suburbs. When it was built in 1904, it was the largest apartment building in the city and a symbol of development patterns, including the expansion of residential life to the hillsides, the role of the streetcar in determining development, and the impact of population growth on residential styles.

Just beyond the apartments is the ❷ **Walnut Hills Branch Library.** This library opened just a couple of years after the Alexandra and was the first in the Cincinnati system to be financed by philanthropist Andrew Carnegie. The front columns and Tyler Davidson Fountain were both shipped from Munich.

Continue on William Howard Taft Road for two more blocks until you reach the Alms Hill Apartments. Originally built as the Hotel Alms in 1925, the expansive modern hotel had 500 rooms and a number of eccentric and glamorous amenities, including the Mermaid Lounge and Tokyo Garden. The towers were also used as a TV broadcasting site for WKRC.

Turn right onto Victory Parkway, where you'll walk through the tree-lined streets for several blocks as you approach Eden Park.

After crossing Cypress Street, a University of Cincinnati campus sits on your left at 2220 Victory Parkway. This site is home to Communiversity, a program of noncredit education programs designed for nonenrolled community members who enjoy ongoing education.

Follow the bend and keep right to continue on Victory Parkway. Take a slight left onto Eden Park Drive and enter Eden Park.

You'll first come upon the iconic **Twin Lakes.** If you'd like to add a short side trip, take the loop around the lakes to Twin Lakes Overlook, where you can find breathtaking views of the city.

Just beyond and opposite Twin Lakes is the **Eden Park Standpipe,** also designed by Samuel Hannaford and listed on the National Register of Historic Places. This historic water tower was erected in 1894 and, at that time, was an active channel in the water supply system in Walnut Hills.

Continue along Eden Park Drive and you'll quickly come upon the ❸ **Krohn Conservatory,** open Tuesday–Sunday, 10 a.m.–5 p.m. The conservatory hosts a variety of seasonal shows but is regionally most famous for the Butterfly Show, which runs mid-March–mid-June. Admission is $4, and if you have the time to visit, it's certainly worth it.

Follow Eden Park Drive around the bend and toward Mirror Lake. At this point, this walk abuts Walk 5: Mount Adams. Continue along Eden Park Drive and you'll pass the ❹ **Spring House Gazebo.** If the weather is nice, you're likely to see anything from engagements to wedding photo shoots at this park icon. Public restrooms are across the street. The gazebo also rests at the center of Cincinnati folklore as the location where famous bootlegger George Remus shot his ex-wife Imogene in the abdomen. Many claim that her ghost still occupies the park and gazebo today.

Stay left on the roundabout and continue along Eden Park Drive. Soon you'll see a bed of solar panels that, along with a wind turbine, power the park's administration building.

Exit the park and turn right onto Gilbert Avenue. Once you cross over Morris Street, you'll continue along Gilbert Avenue in the **Gilbert-Sinton Historic District.** Here you will find a number of Queen Anne and Shingle-style homes built between 1880 and 1900. This area was developed along the main streetcar corridor and offered a number of amenities within a short travel time for wealthy Cincinnatians. The neighborhood was established as a national historic district in 1983.

As you continue up Gilbert to return to your starting location, you'll pass several local businesses that reflect the history of the neighborhood's once-prominent African American Business District. Many African Americans took residency here at the beginning of the 19th century because Reverend Kemper was one of the few property owners to rent and sell land to African Americans.

If you're looking for a snack or a drink after all this walking, a number of great spots line Gilbert Avenue, including ❺ **The Greenwich,** a historic jazz club; ❻ **Gomez Salsa Cantina,** famous for its fresh ingredients and tasty burritos; and just left down McMillan Street, ❼ **Fireside Pizza.**

Walnut Hills

Points of Interest

1. **Walnut Hills Presbyterian Church** 2601 Gilbert Ave.
2. **Walnut Hills Branch Library** 2533 Kemper Ln., 513-369-6053, cincinnatilibrary.org/branches/walnuthills.html
3. **Krohn Conservatory** 1501 Eden Park Dr., 513-421-4086, cincinnatiparks.com/krohn
4. **Spring House Gazebo** Eden Park, cincinnatiparks.com/eden-park
5. **The Greenwich** 2442 Gilbert Ave., 513-221-1151, the-greenwich.com
6. **Gomez Salsa Cantina** 2437 Gilbert Ave., 513-954-8541, gomezsalsa.com
7. **Fireside Pizza** 773 E. McMillan St., 513-751-3473, firesidepizzawalnuthills.com

Connecting the Walks

You can extend this walk by adding Walk 5: Mount Adams. When you reach the Spring House Gazebo, head south, skirting Mirror Lake. Follow the route of Walk 5 back to Mirror Lake and then continue on Walk 6.

7 Clifton Heights, University Heights, and Fairview

Heights, Flights, and Hidden Sights

Above: St. George's is a prominent architectural presence at W. McMillan and Ravine Streets.

BOUNDARIES: Vine St., Calhoun St., Ohio Ave., Park Dr., Warner St., Ravine St., Fairview Rd., W. McMillan St., Clifton Ave.
DISTANCE: 3.3 miles
DIFFICULTY: Strenuous
PARKING: Parking in this part of town is a challenge. If you must drive instead of taking the bus, hailing a car, or riding a bike, there are sidewalk meters in the business district and free spots the farther you get from the center. One of these garages will gladly take your cash in exchange for a covered parking spot: Calhoun Garage (240 Calhoun St.), University Park Apartments Parking (238 Calhoun St.), USquare East Garage (211 Calhoun St.), USquare West Garage (301 Calhoun St.), and 121 West McMIllan St.
PUBLIC TRANSIT: Metro buses (go-metro.com) serve this area. Cincinnati Red Bike (cincyredbike.org) has nearby bicycle rental stations at 123 Calhoun and Dennis Streets and 166 W. McMillan and W. Clifton Streets, and elsewhere closer to UC.

This walk covers the hilltop neighborhood of Clifton Heights, University Heights, and Fairview immediately south of the University of Cincinnati (UC) main campus. It includes captivating views of the Cincinnati skyline, a slew of historic structures, hidden pathways, and food options at a variety of multicultural eateries. CUF, the official acronym used to describe the three communities that compose it, is often confused with Clifton, which is located north of UC and featured separately in this book in Walk 8. CUF is largely a rental area and functions as off-campus student housing. The busy business area of W. McMillan and Calhoun Streets between Vine Street and Clifton Avenue has changed dramatically over the past decade, while the residential sections south of W. McMillan remain remarkably intact and full of Italianate architecture in dense blocks. A generous helping of public space for leisure and recreation rounds out CUF's amenities.

Walk Description

Begin at **Inwood Park** near the southeast corner of Vine and E. Hollister Streets. The 20-acre park is a former stone quarry that was the source for many of the earliest buildings in Clifton Heights, originally an area called Rohs Hill. Walk through here now or explore its features following Walk 4: Mount Auburn. Across the street at 2347 Vine St. is the building that served as the headquarters of the International Union of United Brewery, Flour, Cereal and Soft Drink Workers from 1886 to 1973. Previously, in pre-Civil War days, the site was home to the Rohs and Co. Brewery. Today it is Ikron, a social services nonprofit organization.

Make your way uphill on Vine Street, and turn left at **Pitt Street**, the steepest alleyway in Cincinnati. Motor vehicles have never had through-access to W. McMillan Street above. Note the gaslights and brick sidewalks, including two former alley homes now part of **Hollister Triangle Park.** Nestled within the block bound between W. Hollister, W. McMillan, and Vine Streets, the pocket park was created as an accessible public space in 1979 through a plan to rehabilitate numerous residential properties on the block. Continue uphill on the cobblestone walkway to W. McMillan Street. To the right is **Melbourne Flats** (39 W. McMillan St.), built in 1898 and one of five structures in CUF on the National Register of Historic Places.

Use the crosswalk at W. McMillan Street and continue upward on Scioto Lane to Calhoun Street. Opposite Calhoun is the breathtaking ❶ **St. George's Catholic Church,** built in 1973 as the highest point in CUF for more than 100 years. Acclaimed Cincinnati architect Samuel Hannaford designed the building in the Romanesque Revival style. Due to declining membership, the parish was consolidated with St. Monica's and closed in 1993. A fire destroyed both steeples in 2008. Crossroads Church acquired the property and renovated it, rebuilding the steeples to scale.

Make a left on Calhoun Street and approach this rare collection of surviving 19th-century buildings that serve as a reminder of the historic commercial district that once dominated here. On the left is the second location of 43-year-old ❷ **Mole's Record Exchange.** A few more doors down is ❸ **Floyd's of Cincinnati Restaurant,** which serves Middle Eastern specialties in a casual dining area.

At the end of the block, make a left on Ohio Avenue. **Third Protestant Memorial Church** (2510 Ohio Ave.) is the former location of the first German congregation in Cincinnati that dated back to 1814. Founded in Over-the-Rhine, it relocated several times before moving up the hill to Clifton Heights, due to anti-German hysteria during World War I and a dwindling congregation. The church disbanded in 2001, and the building currently houses retailer Urban Outfitters.

Cross W. McMillan Street to continue on Ohio Avenue. The Italianate Christian Moerlein Residence near Detzel Place was the home of the local beer baron before his death in 1897. It is now rental units catering to students. Continue along Ohio Avenue until you reach the **Ohio Avenue Steps,** a pedestrian connection that dates back to the 1870s. It connects to a lower section of Ohio Avenue before crossing W. Clifton Avenue to Over-the-Rhine as a separate stairway.

Take a right up the primitive stone steps into the park. Named after the incline railway that operated from 1876 to 1926, the 400-foot-high **Bellevue Hill Park** features an extraordinary view of downtown Cincinnati and the surrounding Ohio River Valley. Architect R. Carl Freund designed the park pavilion, an example of organic architecture, built in 1955 as an outdoor dancing venue. Continue along circular Park Drive, and then continue north on Ohio Avenue. Cross Parker Street, and make a left on Warner Street. On the southwest corner of Clifton Avenue and Warner Street is ❹ **Murphy's Pub,** a neighborhood and student gathering spot since 1969.

Walk three more blocks to Chickasaw Street. The massive **Fairview Public School and Annex** was built at Warner Street and Stratford Avenue in 1888. Designed by renowned architect H. E. Siter, the city school was one of several designed in the Romanesque Revival style. Listed on the National Register of Historic Places, the building now contains The Stratford apartments.

Walk a few more blocks and cross Ravine Street. Turn left and follow the sidewalk to Fairview Park Road and turn right into **Fairview Park.** The hillside park, which was added to the city park system in 1931, forms a ridgeline that includes two extravagant overlook areas. Stone features were constructed during the Works Progress Administration, under the presidency of Franklin D. Roosevelt. The first overlook offers views into the West End, Over-the-Rhine, downtown Cincinnati, and distant Northern Kentucky. The second overlook offers an expanse into the west side of Cincinnati, including the Art Deco–style Western Hills Viaduct. Continue around Fairview Park Road to the **Warner Street Steps** off to the left, which connect to a section of well-preserved

Backstory: Spring in Our Steps

Founded in 2012, Spring in Our Steps is a nonprofit organization whose mission is to bring a brighter future mainly to neglected alleys and hillside stairways through cleanup projects, programming, preservation, and advocacy. Spring in Our Steps has led more than 150 cleanup events in 20 neighborhoods, and initiated more than 30 alley pop-up projects, from film screenings to karaoke and lawn bowling to art installations. In 2012, SiOS was able to make its mark on Plan Cincinnati, the city's first comprehensive update in 25 years, giving emphasis to alleys and stairways. In July 2017, a *Cincinnati CityBeat* cover story featured Spring in Our Steps, bringing the strongest attention to the city's walkable public space in generations. The following year, it catalyzed a partnership with ArtWorks and the Pendleton neighborhood, which provided cleanup support of a forgotten central alley corridor for the transformational installation of sanctioned graffiti art. Moving into its eighth year, Spring in Our Steps continues to evolve as a transformational driver of projects and advocacy for walkable public space. Ongoing initiatives include cleanup and preservation of Schorr Alley in Clifton Heights, clearance of the Isaac J. Miller switchback trail in Fairview Park, and support for renewal of stairway connections in South Fairmount.

homes in Fairview. An upper section of the stairs once connected to Fairview Avenue, where streetcars from the Fairview Incline served passengers from 1892 to 1923. Community pressure closed the upper stairway in the 1980s, although the neighborhood association is actively working today to have City Hall rebuild it. Warner Street served as the earliest commercial corridor in CUF, necessitating walking connections.

Continue ahead along Fairview Park Road about 450 feet to the trail extending down from Foxhall Court on the right for a view of the **Isaac J. Miller Residence and Wine Cellar.** It served as storage for a tavern up on Fairview Avenue at Foxhall Court. The former owner pushed for streetcar access to Fairview and the eventual opening of the Fairview Incline. While riders would have more easily accessed the tavern by the 1890s, the cellar could be accessed by the Miller estate (2367 Fairview Ave.) via a switchback trail, which neighborhood volunteers recently cleared and reestablished.

Continue to the end of Fairview Park Road and then turn right on W. McMillan Street. Residents have cleared weeds on the south side of McMillan and are soliciting City Hall to install a paved sidewalk from Fairview Park Road to Ravine Street and Fairview Avenue. **Police Station No. 7,** at W. McMillan and Ravine Streets, is a modest sample of the emblematic repertoire of Samuel Hannaford's architectural legacy. This 1895 building served as a satellite patrol station

Produce beds along W. McMillan Street bring together students and teachers at Hughes STEM High School.

for Cincinnati Police District 8. Today, the National Register–listed building is home to an Asian food market.

Continue walking along W. McMillan Street to ❺ **St. Monica–St. George Parish,** the one remaining active Catholic parish in CUF. It became a fixture at the three-way intersection in 1928 and briefly served as the Cathedral of the Archdiocese of Cincinnati in the 1940s and 1950s.

Continue on W. McMillan Street to Rohs Street, and turn right into the doors of ❻ **Rohs Street Cafe,** which has served the neighborhood since 2003. It functions as an extension of University Christian Church and provides a welcoming place for people to gather. It was the city's first fair-trade coffeehouse featuring locally roasted coffee, poetry readings, musical acts, and wooden tables and chairs primed for conversation, reading, and computer time.

Return to W. McMillan Street and head toward Clifton Avenue. The block ahead is similar to the 100 block of Calhoun Street, visited previously. Here you'll find mostly local businesses catering to students in older commercial buildings, unlike most other blocks on Calhoun and W. McMillan. On the right is ❼ **Campus Cyclery,** which has served students and bicycle nerds since

1975. CUF favorite ❽ **Cilantro Vietnamese Bistro** recently reopened with its original owner back in charge, much to the relief of lovers of this Vietnamese comfort food haven.

Cross Clifton Avenue at the northeast corner of W. McMillan Street. **Hughes STEM High School** (on the left) is the second-oldest public school in the city. The school dates back nearly 200 years to when Thomas Hughes, an Englishman and shoemaker, willed money for a school in 1826. The first incarnation was built at Fifth and Mound Streets downtown in 1853, before relocating to its present location in 1910. Known for its tall, central tower, it is a notable example of Tudor architecture.

Continue north on Clifton Avenue, and turn right on Calhoun Street. On the corner is ❾ **Fortune Noodle House,** a *real* noodle house smack-dab in the middle of CUF. Continue east on Calhoun Street, crossing W. Clifton Avenue. Walk an additional 500 feet across from the sloped lawn of the University of Cincinnati College—Conservatory of Music. To the right is the **University YMCA.** Now defunct, it began as a student-operated chapter as early as 1890. An official branch was dedicated in 1915. Because the school lacked an on-campus venue for spiritual and social activities, the Gamble estate made a considerable donation, which made construction of this location possible in 1930. It is known for its ornate clubroom space and enduring use as a cafeteria. If all goes well, it will (hopefully) find new life soon as the home of the UC Alumni Association.

Walk to W. Clifton Avenue and turn right. Near the corner of W. McMillan Street are three eateries that combine good food with beer for a (mostly) college crowd. They all help offset the increasingly corporate vibe of CUF. ❿ **Chicago Gyros and Dogs** features gussied-up hot dogs, gyros, and plenty of beer. ⓫ **Drunken Tacos Nightlife Café** offers chips and salsa, Mexican street corn, and other Mexican fare. In addition to Drunken Tacos, owner Inho Cha operates Drunken Bento a few doors down on W. McMillan Street. A Clifton Heights institution, ⓬ **Mac's Pizza Pub** effortlessly captures restaurant business during the day and the bar and pizza crowd at night.

Make a left on W. McMillan Street and head back to W. Hollister Street. For a final historic reference, the **Joseph A. Hemann House** (39 W. Hollister St., previously 49 W. McMillan St.) was built in 1870 as the home of the founder of the Cincinnati Volksfreund, a German-American newspaper. He served on the building committee of Old Saint George, one block away. Make a right on W. Hollister Street and return to Inwood Park.

(continued on next page)

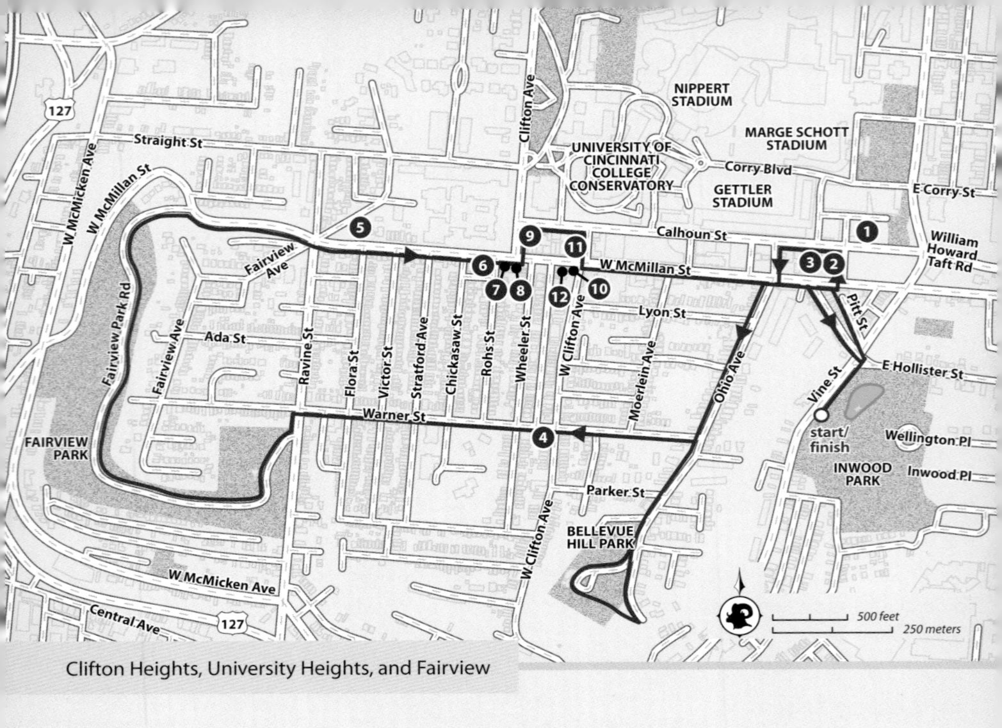

Clifton Heights, University Heights, and Fairview

Points of Interest

1. **St. George's Catholic Church/Crossroads Church** 42 Calhoun St.
2. **Mole's Record Exchange** 111 Calhoun St., 513-861-6291
3. **Floyd's of Cincinnati Restaurant** 127 Calhoun St., 513-221-2434
4. **Murphy's Pub** 2329 W. Clifton Ave., 513-721-6148, murphys-pub.com
5. **St. Monica–St. George Parish** 328 W. McMillan St., 513-381-6400
6. **Rohs Street Cafe** 245 W. McMillan St., rohsstreetcafe.com
7. **Campus Cyclery** 241 W. McMillan St., 513-721-6628, campuscyclery.com
8. **Cilantro Vietnamese Bistro** 235 W. McMillan St., 513-281-1732, eatatcilantro.com
9. **Fortune Noodle House** 349 Calhoun St., 513-281-1800, fortunenoodles.com
10. **Chicago Gyros and Dogs** 201 W. McMillan St., 513-621-3828, chicagogyrosanddogs.com
11. **Drunken Tacos Nightlife Café** 200 W. McMillan St., 513-721-9111
12. **Mac's Pizza Pub** 205 W. McMillan St., 513-241-6227, macsonmcmillan.com

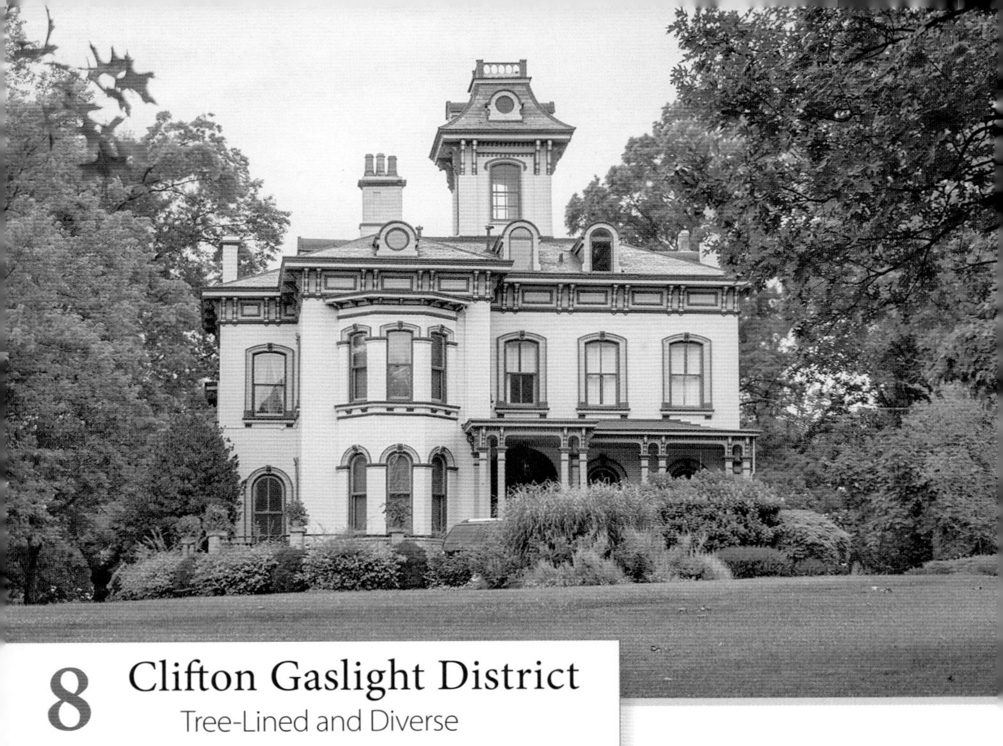

8 Clifton Gaslight District

Tree-Lined and Diverse

Above: Historic mansions set amid gardens and woodlands line the northern section of Clifton.

BOUNDARIES: Brookline Ave., Woolper Ave., Whitfield Ave., Burnet Woods Dr.
DISTANCE: 2.8 miles
DIFFICULTY: Easy
PARKING: Free street parking on Glenmary Ave., Loraine Ave., and Brookline Ave.
PUBLIC TRANSIT: Cincinnati Red Bike (cincyredbike.org) has nearby bicycle rental stations at 321 Howell Ave. and Clifton, Clifton Branch Library, and elsewhere closer to UC. Metro buses (go-metro.com) serve this area.

At night, the old lamps that light the tree-lined lanes of Clifton give the area its name: Gaslight District. Above-shop apartments, lovely old brick houses, and 19th-century mansions create a vibrant community that is racially and socioeconomically diverse, and liberal-leaning politically. Ludlow Avenue is the historic commercial center of Clifton and offers a varied range of fun independent shops, a pharmacy and hardware store, eateries aplenty, and an independent movie theater. The environment feels busy and not overwhelming, and there's something for most everyone.

The first half of this walk surveys a few of the calm gas-lit streets and beautiful old homes before heading to the Ludlow business strip. If you take this walk at twilight, you can watch the gaslights come on and end your evening being entertained on Ludlow. Or, if you are out for the afternoon, the second half makes its way away from the main stretch of shops and heads into Burnet Woods Park—a splash of green, fresh air, and shade in the middle of the city. You can extend the walk—and your own sense of calm—with a loop around Burnet Woods pond.

For Cincinnati residents, the name *Clifton* encompasses many of the nearby neighborhoods, including the University of Cincinnati, the CUF area (Clifton Heights–University Heights–Fairview), and Corryville. Though this tour focuses on Clifton, there's plenty to explore a short distance away.

Walk Description

Begin at the intersection of Glenmary and Clifton Avenues. Stay on the east side and walk a short distance north (toward Resor Avenue) to see the historic **Sir Alfred T. Goshorn House** (3540 Clifton Ave.), a National Register of Historic Places site built in 1888. Its size and Richardsonian Romanesque architecture hint at the wealth and culture that characterized the original settlements in Clifton. James W. McLaughlin designed the house for Goshorn, a businessman who

In the background, the Temple of Love gazebo-pavilion is all that remains of the 19th-century estate of Robert Bowler in Mt. Storm Park.

became internationally famous for his work heading up the Centennial Exposition in Philadelphia in 1876 (he was knighted by Queen Victoria).

Clifton Methodist Episcopal Church and Probasco Fountain are located within 0.25 mile to the south and north, respectively. Continue walking north to see more palatial buildings listed on the National Register. The Clifton Avenue Historic District represents a variety of architectural styles usually reserved for wealthy homeowners during the latter part of the 19th century.

Cross Clifton Avenue carefully (traffic moves quickly here) and walk left (south), back in the direction of Glenmary.

Turn right on Bryant Avenue. On the streets ahead, take note of the sturdy construction and plethora of stained glass windows. Mostly you'll see single-family houses, though a fair number of large old buildings now hold apartments, such as the ones you'll see on your left as you approach Telford Street.

Turn right on Telford Street. You'll see a fine example of a Victorian-era mansion at 3502 Telford St., **Conversa Manor,** home to a rotating bunch of international students, most of whom attend the University of Cincinnati.

Turn left on Thrall Street. On these back streets, continue to notice the decorative details and varied architectural styles. Remembering to be respectful of current residents, you'll particularly want to note **Blenheim** (334 Thrall St.), which is designed in a Dutch style, unlike many of its neighbors, and has a mural of Mespelbrunn Castle in Germany on its facade.

Turn right on Middleton Avenue. As you walk, be sure to look for the gas lamps that give the area its name. Cincinnati Gas Light and Coke Company installed the first gas lamps in the 1840s. By 1875 Cincinnati had more than 5,000 public gas lamps. By 1901, when Cincinnati Gas Light and Coke became Cincinnati Gas & Electric (a forerunner to Duke Energy), it was clear that electricity was the way of the future. Today, more than 1,100 of the gas lamps are still in use all over Cincinnati and collectively comprise a nationally registered historic district.

Detour: If you are interested in the work of American architect Frank Lloyd Wright, you can add a short detour of about 0.5 mile that will allow you to see one of three of his houses in Cincinnati. Turn right on Middleton, go 0.3 mile, and then turn left on Rawson Woods Lane. At the first right, on Rawson Woods Circle, look up ahead through the trees to spot the **Boulter House** (1 Rawson Woods Cir., wrightboulter.com). This two-story Usonian house was built in 1956 (toward the end of Wright's life) for Cedric and Patricia Boulter, who were Greek scholars at the University of Cincinnati. Although not much of the house can be seen from the street, many of Wright's brilliant Usonian details are found here. To get back to the main route, retrace your steps to Evanswood Place off Middleton.

Turn right on Evanswood Place and walk slightly uphill. Turn left on Whitfield Avenue. Like Thrall, this street has low traffic, and more of the especially large and stately homes sit side by side, particularly on the right (west) side. On the porch of 3463, perhaps you can see a bright pink pig statue, a reminder of the 2002 citywide art project known as the Big Pig Gig. Hundreds of the fiberglass pigs are scattered throughout the city, a tribute to Cincinnati's role in the history of the meatpacking industry.

Turn left on Bryant Avenue (again) for one short block, and then turn right on Middleton Avenue (again). Up ahead you'll see the CVS sign on bustling Ludlow Avenue, marking the end of the quiet residential part of your walk.

Turn left on Ludlow Avenue, where residents of Clifton historically came to get their goods. Current residents still do much of their shopping here, while visitors from across the city come here looking for a relaxing afternoon or a nice evening out. Some highlights of the Ludlow strip are mentioned here, though you are encouraged to spend time ducking into other businesses as well.

Across the street on the right is the **Roanoke** apartment building (369 Ludlow Ave.). Built in 1900, the Roanoke is an iconic apartment building in Clifton, with its redbrick facade, courtyard entrance, and three-story portico. It was featured as the apartment for Harry Connick Jr.'s character in *Little Man Tate*, a 1991 film from actress-director Jodie Foster.

On your left you'll see a pair of Indian restaurants, ❶ **Grill of India** and ❸ **Ambar India,** with ❷ **Habanero,** a popular non-chain burrito place, in between. Just past Ambar is the old Ludlow Garage. Originally an automobile shop, for less than two years (between 1969 and 1971), the Garage was a rock-and-roll venue that held pieces of the original Woodstock sound system and hosted big-name acts like The Allman Brothers and Santana. While the first floor holds multiple local businesses, the lower level is a music venue called ❹ **The Ludlow Garage.**

A few more doors down you'll find one of two grocery stores on Ludlow. It is rare these days for an older neighborhood to have one grocery store—let alone two—in a walkable neighborhood business district. First is ❺ **Clifton Natural Foods,** and across the street, ❻ **Clifton Market.**

At Telford Street is a Cincinnati mainstay—❼ **Graeter's** "irresistible" ice cream. The ice creams, made using a French pot process, will certainly melt your heart—if frozen dairy is your thing—after a satisfying dinner on Ludlow. You can take your cones directly across the street and hang out at the tables on quiet **Clifton Plaza,** which features a summer music festival and other events.

Just past Clifton Plaza, a pair of wonderful coffee shops hugs Ludlow on either side: ❽ **Sitwell's Act II,** on the left, and ❾ **Lydia's on Ludlow** on the right. Both are cozy, colorful, and calm places to hang out, with local and organic foods featured.

Just past Lydia's is ⓾ **Toko Baru,** an adorable store crammed with truly fun items that are perfect for gifts—wooden products, fabrics, cards, home goods. Across the street, next to Sitwell's, is ⓫ **Esquire Theatre,** an independent movie theater. Originally opened in 1911 to show silent films, it now has six screens and draws folks from all over the city who are looking for something outside the mainstream.

A little farther down Ludlow on the right side is ⓬ **Arlin's Bar & Restaurant,** another wonderful community cornerstone. It has a lively and comfortable atmosphere, frequent live music, and a large patio out back. Next door is **Cincinnati Fire Department Station 34,** a classic neighborhood fire station built in 1906 to serve the surrounding community. Across the street, on the corner of Clifton Avenue, you'll find **Adrian Durban,** a family-owned florist.

When you reach the Clifton Avenue intersection, cross to the northeast corner (the corner with Skyline Chili) and continue up Ludlow. ⓭ **Skyline Chili** is well known to Cincinnatians, serving up Cincinnati-style chili on hot dogs (coneys) and spaghetti for generations. Open since 1966, it's one of the few locations that maintains the original old-time feel. Whether you pause now to try it or just peek in the steamy window on your way past, keep in mind that Skyline's chili is more than fast food, and the dining experience is more than the chili.

Across Ludlow from Skyline, you'll see **Diggs Fountain Plaza.** Finished in 2002, the center of the 3,000-square-foot community meeting spot is an 8-foot-tall bronze figure of a woman (ArtWorks CEO Tamara Harkavy) with her arms raised, designed by local artist Matt Kotlarczyk, Tamara's husband. The plaza, composed of natural rock walls and a granite walking surface with steps, is named in memory of Matthew O'Brien Diggs III, whose family was a major donor. The perennial garden that runs along Ludlow is named after former Cincinnati Reds owner Marge Schott's family name, Unnewehr.

Continue up Ludlow on the left (north) side. You will notice a few more local businesses, including the back side of ⓮ **Dewey's Pizza,** a popular neighborhood outpost from the local chain known for its inventive pizzas, fresh salads, and seasonal craft beers.

Ludlow becomes more residential again the farther you get from Clifton Avenue. You'll pass the four-story brick **Marburg Hotel** (260 Ludlow Ave.), built in 1902, with its old ghost sign. In 1960, the University of Cincinnati converted the hotel into a women's dorm (Ludlow Hall) until a new dorm was completed. In 1974, UC sold Ludlow Hall, and the dormitory closed at the end of the year. It has remained apartments since.

Also on the left is **Enoch T. Carson Lodge** (218 Ludlow Ave.), a well-maintained brick fraternal lodge that features an annual Laurel and Hardy film festival that amuses fans of this slapstick comedic pair from the early Hollywood era of American cinema.

As you cross Brookline Avenue, ⓯ **Parkview Manor** is on your left. Built in 1894, the sandstone home was designed by notable Cincinnati architect Samuel B. Hannaford for the infamous George B. "Boss" Cox, who controlled Cincinnati politics for more than 25 years in the late 19th century. Boss Cox lived and entertained here until his death in 1916. After the death of his widow in 1938, the building had various uses during the 20th century (including as a fraternity house) and is now home to the Clifton Branch Library.

As you cross Ludlow and walk down Brookline into 90-acre Burnet Woods, you'll see a shaded picnic area with swings that is accessible via stairs just before the ⓰ **Trailside Nature Center.** A wonderful, smooth stone slide next to the stairs offers a quicker descent. The nature center is an impressive fieldstone building, constructed in 1939, with the influence of Frank Lloyd Wright reflected in its design.

Just past the nature center is Burnet Woods Lake. To extend your walk around the lake, enter the trail on the left side of the pond, where people may be fishing. Enjoy a quiet walk or sit on the low brick wall on the left side to enjoy the reflections of the trees and sky in the water.

Follow the trail around the edges of the lake. When you are on the west side of the lake (the opposite side from your starting point), you will find that the trail leads you to a set of steps that will take you up to the paved Burnet Woods Drive.

To return to your starting point, simply follow Burnet Woods Drive west up the hill and to the right around the historic bandstand, and eventually down to Clifton Avenue. Turn right and walk along the western edge of Burnet Woods. Once you cross Ludlow, you are treated to more regal brick homes and a few more gas lamps before reaching Glenmary Avenue and your starting point.

Points of Interest

❶ **Grill of India** 354 Ludlow Ave., 513-961-3600

❷ **Habanero** 358 Ludlow Ave., 513-961-6800, habanerolatin.com

❸ **Ambar India Restaurant** 350 Ludlow Ave., 513-281-7000, ambarindia.com

❹ **The Ludlow Garage** 342 Ludlow Ave., 513-221-4111, ludlowgaragecincinnati.com

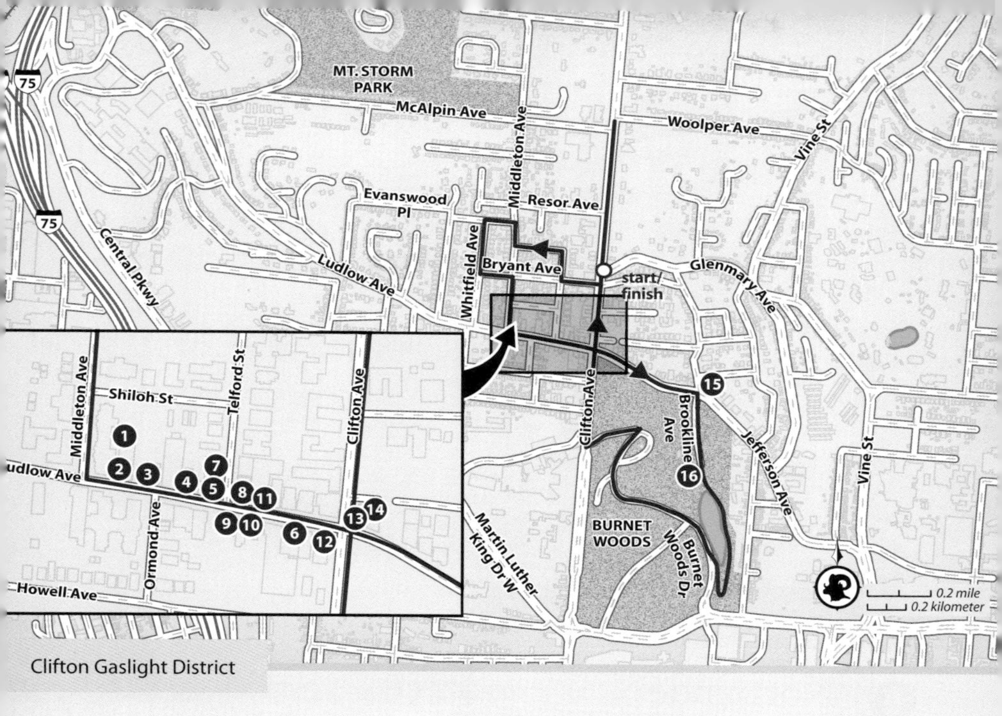

5. **Clifton Natural Foods** 336 Ludlow Ave., 513-961-6111, cliftonnaturalfoods.com
6. **Clifton Market** 319 Ludlow Ave., 513-861-3000, cliftonmarket.com
7. **Graeter's** 332 Ludlow Ave., 513-281-4749, graeters.com
8. **Sitwell's Act II** 324 Ludlow Ave., 513-281-7487, sitwellsact2.com
9. **Lydia's on Ludlow** 329 Ludlow Ave., 513-381-3436, aquariusstar.com
10. **Toko Baru** 325 Ludlow Ave., 513-751-3338
11. **Esquire Theatre** 320 Ludlow Ave., 513-281-8750, esquiretheatre.com
12. **Arlin's Bar & Restaurant** 307 Ludlow Ave., 513-751-6566
13. **Skyline Chili** 290 Ludlow Ave., 513-221-2142, skylinechili.com
14. **Dewey's Pizza** 265 Hosea Ave., 513-221-0400, deweyspizza.com
15. **Parkview Manor/Clifton Branch Library** 3400 Brookline Ave., 513-369-4447, cincinnatilibrary.org/branches/clifton.html
16. **Trailside Nature Center** Burnet Woods Park, 3251 Brookline Ave., 513-751-3679, cincinnatiparks.com

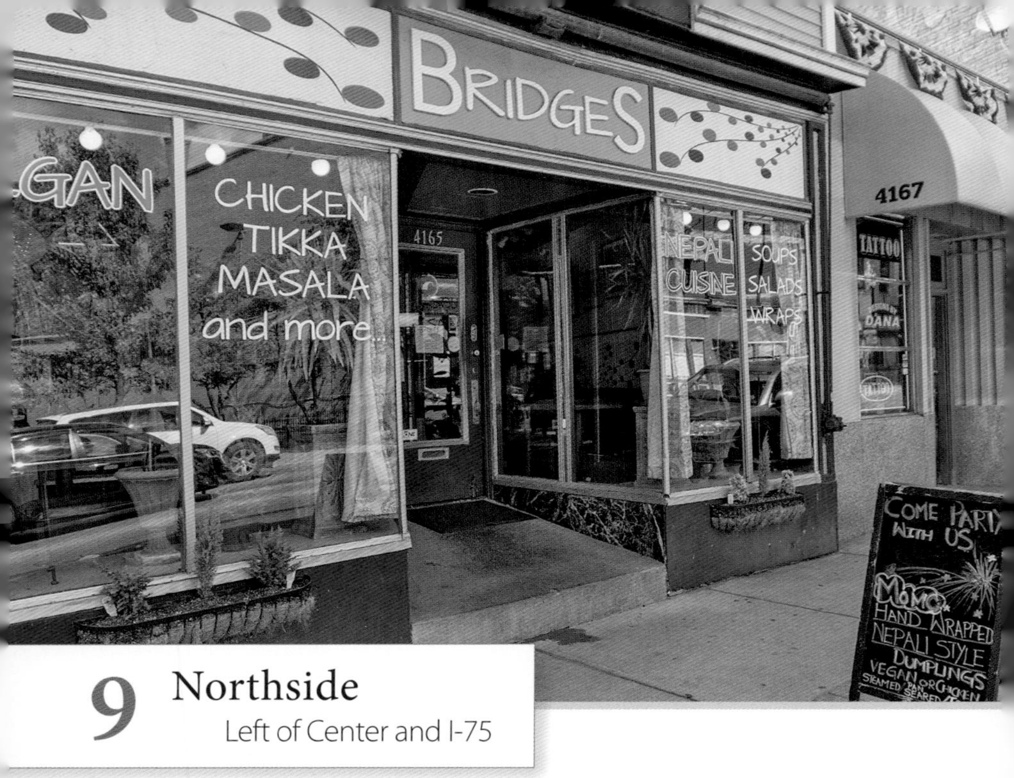

9 Northside

Left of Center and I-75

Above: Bridges Restaurant on Hamilton Avenue serves Nepali cuisine.

BOUNDARIES: Blue Rock St., Hamilton Ave., Stanford Dr., Buttercup Valley Nature Preserve
DISTANCE: 2.8 miles
DIFFICULTY: Moderate–strenuous
PARKING: Northside Business District maintains several metered lots throughout the business district. The closest lot to the start of the walk sits behind the Hamilton Ave. storefronts (Tillie's and SkinCraft, for example) off Blue Rock St. on the southeast corner of the block. Other metered street parking is available on Hamilton or any of the side streets nearby.
PUBLIC TRANSIT: Northside is one of the bus hubs of the city, so it's very easy to get to and from here on a bus. At Hamilton Ave. and Blue Rock Rd. you can find the 15X, 17, 27, 1112, 1712, 1741, 1742, 1791, 2412, 3111, 3114, and 3311. Around the corner on Blue Rock, the 19, 51, 1111, 2111, 2161, 2411, 3112, 3113, 4014, and 4034. Also at Blue Rock and Hoffner is the Hoffner Park Red Bike Station.

Northside residents pride themselves on the neighborhood's balance of locally owned shops, arts and culture, and diversity without the pretentious feel of more gentrified neighborhoods. The annual Fourth of July parade is a shining example of the mix of fun, culture, progressive-leaning tendencies, and *ars gratia artis* that the neighborhood embraces. Northside boasts one of the largest and most active community councils in the city, and its established community endeavors include everything from a farmers market to a bicycle co-op.

The Northside neighborhood was historically a part of Cumminsville, a destination for Cincinnati dwellers in the mid-1800s, and was annexed by the City of Cincinnati in 1873. When I-74 was built in 1974, the neighborhood of Cumminsville was split in two. South Cumminsville retained its name while North Cumminsville became known as Northside.

This walk explores the main commercial corridor of Hamilton Avenue, ventures into a couple of adjacent residential streets, and makes a loop within Buttercup Valley Nature Preserve, which has been undeveloped since the earliest local settlements and is home to 200-year-old trees. Hamilton Avenue follows the paths of trails originally set by the American Indians in the 18th century.

One of the most exciting times to visit Northside is during the monthly Second Saturday event— each month features new art openings, interactive events, extended hours at most businesses, and many special food and drink promotions.

Walk Description

Start at ❶ **Jacob Hoffner Park** at the intersection of Blue Rock Street and Hamilton Avenue. A 2-acre grassy area designed to look like an old-fashioned town green, Hoffner Park hosts the Northside farmers market and other community events. This area was formerly the Hoffner estate, owned by Jacob Hoffner, who came from Pennsylvania to the Cumminsville area in the early 19th century and bought up about 50 acres of land. Hoffner was active in the economic growth of Cumminsville and donated land to the Cincinnati, Hamilton & Dayton (CHD) train station as well as to the Hoffner Masonic Lodge (see below). In 1978 the Hoffner Historic District was officially designated and listed on the National Register of Historic Places.

Begin walking north along Hamilton Avenue, away from Blue Rock. Hamilton Avenue is the main commercial thoroughfare of Northside, lined with historical mixed-use buildings and pedestrian-friendly storefronts. The avenue was named after Alexander Hamilton, as he was secretary of the treasury at the time of its development in the late 18th century.

As you approach Palm Avenue, look across the street to find the ❷ **Hoffner Masonic Lodge,** designed by famous Cincinnati architect Samuel Hannaford and built in 1885. Always an important part of the Northside community, it has at various times contained a Kroger store, a post office, North Side Bank & Trust, and other businesses. It now hosts the full-service bike shop Spun Bicycles and the Listing Loon Craft Beer & Wine Shop, as well as a rentable event space on the second floor.

After crossing Knowlton Street, 100 yards down Hamilton, you'll find ❸ **Northside Tavern.** It may seem small at first, but keep going: you'll find rooms continuing back and back—enough to accommodate two bars, a pool table, free live music almost every night of the week, and a lot of laid-back coziness that perfectly suits Northside.

Just after Northside Tavern is ❹ **Bridges,** a South Asian restaurant with fresh Nepali cuisine. Bridges initially opened as a stall at Findlay Market and moved to this storefront in 2017.

Continuing along Hamilton, you'll find ❺ **Sidewinder,** an independent coffee shop. Sidewinder has all your favorite coffee concoctions, plus its own creative drinks, a food menu, Wi-Fi, and a small gravel patio out back.

At the corner of Hamilton and Chase Avenues, you'll see another nationally registered historic site: the Domhoff Buildings, completed in 1893. Today, the Domhoff commercial space is home to the nonprofit ❻ **Happen, Inc.,** which specializes in awesome art learning experiences, including free parent-and-kid art classes.

Continuing on Hamilton, you'll pass the ❼ **Northside Branch of the Public Library** in a 1908 building that still bears Northside's original name, Cumminsville.

As you continue along Hamilton, you'll find Jergens Park on the left just before the intersection of Hamilton and Bruce Avenues. This site was once home to a beautiful castlelike estate, but owner Andrew Jergens instructed the executors of his estate to tear down the building if none of his heirs chose to live there, so they did. In 1970 the park was named after him.

Climb the hill along a residential stretch of Hamilton Avenue. If you're walking in the summer, you'll pass beautiful gardens, as well as some grandiose Victorian and Colonial historic homes at the intersections.

At 4579 Hamilton you'll find ❽ **The Comet,** a local favorite that manages to combine a chill dive-bar vibe with tacos and outer space. This is a great place for an approximately halfway break.

One block beyond The Comet you'll turn right onto Stanford Drive. This street is a great display of the diversity of single-family homes nestled just outside the Northside Business District. Continue along Stanford until you come to the end of the street and the entry sign for the Buttercup Valley Nature Preserve. This land has been untouched by developers since pioneer days and was donated to the Cincinnati Park Board in 1973 by the Greater Cincinnati Tree Council.

For the next mile, you'll walk along a dirt trail through the beautiful forest of Buttercup Valley Nature Preserve and over some hand-built wooden bridges. If you're not up for this adventure, you can navigate back to Hamilton Avenue, down the hill, and back to the beginning. If you have the time, though, definitely explore this urban park oasis.

Follow the B loop through the Buttercup Valley Nature Preserve and into the Parker Woods Preserve and around to Bruce Avenue. The Parker Woods Preserve was sold to the park board in 1911 by Alexander Langlands Parker, the grandson of the original owner, and has served the neighborhood as protected parkland since. Enjoy the oak trees and wildflowers along the trails.

You'll reenter the neighborhood at Bruce Avenue and Haight Street. Follow Bruce one block to Hamilton Avenue and turn left to trace your way back to where the walk began.

At Chase and Hamilton you'll find Salon Gorgeous, a favorite Cincinnati hair salon owned by longtime Northsider Edgar Gonzalez.

After crossing Lingo Street, you'll find delicious comfort food at ❾ **Blue Jay Restaurant.** Next door is ❿ **Shake It Records,** where creaky wood floors, wall-to-wall vinyl, a stocked-up basement, and plenty of merch will welcome music lovers home like no other place in the city.

After crossing little Moline Court, check out the drink selection at ⓫ **Listing Loon** or ask a bike question at ⓬ **Spun Bicycles.** Next door, the ⓭ **Chameleon** bills itself as your neighborhood nightclub, complete with games, lounge, and umbrella-covered patio.

You'll complete the walk by passing ⓮ **Higher Gravity,** a bar and bottle store with 500-plus beers, and ⓯ **Melt Revival,** a hip dining spot for health-oriented sandwiches, soups, and salads. Melt Revival is owned by Cincinnati's famous mixologist Molly Wellman and is home to a full-service cocktail bar.

(continued on next page)

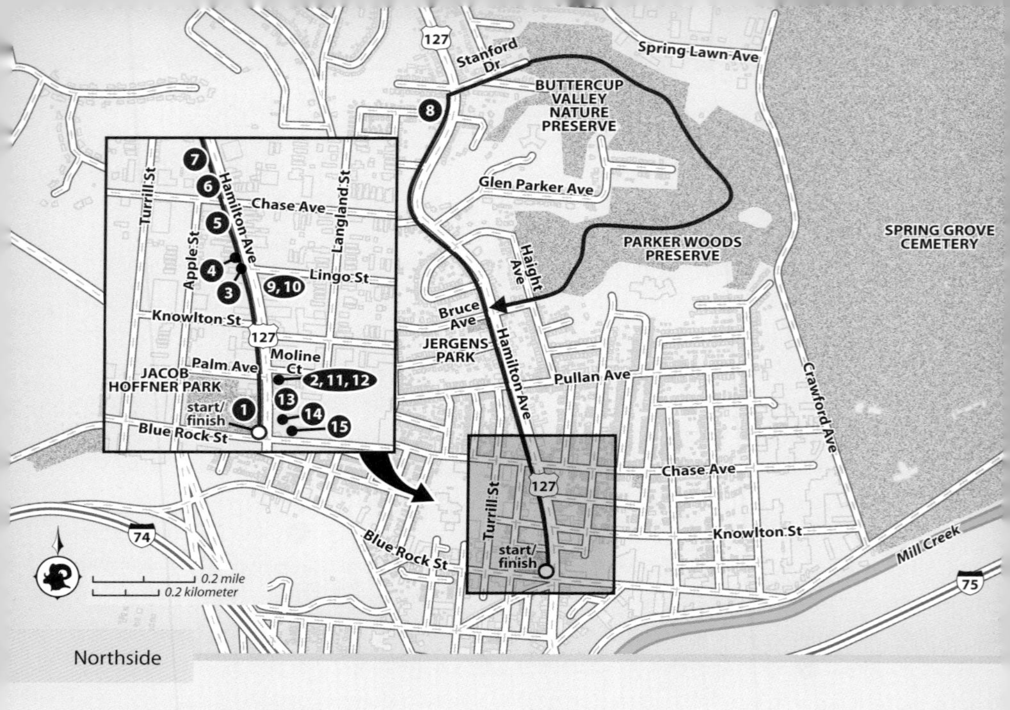

Northside

Points of Interest

1. **Jacob Hoffner Park** 4104 Hamilton Ave., cincinnatiparks.com/jacob-hoffner-park
2. **Hoffner Masonic Lodge** 4120 Hamilton Ave., hoffnerlodge.com
3. **Northside Tavern** 4163 Hamilton Ave., 513-542-3603, northsidetav.com/cincy
4. **Bridges** 4165 Hamilton Ave., 513-374-9354, bridgesnorthside.weebly.com
5. **Sidewinder** 4181 Hamilton Ave., 513-542-8321, sidewindercoffee.com
6. **Happen, Inc. (Domhoff Buildings)** 4201 Hamilton Ave., 513-751-2345, happeninc.com
7. **Northside Library** 4219 Hamilton Ave., 513-369-4449, cincinnatilibrary.org/branches/northside.html
8. **The Comet** 4579 Hamilton Ave., 513-541-8900, cometbar.com
9. **Blue Jay Restaurant** 4154 Hamilton Ave., 513-541-0847
10. **Shake It Records** 4156 Hamilton Ave., 513-591-0123, shakeitrecords.com
11. **Listing Loon** 4124 Hamilton Ave., 513-542-5666
12. **Spun Bicycles** 4122 Hamilton Ave., 513-541-7786, spunbicycles.com
13. **Chameleon** 4114 Hamilton Ave., 513-541-2073, chameleonpizza.com
14. **Higher Gravity** 4106 Hamilton Ave., 513-813-3523, highergravitycrafthaus.com
15. **Melt Revival** 4100 Hamilton Ave., 513-818-8951, meltrevival.com

10 College Hill
Diverse Hilltop Neighborhood

Above: The Peter G. Thomson House, commonly known as Laurel Court, is listed on the National Register of Historic Places.

BOUNDARIES: W. North Bend Rd., Hamilton Ave., Larch Ave., Meryton Pl.
DISTANCE: 3.7 miles
DIFFICULTY: Moderate
PARKING: Metered parking on Hamilton Ave., or park in the public lot at 1555 W. North Bend Rd.
PUBLIC TRANSIT: Take Metro route 17 to Hamilton Ave. and North Bend Rd. (go-metro.com)

Located 6 miles north of downtown, College Hill is the fourth-most populous neighborhood in Cincinnati and a welcoming home to people of all ages, races, and incomes. It's filled with 19th-century cottage-style homes and apartment buildings dating from the 1920s and retains a semirural village atmosphere on the city's northern edge. Originally a wealthy suburb called Pleasant Hill, it was renamed College Hill because of the two colleges (Farmers' College and Ohio Female College) that were established here in the mid-19th century. The most notable early settler was William Cary, who bought 491 acres in 1813 and became known as the founding father of College Hill. College Hill was incorporated as a village in 1866 and annexed into the City of Cincinnati in stages between 1911 and 1923. It features several buildings on the National Register of Historic Places, protected forests on its southern edges, tree-lined and gaslit streets, and a resurgent business district, which locals lovingly call The Avenue, along Hamilton Avenue.

Walk Description

Start your walk at Hamilton Avenue and W. North Bend Road with a cup of coffee at ❶ **College Hill Coffee Co.,** which sometimes appears in *The Dinette Set,* a nationally syndicated comic strip by Julie Larson. (Shop owner Tina Stoeberl's partner, Elizabeth Sherwood, is a fan of the strip and

The Contemporary Dance Theater currently occupies the former College Hill Town Hall, designed by prominent Cincinnati architect Samuel Hannaford.

began exchanging emails with Larson several years ago.) This is the northernmost business in College Hill's historic commercial district. The east side of this block is filled with locally owned businesses that attract residents and visitors alike. Walk south past ❷ **Bacalls Cafe,** ❸ **Schwartz Jewelers,** ❹ **Marty's Hops and Vines,** and ❺ **Silk Road Textiles.**

Cross Elkton Place. Across the street is Hodapp Funeral Home, on the site where William Cary built his first log home. On the left is ❻ **Fern,** a home décor store in a converted gas station. Across Ambrose Avenue, at 6036 Hamilton Ave., is a single-family residence located in the former College Hill Savings and Loan. Continue south on Hamilton Avenue. On the southeast corner of Marlowe Avenue in the former National City Bank is ❼ **Kiki,** a Japanese restaurant from the cofounder and former owner of Over-the-Rhine's Kaze; it features curry doughnuts. Cross Hamilton Avenue, and walk west along Marlowe Avenue. To the left, at 5917 Hamilton Ave., is the region's second location for ❽ **Tortilleria Garcia,** best known for its tortilla machine, which allows customers to see the tortillas being made in front of them.

Continue west along Marlowe Avenue and pass Budmar Avenue. On the right, at 1654 Marlowe Ave., is former Cincinnati Fire Station #51, built in 1914 and later renovated into a single-family home. The fire station moved to new, larger LEED-certified quarters at the corner of Hamilton and Llanfair Avenues. Turn left on Cary Avenue and walk to Cedar Avenue. Look right to 5865 Lathrop Pl. to see the William T. Simpson House, which features an 1880s roofline topped with elaborate ironwork and 20th-century Tudor elements. Turn left on Cedar Avenue and walk past stately College Hill Fundamental Academy (1625 Cedar Ave.).

Return to Hamilton Avenue. This is the business district's most intact intersection. On the southwest corner is a former branch of the Brighton Bank from 1923, which still houses a bank. On the northwest corner is the Dow Corner building (a reminder of the local Dow Pharmacy chain), which the College Hill Community Urban Redevelopment Corporation partly owns and is redeveloping. A newer addition to Hamilton Avenue is ❾ **Brink Brewing Co.** The microbrewery has received multiple medals in the U.S. Open Bar Championship and was named Very Small Brewing Company of the Year in 2018 at the Great American Beer Festival. With a sleek industrial vibe, it has a large menu of beer types.

Like the Dow building, the oldest commercial buildings north of here are set at angles to conform to lot lines. During the 1920s, College Hill residents went to Hollywood Theater (5920 Hamilton Ave.) for good times. It closed in the 1990s. Immediately to the south is Italianate-style Ruthellen Apartments (5906 Hamilton Ave.). Turn right on Hamilton Avenue and walk south to Groesbeck Road. On the left is the impressive ❿ **College Hill Presbyterian Church** from 1889.

Cross Linden Drive and walk to Larch Avenue. Across the street is the Samuel Hayden House (5654 Hamilton Ave.), named for the grocer who originally occupied it in 1869. Turn right on Larch Avenue. This long, narrow street is lined with cottage-style houses that contribute to College Hill's strong residential character. College Hill is one of 13 neighborhoods with gaslights, which are present here on Larch. Walk past Davey Avenue to vast College Hill Park on the left. At its center is the former ⓫ **College Hill Town Hall,** the only public building owned by the village before its annexation. Designed by Samuel Hannaford before he started a partnership with two of his sons, this impressive three-story building from 1886 combines both Greek Revival and Renaissance Revival influences and is listed on the National Register of Historic Places. **Contemporary Dance Theater** (1805 Larch Ave., 513-591-1222, cdt-dance.org) uses the building for rehearsals and performances.

Turn right on Belmont Avenue, where some of College Hill's finest homes can be found. On the right, at 5752 Belmont Ave., is the Charles Cist House. A Cincinnati historian who compiled important reference material on the city's first 50 years, Cist retired here in 1853. Continue walking north on Belmont and cross Llanfair Avenue. On the right is the former Flamm's Grocery (5802 Belmont Ave.), which occupied this building in 1887. The store closed in the 1920s, and the building was later converted into apartments. Cross Cedar Avenue and walk to spectacular ⓬ **Laurel Court.** Designed by James Gamble Rogers for Peter G. Thompson and built between 1902 and 1907, this Beaux Arts Renaissance masterpiece is listed on the National Register of Historic Places. It is one of Cincinnati's most iconic residences. Behind Laurel Court is Mercy-McAuley High School, an all-girls private Roman Catholic high school. Cross Belmont Avenue at Oakwood Avenue, reportedly the highest natural point in Hamilton County.

Past this intersection is ⓭ **The Oaks.** This stately mansion was built around a smaller house. Behind it was once a shed with a concealed hiding place, thought to be used for the Underground Railroad. A lot of movers and shakers have lived in this house, which gives you an idea of what College Hill looked like in the 1880s. Peter G. Thompson lived here until construction of Laurel Court was finished.

Walk west along Belmont Avenue and turn left on Glenview Avenue. A sign at the southeast corner designates it as part of the National Park Service's Network to Freedom. This road was a route of escape for 28 freedom seekers in 1853, fleeing enslavement in Boone County, Kentucky. Abolitionist John Fairfield led the group from Kentucky to downtown Cincinnati, where they met with Levi Coffin, John Hatfield, and others. Buggies containing the 28 created a false funeral procession that skirted the edge of integrated Wesleyan Cemetery in Northside and went up to

College Hill via this back route. After they were hidden safely here, they were sent on to the next station and made it safely to Canada.

On the left is ⓮ **St. George Serbian Orthodox Church,** set back far from the street. This was once stables for The Oaks. To the south is the expansive campus for ⓯ **First United Church of Christ,** which is accessible from Belmont Avenue. Its west side is lined with frame houses from the 1830s to the early 20th century. Glenview is one of College Hill's most idyllic streets, with its well-preserved houses, massive trees, and sweeping views of the surrounding neighborhood and lower parts of the city to the south. The Henshaw House (5831 Glenview Ave.) is the second-oldest house on the street. It is quintessential Italianate circa 1870, though a rear wing is said to date back as early as the 1830s. The next three houses (5807, 5811, and 5819 Glenview Ave.) are Victorian and the result of local builder Andrew Forbes, an officer in the carpenters' union.

Continue walking south along Glenview Avenue. Ahead is ⓰ **Fox Preserve,** a heavily wooded area of more than 15 acres tucked between W. North Bend Road, Kirby Avenue, and Glenview Avenue in the vicinity of Bradford Felter Tanglewood Preserve. Fox Preserve was a gift from Patricia Cass and Edward A. Fox to Cincinnati Parks in 1975 and 1981. Turn right on Meryton Place, a right-angle street that dead-ends into Fox Preserve. On the left, at 5675 Meryton Pl., is a large Victorian house built in 1891. Ahead, at 5673 Meryton Pl., is a stone house; its distinctive look is said to be the result of a promise made to a new bride that she would live in a house like the one she had in Wales. A mix of Victorians, Tudor Revivals, bungalows, and modest midcentury houses line the rest of College Hill's most secluded street, benefiting from the natural riches of the forest that surrounds it.

Turn around at the end of Meryton Place, and return to Belmont Avenue; turn right. Turn left on Cedar Avenue, left again on Lathrop Place, then right on Cedar Avenue. Turn left on Hamilton Avenue to return to the start.

Connecting the Walks

To connect with Walk 9: Northside, drive or take the bus down Hamilton Avenue to the start of the walk, at Blue Rock Street.

(continued on next page)

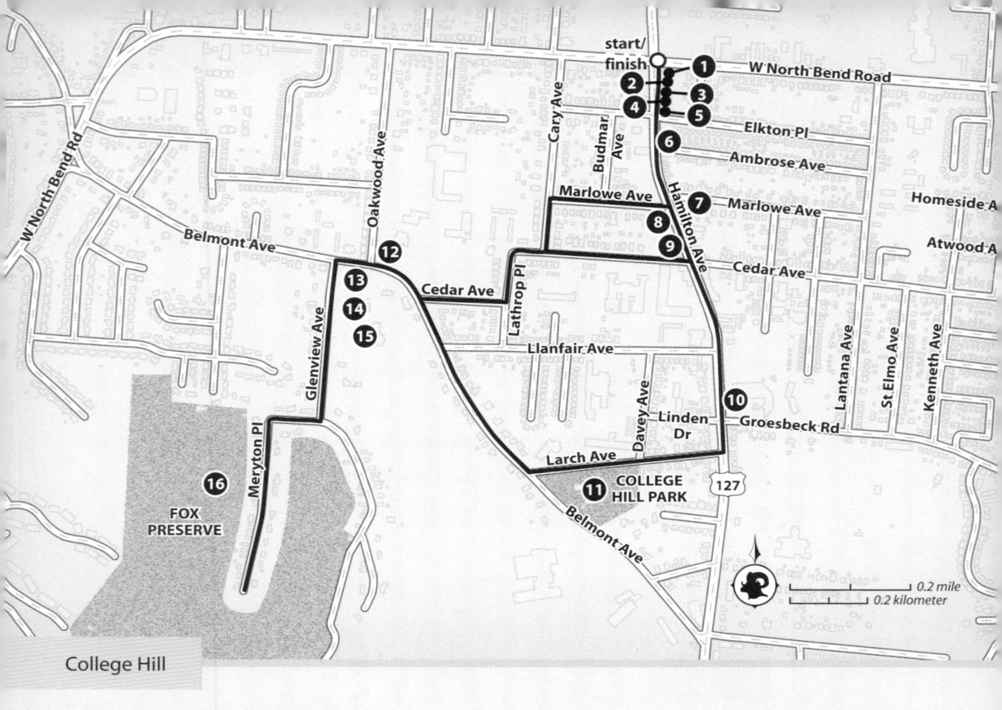

Points of Interest

1. **College Hill Coffee Co.** 6128 Hamilton Ave., 513-542-2739, collegehillcoffeeco.com
2. **Bacalls Cafe** 6118 Hamilton Ave., 513-541-8804, bacallscafe.com
3. **Schwartz Jewelers** 6114 Hamilton Ave., 513-541-5627, schwartzjewelers.net
4. **Marty's Hops and Vines** 6110 Hamilton Ave., 513-681-4222, martys-hopsandvines.com
5. **Silk Road Textiles** 6106 Hamilton Ave., 513-541-3700, silkroadcincinnati.com
6. **Fern** 6040 Hamilton Ave., 513-541-1269, fernstudiocincinnati.com
7. **Kiki** 5932 Hamilton Ave., kikicincinnati.com
8. **Tortilleria Garcia** 5917 Hamilton Ave., 513-671-8678, tortilleriagarcia.us
9. **Brink Brewing Co.** 5905 Hamilton Ave., 513-882-3334, brinkbrewing.com
10. **College Hill Presbyterian Church** 5742 Hamilton Ave., 513-541-5676, chpc.org
11. **College Hill Town Hall** 1805 Larch Ave.
12. **Laurel Court** 5870 Belmont Ave., 513-542-2000, laurelcourt.com
13. **The Oaks** 5907 Belmont Ave.
14. **St. George Serbian Orthodox Church** 5830 Glenview Ave., 513-542-4452, stgeorgecinci.org
15. **First United Church of Christ** 5808 Glenview Ave., 513-541-7302
16. **Fox Preserve** 5801 McCray Ct., 513-352-4000

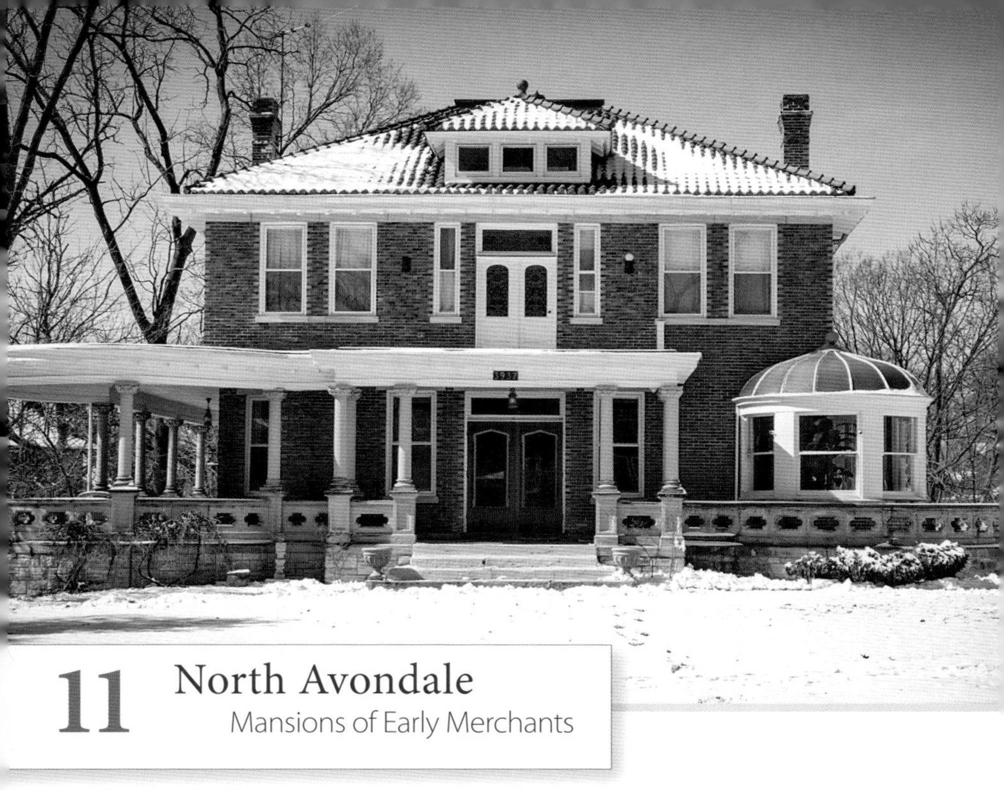

11 North Avondale

Mansions of Early Merchants

Above: The vivid green exterior of the Charles Roth House makes it a neighborhood standout.

BOUNDARIES: Clinton Springs Ave., Red Bud Ave., Paddock St., Reading Rd.
DISTANCE: 2.5 miles
DIFFICULTY: Moderate
PARKING: Free parking lot at North Avondale Recreation Center
PUBLIC TRANSIT: 2411 and 4013 to Clinton Springs and Leyman

North Avondale is a residential gem situated about 3.5 miles north of downtown and surrounded by Clifton to the west, Saint Bernard to the north, and Avondale to the south. The neighborhood has been home to prominent Cincinnatians since its founding, attracting leading architects of the day who created eye-catching houses that range from modest cottages to impressive castle-like mansions. With approximately 7,000 residents, North Avondale features a number of educational institutions, including parts of Xavier University, Burton Public School, Cincinnati Christian College, The New School Montessori, and several others.

In the 1830s, a few wealthy Cincinnati businessmen began building homes in the area. Among the earliest residents and its first mayor was Stephen Burton (1816–1884), whose wife reportedly called the area Avondale because the stream behind their house resembled the River Avon in England. After several attempts, the City of Cincinnati successfully annexed Avondale in 1896. Following annexation, an influx of wealthy German-Jewish families began moving into the northern part of Avondale from the old Jewish neighborhoods of the West End.

While only a few buildings are called out here, this neighborhood is replete with Cincinnati's most extravagant turn-of-the-20th-century homes. Be on the lookout for homes inspired by many different European nations' cultures and building traditions, almost all meticulously maintained.

Walk Description

Start at the ❶ **North Avondale Recreation Center** (617 Clinton Springs Ave.), a City of Cincinnati facility that is made up of ball fields, a fitness center, tennis courts, and more. This rec center is only $2/year for youth and $25 for adults and is open Monday–Friday, 9:30 a.m.–9 p.m., and Saturday, 9 a.m.–1 p.m. Turn right out of the parking lot onto Clinton Springs Avenue and begin the walk.

Turn left onto Burton Woods Lane. You'll quickly see Mitchell Mansion, the stone Victorian castlelike property that is part of ❷ **The New School Montessori campus,** a private school that serves from age 3 through the sixth grade and emphasizes academic excellence, individuality, interdependence, creativity, inner discipline, and self-esteem.

Turn right onto Red Bud Avenue and cross the street to follow the sidewalk.

Turn right onto Rose Hill Avenue. The last house on the left before turning onto Betula Avenue is the ❸ **Flavel F. and Emma Scovill House.** Flavel Scovill (1870–1974) was president of the Sayers-Scovill Company, makers of hearses, ambulances, and limousines. He and wife Emma lived here 50 years.

Turn left onto Betula Avenue, where just two houses down on the left is the ❹ **ToeWater-Joseph House,** a beautiful 1916 Craftsman home wrapped in a pale yellow stucco. A couple houses down, also on the left, is the ❺ **Cantaloupe King Mansion.** Also built in 1916, this 13-room Tudor Revival is listed on the National Register of Historic Places. The original owner, Stephen Gerrard, grew a very successful business by developing systems to transport cantaloupes from Colorado to the Midwest and East Coast.

At the intersection of Rose Hill, Red Bud, and Betula is the ❻ **Nathan and Berenice Levine House.** Built in 1937, this Norman Revival residence has exquisite plasterwork and colorful tile. Note the ogee arch framing the entry within the engaged tower.

Turn right onto Rose Hill Avenue and continue around the circle.

Keep left onto Beechwood Avenue and immediately look right to find a distinctive Spanish Colonial Revival–style residence with an Arts and Crafts flavor, the ❼ **Edward B. and Selma Wertheimer House.** Edward Wertheimer was known as "the dean of the American liquor industry" for his involvement in three distilling companies. He and Selma lived here from 1925 until 1941.

Immediately next door is the ❽ **Thomas Goodwin House,** a rare example of the Prairie Style, which features brick marked with spots of brown and a deeply hooded, hipped roof with Craftsman brackets and an unusual square dormer. Goodwin built and operated the Zoo Clubhouse, a gathering place for socially prominent Cincinnatians, in the early 20th century.

Walk past seven houses and then turn left onto a sidewalk, sometimes signed ROSE HILL LANE. Look for the paved trail between two houses, just before 4003 Beechwood Ave., a redbrick house with white trim and dark shutters. Follow this trail to Rose Hill Avenue.

Turn right onto Rose Hill Avenue and walk past three houses on your right to find the connection pathway for Rose Hill Lane. Turn left on Rose Hill Lane, and then turn right onto Paddock Road.

Turn right onto Reading Road. This block gives passersby a quick glimpse into the historical glamour and serenity that defines this neighborhood. Reading is a busy road, but the buildings hold their own. Across the street, at 3863 Reading Rd., a church wall covers a three-story Indiana limestone castle that the Barney Kroger family once owned. The ❾ **Frank Herschede Mansion** is an uncut-stone mansion with a 6-foot iron fence. The Herschede family, famous for the manufacture of hall and mantel clocks, is this impressive home's most well-known resident.

Turn right onto Clinton Springs Avenue. To see the last two sites, walk around Mitchell Triangle to reconnect with Rose Hill Lane. You can't miss ❿ **The Belvedere,** a 12-story apartment building. Built in 1925, this cast-in-place building with a brick-and-limestone exterior is the epitome of Jazz Age glamour. According to historical newspaper articles, it was the first apartment building of its construction type in America, and it remained Cincinnati's largest apartment building for years. It has a stunning lobby, decorated by Cincinnati mural painter H. H. Wessel, and a rooftop garden.

As you look up Beechwood Avenue, the first house on the left is worth the extra little trek to see the ⓫ **Charles Roth House,** known as the green brick house. The most distinguishing feature of this picturesque home is the exterior, with walls finished in green enameled brick tile. Its intense color contrasts vividly with the gray and brown coloring of neighboring houses. An open porch of rough sandstone with a lily pond and fountain wraps around the house's main section, while a circular conservatory with a green glass roof flanks the other end. This property was built in 1907 by local architect Anthony Kunz Jr.

Return to Clinton Springs Avenue and turn right. Continue along Clinton Springs to return to your starting point.

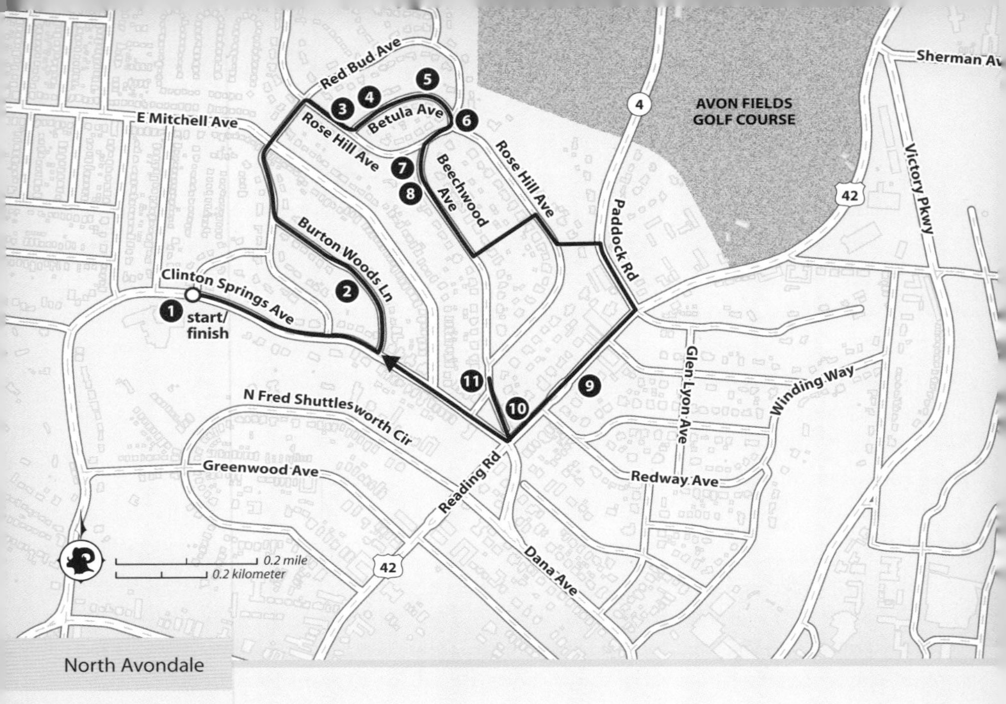

Points of Interest

1. **North Avondale Recreation Center** 617 Clinton Springs Ave., 513-961-1584, cincyrec.org
2. **The New School Montessori** 3 Burton Woods Ln., 513-281-7999, newschoolmontessori.com
3. **Flavel F. and Emma Scovill House** 700 Betula Ave.
4. **ToeWater-Joseph House** 718 Betula Ave.
5. **Cantaloupe King Mansion** 748 Betula Ave.
6. **Nathan and Berenice Levine House** 4098 Rose Hill
7. **Edward B. and Selma Wertheimer House** 4075 Beechwood Ave.
8. **Thomas Goodwin House** 4061 Beechwood Ave.
9. **Frank Herschede Mansion** 3886 Reading Rd.
10. **The Belvedere** 3900 Rose Hill Ave., 513-281-5565
11. **Charles Roth House** 3937 Rose Hill Ave.

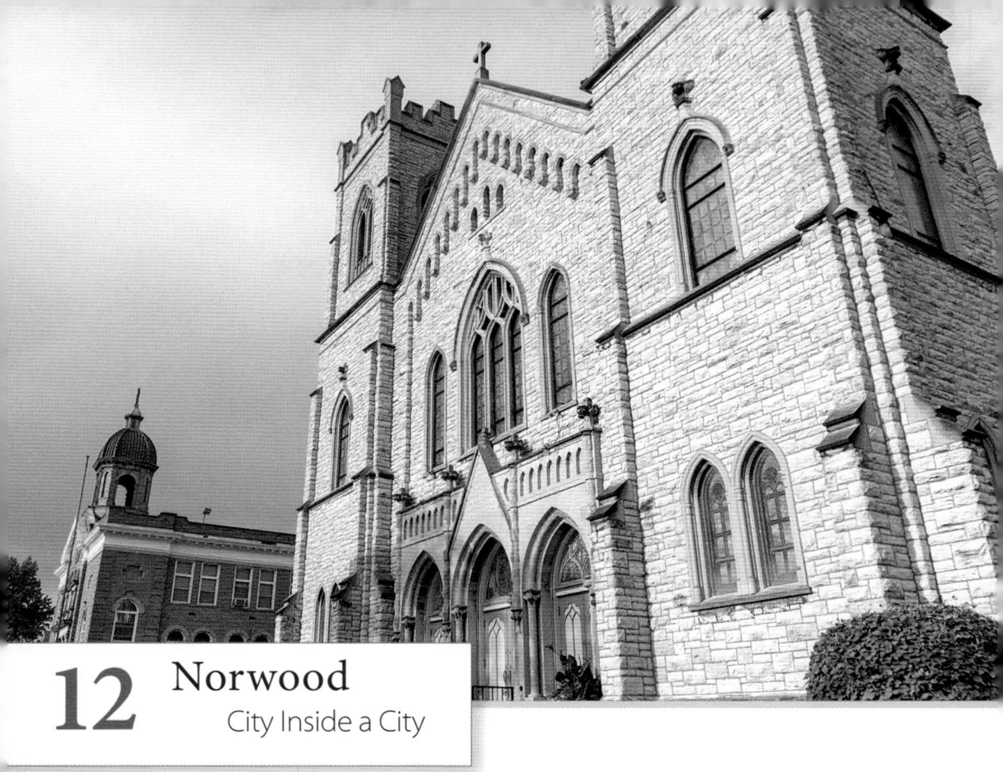

12 Norwood
City Inside a City

Above: Norwood has an impressive collection of historic church buildings.

BOUNDARIES: Montgomery Rd., Allison St., Cameron Ave., Floral Ave., Smith Rd.
DISTANCE: 2.5 miles
DIFFICULTY: Moderate
PARKING: Park on westbound Elm Ave.
PUBLIC TRANSIT: Metro buses (go-metro.com) serve this area. Take route 4 to Montgomery Rd. and Elm Ave.

Engulfed by the city of Cincinnati on all sides, the 3-square-mile area now known as Norwood was settled in the early 19th century as a coach stop along the Montgomery Road turnpike near the present-day intersection of Smith Road. The village was originally named Sharpsburg, after an early settler named John Sharpe. It was informally referred to as Northwood because of its location north of Cincinnati and because it was heavily wooded with horse farms and orchards.

The construction of Marietta & Cincinnati Railroad and Cincinnati, Lebanon & Northern Railway led to increased settlement. In 1873, a local dry goods merchant named L. C. Hopkins subdivided 30 acres of his own land near the intersection of Hopkins Avenue and Montgomery Road. Shortly thereafter, other subdivisions were planned. The area quickly developed into one of Cincinnati's original suburbs. Norwood was incorporated as a village in 1888 and as a city in 1902.

Today, Norwood is the second largest city in Hamilton County. It is home to more than 19,000 people, the headquarters of United Dairy Farmers, and the site of an American Indian burial mound. The mound is one of the highest elevations in southwest Ohio and one of two Norwood sites listed on the National Register of Historic Places. Most people are familiar with Norwood via its main thoroughfare, Montgomery Road; there's so much more to explore on its side streets and hillsides.

Walk Description

Start your walk on the steps of the ❶ **Norwood Municipal Building.** Built in 1915 and added to the National Register of Historic Places in 1980, this Renaissance Revival–style building sits prominently at the northern edge of Norwood's historic commercial district. Continue south past the clock on Montgomery Road. On the right are two longtime local diners, ❷ **Anna's Family Restaurant** and ❸ **Bluebird Restaurant,** where coffee and hash browns are orders of the day. Across the street is the Central Parke complex on the site of the former General Motors assembly plant, which closed in 1986, causing Norwood to rethink its economic base. Mostly restaurants, services, and light industry businesses make up the site.

Cross Sherman Avenue. On the southwest corner of Montgomery Road and Sherman Avenue is the Fidelity Professional Building, a slender midcentury modern bank building. Continuing south on Montgomery Road, cross Lawrence Avenue just past US Bank. Take the stairs on your right into Victory Park. Proceed through the park

Norwood continues to transition from an industrial enclave and early suburb of Cincinnati to a regional business and retail center.

to Mills Avenue and turn right. On the right is the former ❹ **Norwood Market House,** which opened in the early 1900s. According to the Norwood Historical Society, market manager Joseph B. Levingood invited grocers from Cincinnati and Norwood to set up booths on either side of an aisle running through the building's midsection. After the market ceased operations, the building was used as a roller rink, a private ice hockey club, and later an ice-skating rink. It is currently used as a storage building for the city.

Continue walking west along Mills Avenue and turn left on Allison Street. On the right is the impressive Allisonia (4431 Allison St.), a 14-unit, four-story brick apartment building with three sets of bracketed oriel windows protruding from the Allison Street facade. Past the Allisonia, at 1923 Mills Ave., is the former Abrams Brake Shop creatively converted into a single-family home. Continue south on Allison Street.

The next two intersecting streets off Allison Street—Courtland and Weyer Avenues—are lined with several impressive institutional buildings. On the southeast corner of Courtland Avenue is the former Allison Street Elementary School. Looking farther east is the stately Norwood Baptist Church (2037 Courtland Ave.); originally Harmon Memorial Church, the building bears the name of Reverend B. F. Harmon in the pediment. Continue south on Allison Street. On the northeast corner is the older of the two Allison Street elementary school buildings. Built in 1894, the building has a magnificent facade featuring fine stone and brick work.

Turn left in front of the school and continue on Weyer to Montgomery Road. On the right is the former Word of Truth Ministries building (2039 Weyer Ave.). The empty building was built in 1923 and is a nice Greek Revival example. Past the adjoining parking lot is the ❺ **Norwood Branch Library.** Completed in 1907 with funds from the Andrew Carnegie Foundation, the Italian Renaissance Revival building features two Rookwood urns inside near the front entrance and two bas-relief sculptures by celebrated Cincinnati artist Clement J. Barnhorn. Across from the library is ❻ **Gordo's Pub & Grill,** a popular restaurant known for its pub fare and beer selection.

Cross Montgomery Road in front of the library and then turn left. At Monroe Avenue turn right toward Norwood's residential core. Here you will walk multiple blocks featuring a variety of building types and architectural styles. Cross Lafayette Avenue. On your left at 2216 Monroe Ave. is a Swiss Chalet–style house. Across the street is ❼ **Christ the Savior Orthodox Church,** and likely a manse next door. Built in 1913 as an Episcopal church, the current parish purchased it in 1985 and began restoration in 1986, blending original hand-carved wood furnishings and stained glass with Orthodox iconography.

Take a sharp right on Ashland Avenue for a view of four houses with interesting architectural details; 4296 Ashland Ave. is Shingle style. Next door at 4292 is an elaborate stone Queen Anne house. Nearby 4288 has a dramatically steep roof pitch and a storybook faux-Tudor style that resembles a Hobbit house. Before turning left on Elsmere Avenue, note the amazing leaded glass window and door at 4278. There is an impressive amount of leaded glass throughout this part of the walk. Turn left and see two more examples at 2207 and 2218 Cameron Ave., two lovely Queen Anne houses with front bay turrets. The house at 2207 Cameron Ave. is an unusual style; the central bay confidently breaks the roofline. Continue along Cameron to Floral Avenue, where you will discover 4141 Floral Ave., an impressive Colonial Revival–style frame house.

Turn left on Floral Avenue. Here, Hamilton County feels like the working- and middle-class neighborhoods of Chicago, and presidential street names (Monroe, Madison, Jefferson, Adams, Washington) prevail. Many of the homes here are the result of the housing boom associated with manufacturing enterprises that dominated Norwood in the late 1800s and early 1900s. In 1898 George Bullock relocated Bullock Electric Manufacturing Company to 4620 Forest Ave. It became one of Norwood's first industrial plants, following McFarlan Lumber Company and Cincinnati Brick Company on Duck Creek. German-based Siemens eventually acquired Bullock, which remains in operation in the same building.

The next six blocks of Floral Avenue are filled with American Foursquare, Colonial Revival, and late Italianate homes. At 4305 Floral Ave. is a fine example of Eastlake architecture. Next door (4311) is a good example of American Craftsman. Continue to Smith Road and cross to the other side of Floral Avenue at the light. Then cross Smith toward the church. ❽ **Immaculate Conception Church,** originally founded as St. Matthew Catholic Church and built in 1922, dominates this intersection with its Gothic-style facade. North of the adjacent parking lot is Immaculate Conception Academy (formerly St. Matthew School), erected in 1909 in the Renaissance Revival style.

Continue north on Floral Avenue and walk to westbound Park Avenue on the north side of the parkway. Note the large yellow-brick building to the right in the distance. Founded in 1867, **United States Playing Card Co.** moved to this huge factory at 4590 Beech St. in 1901. As its name suggests, the company is a large producer and distributor of playing cards. Popular brands include Bee, Bicycle, Aviator, and Hoyle. The global company relocated its headquarters to Erlanger, Kentucky, in 2009, taking hundreds of jobs with it.

Continue west on Park Avenue. Turn right on Smith Road, cross Sherman Avenue, and turn left on Elm Avenue to return to the start of this walk at Montgomery Road.

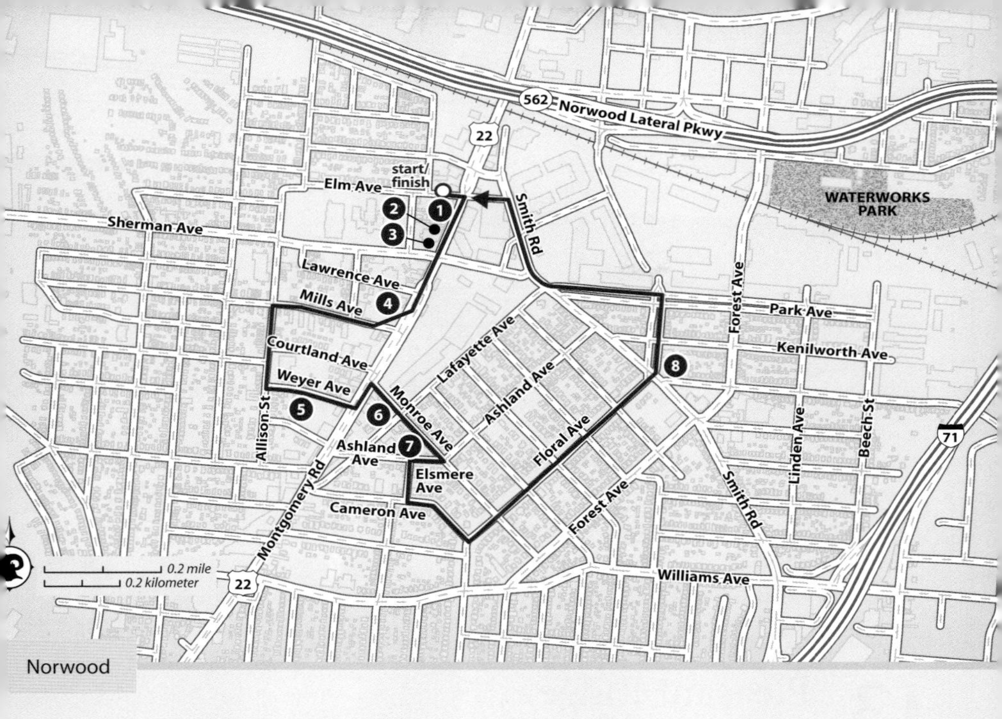

Points of Interest

1. **Norwood Municipal Building** 4645 Montgomery Rd., 513-458-4500, norwood-ohio.com
2. **Anna's Family Restaurant** 4633 Montgomery Rd., 513-731-1100
3. **Bluebird Restaurant** 4629 Montgomery Rd., 513-351-2427
4. **Norwood Market House** 2054 Mills Ave.
5. **Legacy Lofts on Courtland** Allison St. and Courtland Ave.
5. **Norwood Branch Library** 4325 Montgomery Rd., 513-369-6037, cincinnatilibrary.org/branches/norwood.html
6. **Gordo's Pub & Grill** 4328 Montgomery Rd., 513-351-1999, gordospub.com
7. **Christ the Savior Orthodox Church** 4285 Ashland Ave., 513-351-0907, christthesavioroca.org
8. **Immaculate Conception Church** 4510 Floral Ave., 513-731-8863

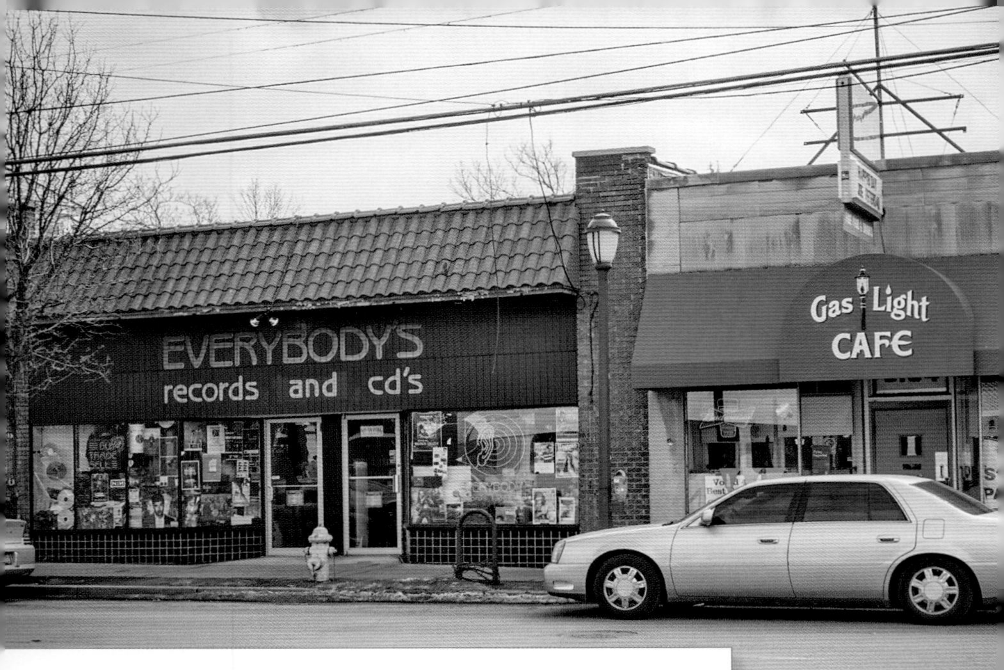

13 Pleasant Ridge

Beer and Peanuts, Wine and Cheese

Above: Local businesses attract residents and visitors alike in Pleasant Ridge.

BOUNDARIES: Montgomery Rd., Ridge Ave., Beredith Pl., Grand Vista Ave., Woodford Rd.
DISTANCE: 2.7 miles
DIFFICULTY: Easy, with an ascending walk up Grand Vista Ave.
PARKING: Park on Orion Ave. or in lot behind Everybody's Records (6106 Montgomery Rd.).
PUBLIC TRANSIT: Take Metro route 4 to Montgomery Rd. and Ridge Ave. (go-metro.com)

Pleasant Ridge is a historic gaslight neighborhood with a small, vibrant business district along Montgomery Road, about 9 miles northeast of downtown Cincinnati. This hilltop area was first settled in 1795 and was named Pleasant Ridge because of its pleasant ridgetop views. During the early 1800s, the Wood family acquired much of the land in the area and renamed the settlement Crossroads around 1825. When the area was surveyed for construction of a railroad during the mid-1800s, the community was once again referred to as Pleasant Ridge. It was incorporated in 1891, and the City of Cincinnati annexed the village in 1912.

Today, Pleasant Ridge is one of the most diverse and durable communities in the region, according to a 2008 study of 122 communities commissioned by the Cincinnatus Association. It has its own library and elementary school, and the business district along Montgomery Road was the first in the region to be granted the designation of Community Entertainment District. Pleasant Ridge is one of 16 communities participating in Go Vibrant (govibrant.org), the largest network of urban walking routes in the country. Look for the Pleasant Ridge map on the website and incorporate the suggested routes into your walk.

Walk Description

Start with a burger that consistently rates as one of the best in the city, according to *Cincinnati Magazine*, at the ❶ **Gas Light Cafe.** There are a lot of old photos featuring local athletes and celebrities, and mirrors at each booth offer creative photo opportunities with friends. Flip through record bins next door at ❷ **Everybody's Records,** which turned 40 in 2018. If you're around during lunchtime or dinner, check out ❸ **Casa Figueroa** for a margarita and Latin-inspired food in a vividly decorated house with outdoor seating. Be sure to use the fun restroom upstairs.

It is worth exploring and supporting the range of businesses along Montgomery Road between Lester Road and Grand Vista Avenue. From half-century-old ❹ **Pleasant Ridge Chili,** known for its gravy-covered fries and late-night hours (Monday–Saturday, 9 a.m.–4:30 a.m.), to all-vegan ❺ **Loving Hut** (which this route passes later), you will discover a core group of merchants that sustain it during the ups and downs of the economy.

Cross Montgomery at Ridge Avenue, heading north, and pass ❻ **Queen City Comic & Card Co.** (open since 1987) on the right. Across the street is ❼ **Share: Cheesebar,** a cheese shop from the uproarious founder of C'est Cheese Food Truck. Local businesses stretch around the corner along Montgomery Road to Losantiville Avenue. Most Cincinnati neighborhoods have a brewery these days, and ❽ **Nine Giant** stakes this claim for Pleasant Ridge. A few more doors down, ❾ **The Overlook Lodge** takes its theme from Stephen King's book *The Shining.*

Continue north on Ridge Avenue past ❿ **St. Peter's United Church of Christ,** one of a few churches in Pleasant Ridge. Across the street at Woodsfield Street and Ridge Avenue is ⓫ **Cincinnati Yoga School,** home of Lotus Yoga Temple, which offers a variety of classes, including teacher training, Thai yoga massage, and special events. It is housed in the former Columbia Township government offices building, constructed in 1884. It became Pleasant Ridge Town Hall in 1891, when the village was incorporated. It housed a jail and the library before being sold to Pleasant Ridge Masonic Lodge in 1912, when the City of Cincinnati annexed Pleasant Ridge.

As you walk along Ridge Avenue, on the west side (past Troy Avenue) are several beautiful Victorian-era houses set far back from the road. They are difficult to see in the summer because there are so many tall trees. Before proceeding north of Harvest Avenue, look for the eclectic blue wooden cottage with decorative outdoor art at 3221 Harvest Ave. The face art in the front yard is from the razed Palace Theatre downtown. Built in 1932, the house was once a sales office in Golf Manor before it ended up here. One might say that this was a tiny home—living large in a small space—long before it was cool.

Continue north on Ridge Avenue, and then turn right on Beredith Place. On the right at 6336 Ridge Ave. is a bell (to the left of the house) that came from an old Presbyterian church. The bell was purchased for about $350 (in pennies) from children at Pleasant Ridge Presbyterian Church and installed in the old church bell tower. In 1960, the old church was razed and replaced with a new structure. Clayton Werden, a local electrician, purchased the bell and the tracker pipe organ. In 1984 Clayton offered the bell back to the church, which declined, so he installed it here.

Beredith Place was originally called Schumann Street. During World War I it was renamed as part of an effort to banish German titles from the community. Beredith merges the first names of two sisters, Beryl and Edith, who lived in the neighborhood. Veer left as Beredith crosses Kincaid Road, and continue east toward Parkman Place, which curves to the right. Just after the jog in the road at Kincaid, look to your left to find a marker on a telpehone pole listing the road's original name. The house at 6341 Parkman Pl. is modeled after the Taft Museum of Art house downtown (see Walk 2).

Continue south on Parkman, and walk to the next intersection; note ⓬ **All Saints Episcopal Church** on the right, which describes itself as a "radically inclusive, just, and loving community." Steer sharply to the left, ascending along Grand Vista Avenue, a gorgeous stretch of homes that could be a historic district at both the local and national levels. Lined with grand homes and massive shade trees, this ridgetop street epitomizes opulent living. Tucked away from busy Montgomery Road, houses on the west side have sweeping views of Mill Creek Valley. A variety of architectural styles are abundant here. Start on the west side and head north. A nice bungalow is situated at 6311. A grand Georgian Revival house is perched in all its glory at 6331. A stately Colonial Revival can be found at 6345, while 6371 has an early Frank Lloyd Wright/Louis Sullivan Chicago School appearance. At 6433 is a renovated brick-and-stucco Tudor Revival. The oldest house on Grand Vista, 6463, was originally part of a farm. An outstanding Norman Revival residence sits at 6475. After reaching the dead end (the last four houses are in Amberly Village), circle back along the other side past 6456, a huge Spanish-style hacienda. The blog "Sears Houses in Ohio" notes that 6416 is historically called ⓭ **Sears Aurora House,** one of 26 Sears Catalog Homes in Pleasant Ridge. It is a rare Prairie residence with horizontal lines and a low-pitched hipped roof. A lovingly preserved Tudor house is located at 6370, and there's another cute bungalow at 6338.

Head to 6272 Grand Vista Ave. and look for a walkway on the left. Take the shaded passageway back to Montgomery Road. Turn right on Montgomery Road and work your way to the other side at Woodmont Avenue. (Crossing at Grand Vista is risky, as there is no sidewalk and traffic really hauls through here.) On the right is ⓮ **Pleasant Ridge Branch Library,** which opened here in 1929. In 2011 a new entrance was added and modifications were completed to make the building compliant with the Americans with Disabilities Act. Walk past Loving Hut to the building at 6225 Montgomery Rd., where Beresford Plumbing-Heating-Cooling has operated since 1985. The building has seen many iterations since it was built in the 1960s and is worthy of a photo. It stands out from its neighbors due to the tall midcentury modern projecting bay. It was originally Dandees Hamburgers, then Pasquale's Pizza in the late 1960s and early 1970s, and then LaRosa's.

Cross the street at Woodmont Avenue, return to Grand Vista Avenue, and turn right. Along this stretch are numerous apartment buildings on large subdivided lots. The apartment building at the corner of Grand Vista and Montgomery Road was built in 1967. The ones running north of it on Montgomery were built in the 1950s and 1960s. There is one house left amid all these apartment buildings—at 6336 Montgomery Rd.—that was built in 1909. Some locals call this the beer-and-peanuts side of Grand Vista, versus the just-visited wine-and-cheese section. Some very nice bungalows, Craftsman-style houses, and a modest Swiss Chalet–style house are found here. As you cross Arrow Avenue, look right. The house on the southwest corner has a large tree house visible from the street.

Turn right on Orion Avenue and enjoy the gaslights that represent 19th-century technology. Cross Woodmont Avenue to briefly check out two more Sears Catalog Homes, 3265 and 3281 Orion Ave., then swing back and turn right on Woodmont Avenue. Take one more right on Woodford Road. ⓯ **Nativity Church** is on the left and hard to miss. Art Deco in style, it combines a low-slung main building topped with a soaring spire right out of the Machine Age of the 1930s. Its spire is eclectic, bold, and lavish in design. It sneaks up on you in other parts of the neighborhood when you least expect it. In addition to offering traditional church services, the church is home to a seasonal farmers market every Monday, June–October. Turn right on Ridge Avenue. At the corner is the former Pleasant Ridge United Methodist Church, built in 1919 and now home to TCP World Academy.

The walk ends here. You might want to get something to eat or drink, or reward yourself with a little shopping, before you leave.

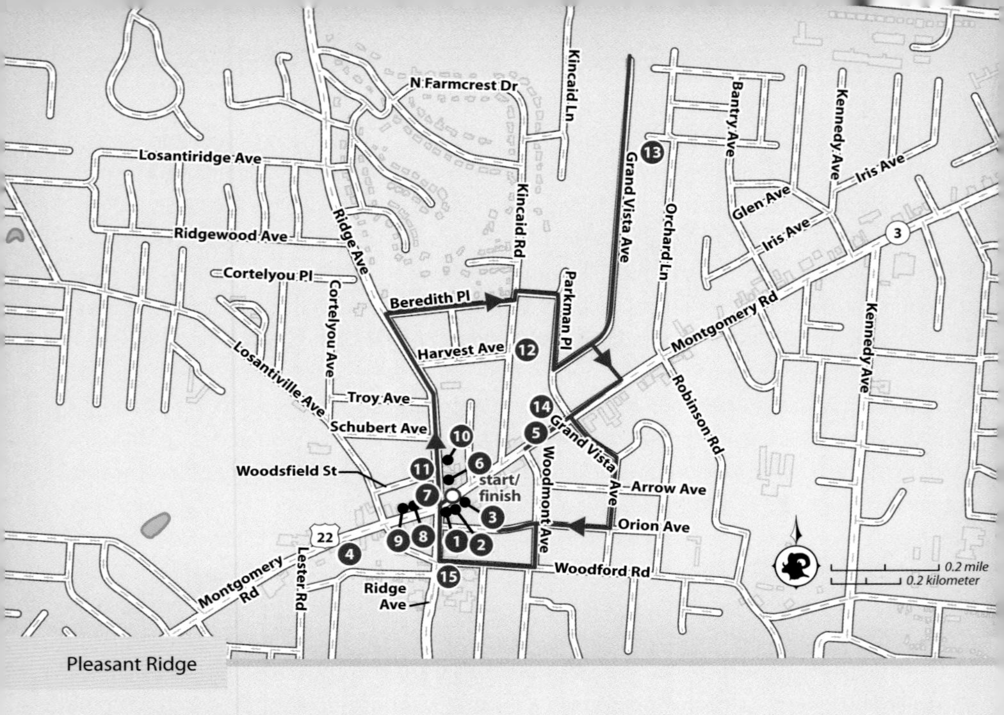

Points of Interest

1. **Gaslight Cafe** 6104 Montgomery Rd., 513-631-6977, gaslightcincy.com
2. **Everybody's Records** 6106 Montgomery Rd., 513-531-4500, everybodysrecords.com
3. **Casa Figueroa** 6112 Montgomery Rd., 513-631-3333, casafig.com
4. **Pleasant Ridge Chili** 6032 Montgomery Rd., 513-531-2365, pleasantridgechili.com
5. **Loving Hut** 6227 Montgomery Rd., 513-731-2233
6. **Queen City Comic & Card Co.** 6101 Montgomery Rd., 513-351-5674, queencitycomics.com
7. **Share: Cheesebar** 6105 Ridge Ave., 513-351-3063, sharecheesebar.com
8. **Nine Giant** 6095 Montgomery Rd., 513-366-4550, ninegiant.com
9. **The Overlook Lodge** 6083 Montgomery Rd., 513-351-0035, thatshiningbar.com
10. **St. Peter's United Church of Christ** 6120 Ridge Ave., 513-621-8549, stpetersucc.net
11. **Cincinnati Yoga School** 6125 Ridge Ave., 513-247-9642, cincyoga.com
12. **All Saints Episcopal Church** 6301 Parkman Pl., 513-531-6333, allsaintscincinnati.org
13. **Sears Aurora House** 6416 Grand Vista Ave., searshousesinohio.wordpress.com
14. **Pleasant Ridge Branch Library** 6233 Montgomery Rd., 513-369-4488, cincinnatilibrary.org/branches/pleasantridge.html
15. **Nativity Church** 5935 Pandora Ave., 513-531-3164, nativity-cincinnati.org

14 Oakley

Mecca for Independent Business

Above: Oakley Square is filled with a variety of local businesses, including restaurants and bars with outdoor seating in warmer months.

BOUNDARIES: Madison Rd., Markbreit Ave., Eileen Dr., Isabella Ave., Brazee St., Allston St.
DISTANCE: 2 miles
DIFFICULTY: Easy
PARKING: Park along Markbreit Ave. or Allston St., or lock your bike at a parking meter.
PUBLIC TRANSIT: Metro buses (go-metro.com) serve this area. Take route 11 to Oakley Square.

Located 8 miles northeast of downtown Cincinnati, Oakley is a walkable and prosperous neighborhood that borders Hyde Park, Madisonville, Pleasant Ridge, and Norwood. In the heart of it all is Oakley's historic commercial district, Oakley Square. It is filled with one of the most lively clusters of locally owned businesses in the city along Madison Road. North and south of the business district is a mix of charming homes and apartments within easy walking distance.

A popular stop in the mid-19th century for wagon drivers on the Madisonville Turnpike (now Madison Road), Oakley was originally known as Four Mile. (Oakley was once the home of famed markswoman Annie Oakley, who made her public debut in 1876.) The village of Oakley, a name referring to the many oak trees in the area, was officially registered with the Hamilton County Courthouse in 1869, and the village was incorporated in 1898. Although Oakley was not annexed into the City of Cincinnati until 1913, the real growth started here in the 1890s when the Oakley Race Course (1889–1905) opened and continued when Cincinnati Milling Machine moved here in 1905. One of Oakley's iconic businesses, Aglamesis Bros. Ice Cream Parlor, opened the same year as annexation.

Walk Description

Start your walk with something to eat and drink at ❶ **Habits Cafe,** a neighborhood landmark since 1980. Vegetarian and vegan fare is available for herbivores, who often dictate the restaurant of choice for an evening out. When you're finished, turn right on Markbreit Avenue. On your right is the Rickard Building (2930 Markbreit Ave.), an unpretentious example of an early-20th-century brick apartment building common throughout Oakley. Next is a long row of two-story, brick apartments (2910–2926 Markbreit Ave.). Continue walking west on Markbreit past a series of simple houses (including ones with subtle American Foursquare influences) dating from the mid-1890s. One exception is a cute brick cottage (2847 Markbreit Ave.).

Cross Markbreit Avenue and turn left on Eileen Drive. This is one of the loveliest residential streets in Oakley, lined with mostly large Tudor Revival-style houses and massive trees shading a curving street. Cross Romana Place, walk to Madison Road, and turn left. Cross the other end of Romana Place, and head back to Oakley Square. On the left are two popular eateries with multiple locations around Cincinnati that add to the value of living in Oakley. ❷ **Rooted Juicery + Kitchen,** which specializes in plant-based foods and juices, opened its first location here in 2015. Additional locations opened in Mariemont and downtown. The original ❸ **Dewey's Pizza** started at this location in 1998. It is known for its gourmet pizza, inventive salads, and craft beer and wine menu.

Despite the general walkability of Oakley, vehicular traffic uses its might to pass through Oakley Square. Pedestrian safety was an issue for a long time, especially at the six-point intersection at the northeast end of Markbreit Avenue and Madison Road. After a recent redesign, streets were realigned, the intersection was simplified, traffic signals were upgraded, and new crosswalks were created. Still, always use caution when entering crosswalks and intersections.

Use the crosswalk in front of Dewey's to enter **Geier Esplanade,** a 350-foot linear park in the middle of Madison Road between Markbreit Avenue and Romana Place. This small parcel was converted into green space in 1932. Today it's a respite in the middle of Oakley, and a staging area for summertime events like Oakley After Hours and Oakley Fancy Flea. Through the generosity of the Geier family, flowers and bulbs are planted each year in memory of Mr. Fred Geier and Mr. Philip O. Geier, Sr. Veer left and walk to ❹ **20th Century Theater,** the most distinctive building in Oakley. With its 72-foot tower looming overhead, the former neighborhood movie theater is now a concert, wedding, and special events venue. Listed on the National Register of Historic Places in 1993, this impressive Art Deco building escaped demolition efforts in the early 1990s. Continue east on Madison Road back to Markbreit Avenue.

Around the bend is ❺ **Oakley Pub & Grill** inside the former Oakley Improved B. & L. Co. building, which holds together the busy three-way intersection of Isabella Avenue, Markbreit Avenue, and Allston Street. The popular neighborhood bar serves pub fare and has an outdoor patio even during colder times. Cross Madison Road. At the northeast corner is the second location of **Oakley Bank.** The Renaissance Revival–style bank serves as a major landmark on the square.

Continue north on Madison Road into the core of the Oakley business district, ground zero for a slew of independent retailers, restaurants, bars, and service businesses. Longtime retailer ❻ **Bona Decorative Hardware** offers a complete line of fine hardware for kitchen, bath, and fireplaces. Next door is another established retailer, ❼ **Flaggs USA,** which specializes in custom banners and flags for various teams, countries, and causes, as well as a variety of kites to take for a test run at a nearby park.

Walk to the corner for ❽ **Oakley Branch Library,** which opened here in 1989. Library service began in Oakley in 1910 with a deposit station inside Barton's Drug Store. A full-service branch opened near the 20th Century Theater in 1926 before moving to a new building in 1940 at Madison Road and Gilmore Avenue. Architect Bernard Fields designed the current 7,100-square-foot facility with skylights and cathedral windows. Across the street is ❾ **St. Cecilia Catholic Church,** an impressive Gothic-style structure. St. Cecilia Parish Festival in July is where Oakley kids let off midsummer steam. There are lots of games, rides, and a petting zoo. Like other local church festivals, there is also plenty of beer and harmless gambling for the adults.

Walk the next two blocks (which are rather barren from a walking standpoint) to Brotherton Road. Cross Brotherton and Ballard Avenue to get to the other side. Here begins the easternmost stretch of Oakley's business district. On the right is Voltage Lofts. ❿ **Voltage** furniture store is at street level, while other design-oriented tenants take residence upstairs. A few more steps and there are two more home furnishing stores: ⓫ **Fine European Furnishings,** inside a traditional commercial district building, and ⓬ **House of France,** which specializes in English and country French-style furnishings.

Built in 1941 and saved from demolition in the 1990s, 20th Century Theater is a registered historic building used for special events and concerts.

Look north past the Madison Road median and walk underneath the elevated railroad tracks and pedestrian bridge to reach ⓭ **MadTree Brewing.** The popular brewery relocated here in 2017 after four fast and furious years in Kennedy Heights. The massive complex includes a 64-tap taproom, 10,000-square-foot beer garden, Catch-A-Fire Café, and private event space. The Oakley location quadrupled their production and transformed this otherwise bleak stretch of Madison Road into something far more interesting. Return to the safety of the pedestrian bridge over Madison Road to get to the other side. **Oakley Station**—the former home of Cincinnati Milacron—is on the other side and mentioned here just as a point of reference. The 74-acre mixed-use development features 650,000 square feet of retail and office space, more than 450 residential units, a 14-screen Cinemark Theatres, and, ironically, no station. This area is designed to navigate in a car, and not the friendliest for pedestrians. It feels out of place in tight-knit Oakley.

Cross under the pedestrian bridge and reenter the friendly confines of old Oakley. Locally owned businesses dominate this block. ⓮ **Essencha Tea House & Fine Teas** offers more than 80 varieties of loose-leaf teas, bubble tea, and masala chai, in addition to pastries and vegan pancakes. After a short stint around the corner on Brazee Street, ⓯ **Redtree Art Gallery and Coffee**

Shop relocated into this larger space, which allows for bigger gallery shows and more seats for lingering. ⓰ **Red Feather Kitchen** opened in the former Boca space in 2014 and serves dishes that are both bold and delicate. The extensive wine list will encourage you to linger in the soft dining area with its transparent white curtains.

Before turning right on Brazee Street, look across the street atop Voltage Lofts (3211 Madison Rd.) for a view of *Little Sure Shot,* the mural designed by Nicole Trimble in 2016 for Artworks, which partnered with Voltage Furniture to celebrate Annie Oakley. Known as "Little Sure Shot," Oakley was born in Oakley and became a world famous sharpshooter for Buffalo Bill's Wild West Show.

Now, walk to ⓱ **Brazee Street Studios,** which Blue Manatee and Sleepy Bee co-owner Sandra Gross created as an uplifting artists' colony devoted to glassmaking, professional art studios, and gallery space on the site of an old tool and die factory. Turn around and walk back toward Madison Road, passing ⓲ **Cincinnati Ballroom Company.** Located in the back room of the Oakley Bank Building, the dance studio comes to life with fiery red walls in between a vaulted ceiling and worn wood floors.

Turn right on Madison Road, cross Appleton Street, and walk to ⓳ **Oakley Paint & Glass Co.,** which replaced 91-year-old Loesch Hardware in 2016. The brightly painted store features the ArtWorks mural *Morning, Noon, and Night* on its southern elevation with partial underwriting from Loesch Hardware. The mural invites viewers to experience a day in the life of Oakley. Next up is ⓴ **Baba India Restaurant,** which has the same menu as Ambar in Clifton. Cross Brownway Avenue to reach ㉑ **Sleepy Bee Cafe,** the popular breakfast-and-lunch restaurant with additional locations in Blue Ash and downtown Cincinnati. Opened in 2013, the café is known for food that appeals to the conscious eater, allowing options for dietary restrictions, with chef Frannie Kroner overseeing the menu. Next door is ㉒ **Blue Manatee Bookstore and Literacy Project,** a nonprofit that provides reading instruction and mentoring to local children ages 4–8. For every book you buy, they will donate another book to a child in need.

Walk a bit more to ㉓ **Quince & Quinn,** another Oakley furniture store. It's housed in a renovated Baptist church and offers 9,000 square feet of stuff for the home, including design services. ㉔ **Deeper Roots Coffee** opened its first location here in 2015. The company got its start in 2006 and began roasting and distributing in 2011, with a commitment to ethical sourcing and specialty brews. An outsider artist from V+V designed *Building Inclusive Communities: A Mural Project of Visionaries + Voices and ArtWorks,* which was installed on the north side of Deeper Roots' building in 2018. The nonprofit for creatives with disabilities opened its ㉕ **V+V Visionarium** studio and gallery next door in 2017.

Next is Kid's Row, a small cluster of local businesses geared toward families with—you got it—kids! 26 **The Spotted Goose** is a colorful kids' clothing store with outfits from different designers. Dark chocolate opera creams, cherry cordials, and French-style ice cream fill cases in brightly lit 27 **Aglamesis Brothers,** which celebrated its 110th anniversary with single-dipped sugar cones for $1.10. 28 **King Arthur's Court Toys** has served Oakley and surrounding communities for 35 years. It's a stalwart retailer in a rapidly changing landscape. Find hundreds of toy brands for the kids, as well as games and puzzles for the older set.

Return to Oakley Square. Allston Street to the right is a secondary commercial street. 29 **Oakley Wines** houses The Cellar, a 2,000-square-foot bar beneath the shop featuring beer, cocktails, and wine, and is a good place to wrap this walk.

Points of Interest

1. **Habits Cafe** 3036 Madison Rd., 513-631-8367, habitscafe.com
2. **Rooted Juicery + Kitchen** 3010 Madison Rd., 513-351-2900, rootedjuicery.com
3. **Dewey's Pizza** 3014 Madison Rd., 513-731-7755, deweyspizza.com
4. **20th Century Theater** 3021 Madison Rd., 513-731-8000, the20thcenturytheatre.com
5. **Oakley Pub & Grill** 3924 Isabella Ave., 513-531-2500, oakleypubandgrill.com
6. **Bona Decorative Hardware** 3073 Madison Rd., 513-321-7877, bonahardware.com
7. **Flaggs USA** 3075 Madison Rd., 513-533-0330, flaggsusaohio.com
8. **Oakley Branch Library** 4033 Gilmore Ave., 513-369-6038, cincinnatilibrary.org
9. **St. Cecilia Catholic Church** 3105 Madison Rd., 513-871-5757, stceciliacincinnati.org
10. **Voltage** 3209 Madison Rd., 513-871-5483, voltagefurniture.com
11. **Fine European Furnishings** 3223 Madison Rd.
12. **House of France** 3225 Madison Rd., 513-871-9800, houseoffrance.com
13. **MadTree Brewing** 3301 Madison Rd., 513-836-8733, madtreebrewing.com
14. **Essencha Tea House & Fine Teas** 3212 Madison Rd., 513-533-4832, essenchatea.com
15. **Redtree Art Gallery and Coffee Shop** 3210 Madison Rd., 513-321-8733, redtreegallery.net

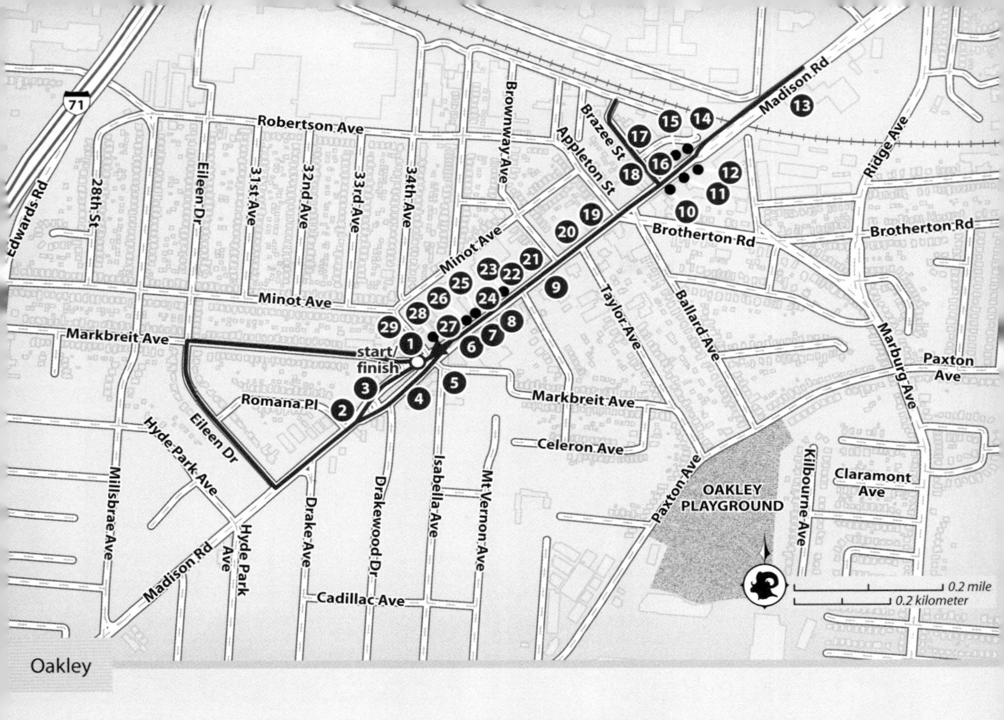

Oakley

16 **Red Feather Kitchen** 3200 Madison Rd., 513-407-3631, redfeatherkitchen.com

17 **Brazee Street Studios** 4426 Brazee St., 513-321-0206, brazeestreetstudios.com

18 **Cincinnati Ballroom Company** 4409 Brazee St., 513-321-2801, cinciballroom.com

19 **Oakley Paint & Glass Co.** 3142 Madison Rd., 513-871-5036, oakleypaintandglass.com

20 **Baba India Restaurant** 3120 Madison Rd., 513-321-1600, babarestaurant.com

21 **Sleepy Bee Cafe** 3098 Madison Rd., 513-533-2339, sleepybeecafe.com

22 **Blue Manatee Bookstore** 3094 Madison Rd., 513-731-2665, bluemanateebooks.com

23 **Quince & Quinn** 3066 Madison Rd., 513-321-3343, qandqhome.com

24 **Deeper Roots Coffee** 3056 Madison Rd., 513-913-9489, deeperrootscoffee.com

25 **V+V Visionarium** 3054 Madison Rd., 513-417-8491, visionariesandvoices.com

26 **The Spotted Goose** 3048 Madison Rd., 513-351-9600, thespottedgoose.com

27 **Aglamesis Brothers** 3046 Madison Rd., 513-531-5196, aglamesis.com

28 **King Arthur's Court Toys** 3040 Madison Rd., 513-531-4600, kingarthurstoys.com

29 **Oakley Wines** 4011 Allston St., 513-914-5735, oakleywines.com

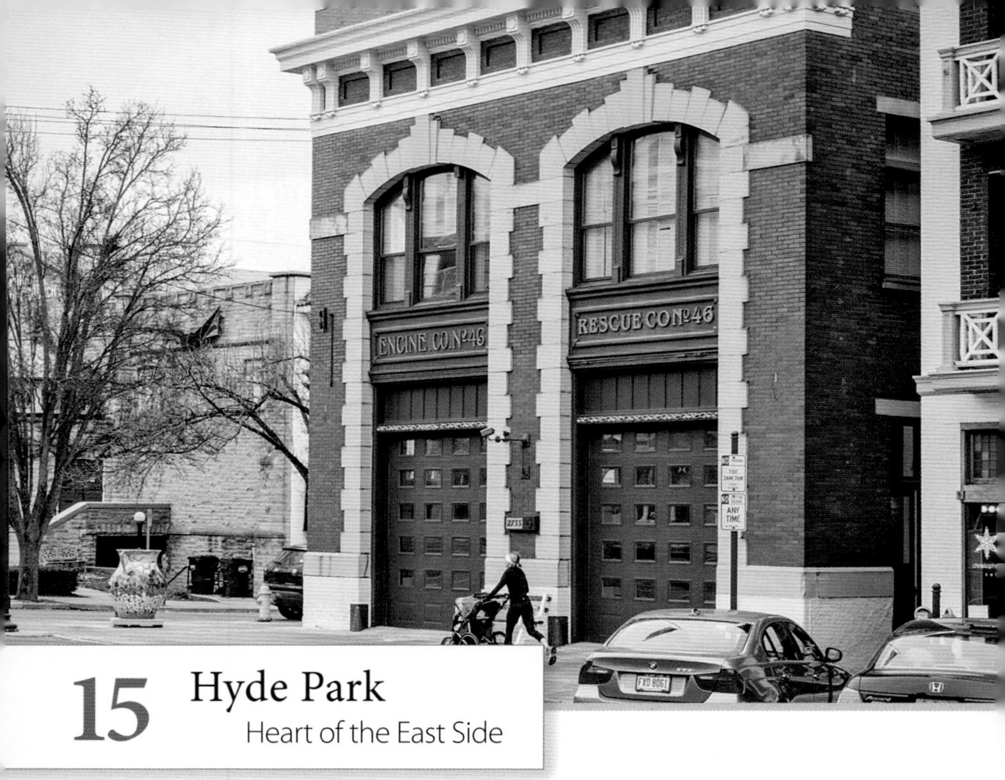

15 Hyde Park

Heart of the East Side

Above: Firehouse Engine Co. No. 46, across from Hyde Park Square, has been in service since 1908.

BOUNDARIES: Stettinius Ave., Erie Ave., Kilgour Ln., Observatory Ave.
DISTANCE: 2.4 miles
DIFFICULTY: Easy
PARKING: Public lot on east side of Edwards Rd., just north of Erie Ave.
PUBLIC TRANSIT: Take Metro (go-metro.com) bus route 11 to Hyde Park Square.

Hyde Park is one of Cincinnati's most desirable neighborhoods, with its lovely older homes, busy historic square, and shaded streets filled with walkers, runners, and bicyclists. Located 5 miles northeast of downtown Cincinnati, Hyde Park could easily take up multiple chapters in this book because it's such a wonderful place to explore.

A group of prominent Cincinnati businessmen (Charles Kilgour, John Kilgour, James E. Mooney, Albert S. Berry, Wallace Burch, Simeon Johnson, John Zumstein, and Thomas B. Youtsey) established Hyde Park in 1892 as an exclusive neighborhood for Cincinnati's wealthy. Together, they formed what was known as the Mornington Syndicate and purchased the triangle of land bounded by Edwards Road, Observatory Avenue, and Madison Road, along with a large stretch of ground to the east of Edwards. This section contains Hyde Park's oldest houses and its heart, Hyde Park Square. Later annexed to the City of Cincinnati in 1903, the neighborhood is named after New York's Hyde Park community.

Walk Description

For a walking tour of Hyde Park's original section and a little beyond, start at **Hyde Park Square,** which features a narrow park with seating raised above passing traffic. The centerpiece is **Kilgour Fountain,** originally installed in 1900 as a gift to the city. The work of Cincinnati-born sculptor Joseph Cronin (1859–1923), the fountain was restored and redesigned by Eleftherios Karkadoulias in 1976. Karkadoulias, who lowered the lamps and added a large concrete pool, was responsible for the restoration of Tyler Davidson Fountain at Fountain Square downtown too. Surrounding the block-long square are more than 100 retail stores, restaurants, galleries, fitness studios, and small offices housed in mixed-use buildings. Several regular events attract people from all over the city. Hyde Park Farmers Market takes place every Sunday, June through October. (It's the only local farmers market in Cincinnati where streets are closed to vehicles.) Hyde Park Blast is a nationally ranked cycling race, run, and street party in June, and the Hyde Park Art Show in October is the largest juried art show in the Midwest. Everything comes together to form a lively and relaxed neighborhood business district.

Use one of the two crosswalks connecting the square to the north side of Erie Avenue, and turn left. On the right is ❶ **Teller's of Hyde Park,** a retrofitted eatery and cocktail bar since 1995 inside the former Hyde Park Savings and Loan building. Next door is ❷ **Delamere & Hopkins,** a local retailer specializing in outdoor gear for field and stream. The oldest ❸ **Graeter's Ice Cream** in the regional chain has scooped its addictive handcrafted "French Pot method" ice cream, baked goods, and candy in this location since 1922. Around the corner on Edwards Road are two 1940s diners, ❹ **The Echo** (1945) and ❺ **Arthur's** (1947). Cross Erie Avenue, head south along Edwards Road, and turn left once you reach the other side. As with any commercial district intersection, check all directions before crossing. In the middle of the block is ❻ **Miller Gallery,** which represents emerging and established contemporary art. Continue to the end of the block where ❼ **Firehouse Engine Company No. 46** has served the community since 1908. To the right, on Michigan Avenue, is a half-block stretch of local businesses worth visiting, including ❽ **Poême** stationery shop, ❾ **Patty's Old Fashioned Popcorn,** and ❿ **Unwind Wine Bar & Light Fare.**

Leaving the square behind, continue walking east along Erie. ⓫ **Hyde Park Branch Library** (on the right) was built with funds from the Andrew Carnegie Foundation in 1912 and is one of the seven remaining Carnegie libraries in Hamilton County. In 1970, the branch underwent an extensive expansion and renovation project, which explains its understated appearance compared to other Carnegie libraries. Cross Shaw Avenue. At Shady Lane on the right is ⓬ **St. Mary Church.** Built in 1917, it is the second of several churches along this walk (Hyde Park Baptist Church at 2753 Erie is the first). As for the number of churches in Hyde Park, its founding as a village away from the city necessitated the need for places of worship to be within walking distance. Across the street at 2872 Erie Avenue is a modern house built following Leadership in Energy and Environmental Design (LEED) standards. Standing in contrast to its neighbors, the 4,200-square-foot house was featured in singer-actress Mariah Carey's directorial debut, *A Christmas Melody,* in 2015. (Hyde Park and adjacent Mount Lookout are increasingly popular East Side destinations for home buyers, putting pressure on existing homeowners to sell, which has led to an increasing number of teardowns. Residents are working with city officials to calm the teardown trend.) More typical for Hyde Park is the grand Swiss Chalet house at 2919 Erie Avenue.

Continue walking east. On the northeast corner of Erie and Paxton Avenues is ⓭ **Church of the Redeemer,** an Episcopal congregation founded in 1908. Still on the north side of Erie Avenue and past Grace Avenue are six new houses with main entrances off Raymar Boulevard in the back. They replaced a monastery built in the 1950s and demolished in early 2014. To the east beyond a long tree hedge is **Clark Montessori,** a junior and senior high school that sits on the former estate of Ohio Governor Myers Y. Cooper (1929–1931).

Just past 3049 Erie Avenue on the right is the unmarked **Kilgour Lane.** Follow this secluded and shaded walkway to Observatory Avenue. (Before this area became Hyde Park, it was part of two townships, Columbia to the north and Spencer to the south, in 1869. Observatory—then called City Road—was the dividing line.)

Bicycling is a popular form of transportation around Hyde Park.

Detour a smidge to your left and look across Observatory at the **George N. Stone House** (3025 Observatory Rd.). Built in 1880, it's an extremely vertical Stick Style house with Gothic Revival elements that was listed on the National Register of Historic Places in 1980. Architect Samuel Hannaford designed the house for George Stone (1839–1901), a prominent figure in the 19th century. After serving as a lieutenant and general in the Civil War, Stone moved from Colorado to Cincinnati with his family. He held stock in the Bell Telephone Company, where he became a director and eventually president and general manager. He was director and one of the largest owners in the street railway, gas, and coke companies; a member of multiple local clubs; a councilman and alderman; and a board of education member.

Walk back past Kilgour Lane and continue west toward Grace Avenue to ⓮ **Hyde Park Community United Methodist Church.** Completed in the Gothic style in 1927, the church is listed on the National Register of Historic Places. Walk three more blocks and take note of the many small apartment buildings and two-family houses along this stretch of Observatory. Monteith Apartments (3405 Monteith Ave.) is a well-preserved example of apartment living. Next door is ⓯ **Carl's Deli,** a classic neighborhood deli since 1938 known for its made-from-scratch sandwiches and sides, walk-in beer and wine cooler, and intimate neighborhood vibe.

Continue walking several blocks west on Observatory Avenue, crossing the busy Shaw and Linwood Avenues intersection. Five apartment buildings from the 1930s, '40s, and '50s were cleared from the northwest corner in late 2013 to make way for a new condominium complex.

On the right is another church, ⓰ **Knox Presbyterian Church,** finished in 1929 at an initial cost of $360,000.

Before reaching Edwards Road, you'll pass a series of former houses converted into offices. On the south side of Observatory Avenue at Edwards Road are two corner commercial buildings with numerous retail shops. On the northeast corner is La Tosca Flats, an American Craftsman apartment building listed on the National Register of Historic Places for reasons unknown to us. On the northwest corner is the restored **Hyde Park School** (1902). Another Samuel Hannaford–designed building, the school has a fascinating story. After the school closed in 2005 due to declining enrollment, parents presented proof that there was demand for the school and in 2012 successfully convinced Cincinnati Public Schools to reopen the historic building as a neighborhood school.

Cross Observatory Avenue at Edwards Road and continue west. Edwards Road is named for Jonathan Edwards, a Spencer Township pioneer from the early 1800s. Across the street at 2618 Observatory Avenue (immediately west of Hyde Park School) is an adorable cottage that resembles a Smurf house, for lack of a better description. Turn left on Westside Avenue, and then right on Perkins Lane. Follow Perkins to Stettinius Avenue. On the left is the **John Stettinius House**

(Oatfield), the last remaining home from the original Longworth Rookwood property, according to the *Digging Cincinnati History* blog (diggingcincinnati.com). John Longworth Stettinius was the son of John and Mary (Longworth) Stettinius and the grandson of wealthy Cincinnatian Nicholas Longworth. John L. Stettinius's grandson, John Longworth Stettinius II, was a lawyer and one of the founders of the Taft Stettinius & Hollister law firm in 1885.

Turn right on Stettinius and cross Observatory Avenue. The blocks north of Observatory to Erie Avenue between Madison and Edward roads are some of the most intact in Hyde Park. Remarkably, no local historic district is in place to protect the well-maintained old homes here. Walk one block to Erie Avenue. At the northwest corner is **Madison Park,** a triangular green space with considerable frontage along Madison Road that is rarely explored.

Before returning to Hyde Park Square along Erie Avenue, consider walking one block north to the **Grace and Wilfred Rush House** (3574 Burch Ave.). According to Cincinnati food etymologist Dann Woellert, this is where Martha Ann fruit cake—"one of the booziest and most gourmet fruitcakes distributed in the U.S. for more than 60 years"—got its start. The house was later known as Ivy Manor because most of the house was covered in English ivy.

Points of Interest

1. **Teller's of Hyde Park** 2710 Erie Ave., 513-321-4721, tellersofhydepark.com
2. **Delamere & Hopkins** 2708 Erie Ave., 513-871-3474, dhoutfitters.com
3. **Graeter's Ice Cream** 2704 Erie Ave., 513-321-6221, graeters.com
4. **The Echo** 3510 Edwards Rd., 513-321-2816, echo-hydepark.com
5. **Arthur's** 3516 Edwards Rd., 513-871-5543, arthurscincinnati.com
6. **Miller Gallery** 2715 Erie Ave., 513-871-4420, millergallery.com
7. **Firehouse Engine Company No. 46** 2731 Erie Ave.
8. **Poême** 3446 Michigan Ave., 513-321-4999, poeme-online.com

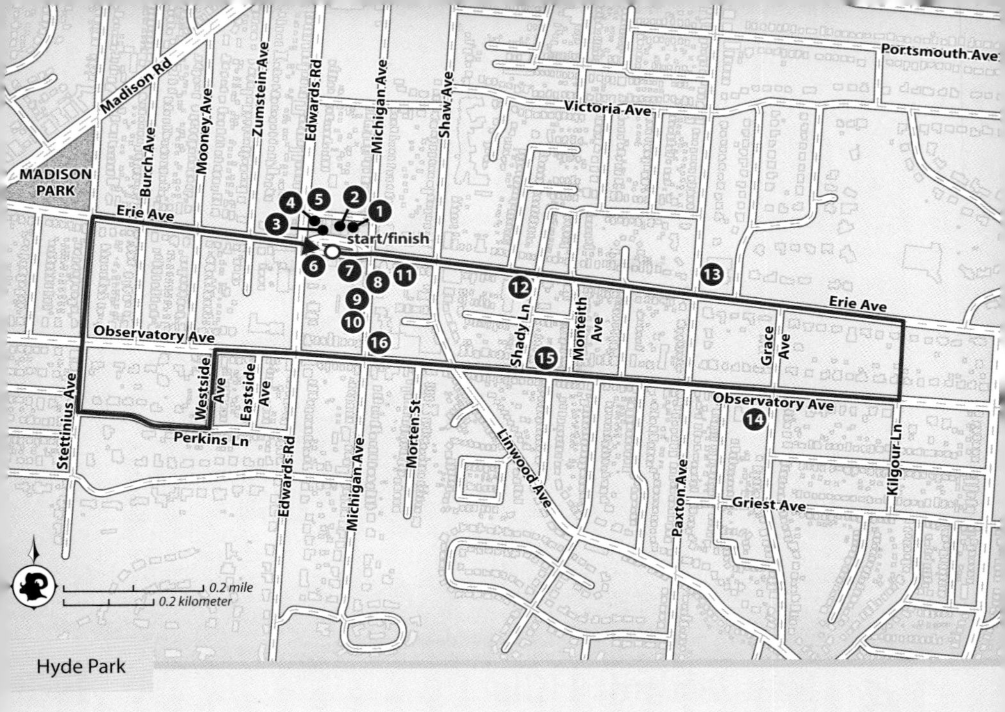

9 **Patty's Old Fashioned Popcorn** 3437 Michigan Ave., 513-533-2676, pattysoldfashionedpopcorn.com

10 **Unwind Wine Bar & Light Fare** 3435 Michigan Ave., 513-321-9463, unwindhydepark.com

11 **Hyde Park Branch Library** 2747 Erie Ave., 513-369-4456, cincinnatilibrary.org/branches/hydepark.html

12 **St. Mary Church** 2853 Erie Ave., 513-321-1207, smchp.com

13 **Church of the Redeemer** 2944 Erie Ave., 513-321-6700, redeemer-cincy.org

14 **Hyde Park Community United Methodist Church** 1345 Grace Ave., 513-871-1345, hydeparkchurch.org

15 **Carl's Deli** 2836 Observatory Ave., 513-871-2275, carlsdeli.com

16 **Knox Presbyterian Church** 3400 Michigan Ave., 513-321-2573, knox.org

16 East Walnut Hills

From Midcentury Suburb to Diverse Neighborhood

Above: Homes in East Walnut Hills, representing a variety of architectural styles, were built primarily between 1880 and 1930.

BOUNDARIES: E. McMillan St., Ashland Ave., Upland Pl., Woodburn Ave., Madison Rd., Cleinview Ave., Ingleside Ave.
DISTANCE: 2 miles
DIFFICULTY: Easy
PARKING: Parking lot on Woodburn Ave. between Clayton Ave. and Madison Rd.
PUBLIC TRANSIT: Take Metro (go-metro.com) bus route 11 or 24 to DeSales Corner.

East Walnut Hills is a diverse neighborhood, both ethnically and economically. It developed in the mid-19th century, as wealthy professional people—seeking relief from the soot and blight of the densely populated basin area near the Ohio River—developed great estates in the hillsides. Their 5- and 10-acre properties were located largely around the O'Bryonville and Grandin Road areas, reached by what was then called Madison Pike, a toll road. A German community congregated along what is now Woodburn Avenue. Eventually this part of East Walnut Hills was incorporated as the village of Woodburn, and both areas remained independent until the City of Cincinnati annexed them in 1870 and 1873, respectively. This walks focuses on the areas primarily around Woodburn Avenue from E. McMillan Street to Madison Road and excludes the large East Walnut Hills Historic District east of Cleinview Avenue.

Walk Description

Start your walk in front of the former **William J. Williams YMCA,** a Tudor Revival building constructed in 1930 on the property where Williams lived. Across E. McMillan Street is ❶ **Walnut Hills Methodist Episcopal Church,** a fine Gothic Revival built in 1872. The building now houses the Cincinnati Early Learning Centers and Echo Church. Turn right on Ashland Avenue, walking past the four Second Empire houses on the left (2402–2414) featuring entrance towers, mansard roofs, and decorative iron railings. Turn left on Fleming Street. On the opposite corner is the **William Griffith House** (2344 Ashland Ave.), an exceptional example of Stick style built in 1875. Griffith was—appropriately—the owner of a lumberyard and construction company, James T. Griffith Company, which worked on Music Hall, City Hall, and Shillito's Department Store.

Walk to Upland Place and turn right. This is the center of the **Uplands Historic District,** notable for its high concentration of late-19th-century residential architecture. Locally and nationally prominent architects designed houses here. **William Watts Taylor House** (2333 Upland Pl.), a Queen Anne with half-timbered gables, was built in 1885. Taylor succeeded Maria Longworth Nichols Storer as director of Rookwood Pottery when she retired in 1890. Another Queen Anne is the **Joseph A. Jones House** (2315 Upland Pl.), built circa 1875. Samuel Hannaford designed this richly detailed house for Jones, who worked for Robert Jones & Co., a 19th-century manufacturer of steam boilers and lard tanks.

Cross to the other side of Upland at Cypress Street. Ahead is a magnificent Swiss chalet, likely the best example in Cincinnati. The **Albert and Alice Fisher House** (2214 Upland Pl.) was built in 1892 after the couple had honeymooned in the mountains of Switzerland and wanted a home to preserve their memories. Architect Lucian Plympton used traditional Swiss folk art in the design, including handmade pegs in its interior. Plympton also designed the **Cordelia A Plympton House** (1885) for his mother at the end of the street. The Willis Kemper House (1895) next door is attributed to Plympton too. Heading north, the **Harvey/Graveson House** (2326 Upland Pl.) is brazenly Châteauesque. William Harvey is listed in *The Inland Architect and Building News* in 1884 as commissioning the house, which was finished in 1883.

Cross Fleming Street and return to E. McMillan Street. On the left at 1339 E. McMillan St. is the **Macneal-Joseph Thomas House.** Now the St. Ursula Fine Arts Building, the Italianate house was built mid-19th century with an addition circa 1893 by James W. McLaughlin for department store magnate Joseph Carew. Turn right on E. McMillan Street and walk alongside the ❷ **Saint Ursula Academy** complex established by Ursuline nuns in 1910. Over time, the historic Worcester residence, the Schuster-Martin building, and Bellamy Storer house would form the nucleus of the campus. The easternmost Worcester residence and the center Schuster-Martin building were connected in 1915. The far west building became the property of the school in the early 20th century when the residents, Maria Longworth Nichols Storer and her husband, U.S. Ambassador Bellamy Storer, died and left their home to the Ursuline order.

Continue east to where Woodburn Avenue intersects E. McMillan Street, which becomes a two-way street at Grandview Avenue. On the right is ❸ **New Thought Unity Center,** a Neoclassical Revival structure built in 1926. Garber & Woodward is responsible for the design, which features Corinthian columns, classical pilasters, and a massive pediment similar to those of the two high schools for which the firm is better known—Walnut Hills (2700 Ashland Ave.) and Withrow High School (3250 Victory Pkwy.). Cross E. McMillan Street in the crosswalk that connects with Woodburn Avenue. On the northeast corner is **The Clermont** (1404–1406 E. McMillan St.), one of many apartment buildings that Thomas Emery & Sons developed with the Steinkamp firm. Built in 1906, the Colonial Revival building is noted for its colonnaded entrance on E. McMillan Street and multiple porches across its facade.

Ahead is the **Woodburn Avenue Historic District,** also known as DeSales Corner. Most of the historical buildings date from 1880 to 1910, when East Walnut Hills was developing as a streetcar suburb. It remains as an outstanding example of the development of a late-19th-century business district expanding from a centrally located Catholic church along busy

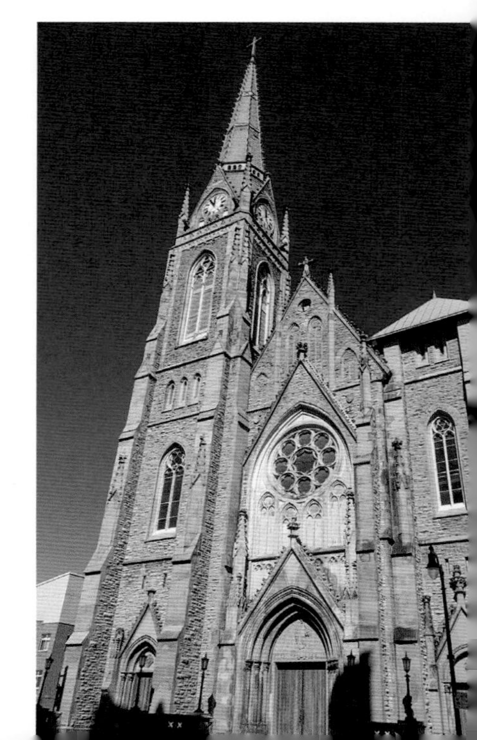

St. Francis de Sales Catholic Church

transportation corridors. Walk north past Locust Street to William Howard Taft Road. Ahead is the imposing **Eckert Building** (2600 Woodburn Ave.), erected in 1896. Merchants Valentine and Joseph Eckert financed the construction. The corner tower is a distinctive Queen Anne feature, along with the decorative cornice, stone trim banding, and a Palladian window in the gable. Walk past Burdette Avenue to Clayton Avenue. The **Krug Buildings** (2714–16 Woodburn Ave.) on the southeast corner are emblematic of distinctive corner towers common on apartment buildings in East Walnut Hills. ❹ **Urbana Cafe,** a coffee shop with locations in Findlay Market and Pendleton, opened here in 2018. Across the street is ❺ **Schulhoff Equipment Rental & Sales,** which opened in 1935. The original 1922 building on the west side included an auto repair shop and parking garage. The shop was expanded in the 1930s to include a paint shop and another repair building across the street. In 1973, the current Western look was introduced, covering all exterior walls with cedar siding. Next door, **Felix Flats** (2723 Woodburn Ave.) was built in 1906 and is exalted for its elaborate stone carvings and iron railings on the balconies. It is one of eight apartment buildings on Woodburn, evidence that apartment living was popular here in the early 20th century.

Cross Myrtle Avenue. ❻ **Argos,** an all-natural pet food and supply store, occupies the first floor of **Amelia Flats,** a corner Italianate town house from the 1880s that was expanded in 1898. Find selective vintage and modern clothing, housewares, vinyl records, and crafts at ❼ **Hi-Bred,** which has one of the most creative window displays in the city. Across the street is ❽ **Woodburn Brewery,** which opened in 2016 inside a former movie theater. Immediately to the north is **Lutmer Flats** (2804–06 Woodburn Ave.), where builder Henry Lutmer operated a grocery store until his death in 1915. Built circa 1895, the impressive Queen Anne facade includes a two-story oriel window, a bracketed cornice, and stone banding at each window level.

Holding down the southeast corner of Madison Road and Woodburn Avenue is the **San Marco Apartment Building** (1893). It is seven stories high with gables, pinnacles, diagonal chimneys, and cone-roofed turrets moving the eye along the roofline. On the southwest corner is a handsome Art Deco bank building that was built after Madison Road was extended to meet up with Victory Parkway in 1930. ❾ **The Littlefield** opened its second location here in fall 2018 after an extensive renovation and considerable community support. It joins several other culinary businesses, including Mardi Gras on Madison (1524 Madison Rd.), O Pie O (1527 Madison Rd.), The Growler House (1526 Madison Rd.), and Suzie Wong's (1544 Madison Rd.). Across the street on the northwest corner is Residences at DeSales Plaza (1550 Madison Rd.), the first in a series of contemporary apartment complexes built north along Woodburn Avenue.

Completing the trifecta is ⑩ **St. Francis de Sales Catholic Church,** on the northeast corner. Completed in 1879 for a parish founded in the area in 1849, it served a growing German population. The highly expressive neo-Gothic building, designed by Francis Himpler, includes a dominating corner tower whose bell, Big Joe, was installed in 1895. At the time, it was the largest church bell and largest swinging bell ever cast in the United States.

Turn right on Madison Road. ⑪ **indigenous,** a contemporary craft store, relocated here from O'Bryonville in 2017. Cross Moorman Avenue and walk to Hackberry Street. Across the street is **Purcell Marian Catholic High School** (2935 Hackberry St.), one of three Catholic high schools built in 1928 and designed by prominent local architects Crowe & Schulte. Purcell was all boys until the 1981–82 school year, when it merged with the all-girls Marian High School. **Engine Co. #23** (1700 Madison Rd.) was one of a number of firehouses built in the last decade of the 19th century with funding from a city bond. Company #23 was organized in 1885 and remained at this location until 1980, when it moved to 1623 Madison Rd. Walk one more block to Cleinview Avenue. All that remains of **Seventh Presbyterian Church** (built in 1886) is the Romanesque Revival facade and soaring tower that can be seen from DeSales Corner. The early congregation included prominent East Walnut Hills families, all of whom established large estates in the community. After a fire in 1971, a new church in a modern style was built within the ruins. A developer cleared most of the property in 2015 to prepare it for a nine-home residential site.

Turn right on Cleinview Avenue and enter the small **Cleinview-Hackberry Historic District,** a community that developed in the 1870s as people left the overcrowded city. This tucked-away street benefits from the openness of mature trees and landscaped yards. The six brick houses on the left share a similar setback and height. At the south end of the street are the Cleinview Avenue Steps, which lead to William Howard Taft Road. Follow Cleinview Avenue to E. McMillan Street, and turn right for a quick glance at three more impressive residences and a church before returning to your starting point.

Opposite Cleinview Avenue is the 1910 **Goodman Residence** (1707 E. McMillian St.), an eclectic design by William Martin Aiken. Walk two blocks west to the **Bernard Moorman Residence** (1514 E McMillan St.), an early Italianate home designed by Johann Bast and constructed for the dry goods merchant in 1860. Opposite here and just south of E. McMillian Street is the **George Pohlman Residence** (2431 Ingleside Ave.), an exuberant example of Queen Anne built in 1889. Alfred O. Elzner designed this house, along with others on Cleinview Avenue and Hackberry Street. Back on E. McMillan Street at the northwest corner of Ingleside Avenue is the Gothic Revival–style ⑫ **Walnut Hills Christian Church** by Samuel Hannaford & Sons, constructed in 1925.

Continue west on E. McMillan Street to return to your starting point.

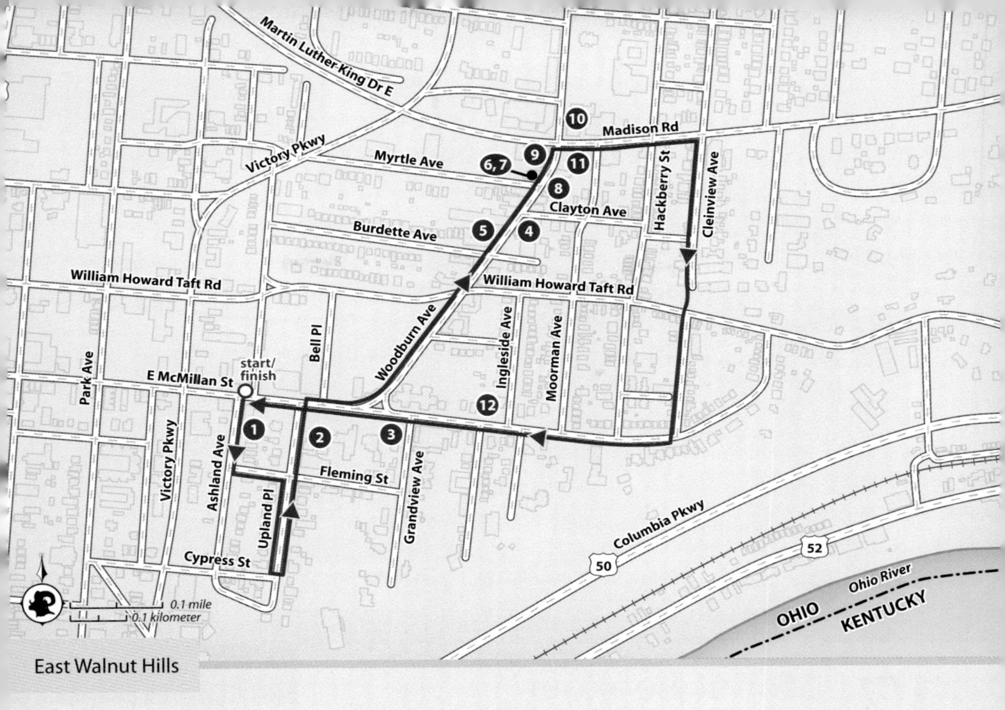

Points of Interest

1. **Walnut Hills Methodist Episcopal Church** 1301 E. McMillan St., celcinc.org
2. **Saint Ursula Academy** 1339 E. McMillan St., 513-961-3410, saintursula.org
3. **New Thought Unity Center** 1401 E. McMillan St., 513-961-2527, ntunity.org
4. **Urbana Cafe** 2714 Woodburn Ave., 513-813-3133, urbana-cafe.com
5. **Schulhoff Equipment Rental & Sales** 2709 Woodburn Ave., 513-961-1122
6. **Argos** 2801 Woodburn Ave., 513-221-4451, argospet.com
7. **Hi-Bred** 2807 Woodburn Ave., 513-240-4664, hibred.life
8. **Woodburn Brewery** 2800 Woodburn Ave., 513-221-2337, woodburnbrewery.com
9. **The Littlefield** 1535 Madison Rd.
10. **St. Francis de Sales Catholic Church** 1600 Madison Rd., 513-961-1945, stfrancisds.com
11. **indigenous** 1609 Madison Rd., 513-321-3750, indigenouscraft.com
12. **Walnut Hills Christian Church** 1438 E. McMillan St., 513-961-4084

17 Mount Lookout

Birthplace of American Astronomy

Above: The Cincinnati Observatory is home to the world's oldest telescope still in use.
Photo by Warren LeMay

BOUNDARIES: Linwood Ave., Lookout Cir., Heekin Ave., Avery Ln., Inglenook Pl.
DISTANCE: 3.6 miles
DIFFICULTY: Strenuous
PARKING: Park your bike or car in the Mount Lookout Square metered parking lot or southwest of the square along Delta Ave.
PUBLIC TRANSIT: Metro buses (go-metro.com) serve this area. Take route 24 to Mount Lookout Square.

One word can describe Mount Lookout: *enchanting*. Located 5.5 miles east of downtown Cincinnati, Mount Lookout is tucked in between Hyde Park and Columbia-Tusculum. It is named for Mount Lookout Observatory, which moved from Mount Adams to this part of the city in 1873 and was later renamed Cincinnati Observatory. Mount Lookout's lively business district,

Mount Lookout Square, is lined with restaurants and bars, contributing to a vibrant nightlife. Revival-style houses dominate its rugged peaks and wooded valleys, while hidden walkways and steps connect its streets. Its crown jewel is Ault Park, which the City of Cincinnati recognizes as being in Mount Lookout, although nearby Hyde Park claims it as its own.

Walk Description

Begin your adventure with a cup of coffee at ❶ **Lookout Joe,** on the northwest corner of Mount Lookout Square. What could easily be a chaotic mess of traffic is instead Delta and Linwood Avenues flowing seamlessly through the center of Mount Lookout with a series of traffic signals, pedestrian islands, bike lanes, and a central parking square. Mount Lookout Square remains a thriving neighborhood center with a mix of businesses that cater to daytime and nighttime visitors.

Walk south on Delta Avenue to ❷ **The Redmoor,** the former Mount Lookout Theater built in 1928, and cross Linwood Avenue into the parking lot at the crosswalk in front of the theater. Looking southeast, you can see the steeple of ❸ **Christ the King Church,** designed by Edward J. Schulte, a midcentury modernist architect known for combining modern details with traditional church functions.

Restaurants dominate this side of the square. At the north end is ❹ **Zip's Cafe,** which opened in 1926 and is known for its burgers. ❺ **Ichiban Restaurant** is one of two sushi restaurants on the square. Treat yourself at the end of this walk. Cross Delta and turn right, heading up the Lookout Lane Steps (to the left of 1010 Delta Ave.). Turn around once you reach the top for a dramatic view of the square below.

As you enter Lookout Circle, continue east, keeping to the left sidewalk and passing one tidy house after another. Just past Van Dyke Drive, the street becomes fully shaded thanks to the canopy of trees along the block before Herlin Place. Turn left on Herschel Avenue and then right on Beverly Hill Drive, which slopes downward. Most houses here were built between 1925 and 1935. At the bottom of the hill on the right is Salisbury Walkway, a lovely pedestrian oasis in a dry creekbed that reaches Salisbury Drive. This could be a good side trip for another day.

Heading back up the hilly street, just past 1154 Beverly Hill Dr., on the left, are the Arnold Street Steps. Follow them to Arnold Street above. To the left is gaslit Hayward Avenue. Continue on Arnold Street and follow it to Le Blond Avenue. Turn left and walk to Heekin Avenue. A sign on Heekin reads WELCOME TO HISTORIC LINWOOD. For this short stretch up to Shattuc Avenue, you're straddling the neighborhood lines of Mount Lookout and Linwood. Heekin Avenue is super-steep, so breathe through your nose and suck in all the oxygen you can get from the surrounding hillside while climbing all the way to the top at Principio Avenue.

To the right is ❻ **Ault Park,** the fourth-largest park in Cincinnati at 224 acres. Landscape architect A. D. Taylor designed the figure eight layout of the drive and the formal gardens within the park. It is an ideal place for taking a walk, especially at sunrise and sunset, when the extensive panoramic views of the Little Miami River valley from the grand Italian Renaissance–style pavilion are most stunning. To the west, Mount Adams and the tops of downtown buildings are visible.

Turn left on Principio Avenue and walk downhill back to Herschel Avenue. Turn right on Herschel Avenue and head toward ❼ **Kilgour School,** built in 1928. To the left of the school, walk to the back of the property, to the right of the playground, and follow the chain-link fence to a gate hidden behind the school's new gym. Go through the gate and down the path to the Griest Avenue Steps. This hidden path is an enchanting ravine shortcut to Griest Avenue. At the top of the steps, turn right on Suncrest Drive, a delightfully narrow street where traffic moves slowly enough that children can play freely. Turn left on Herschel Avenue and walk to Observatory Avenue.

Turn left and walk to gaslit Observatory Place. Turn right and walk past the houses that make up the single-block **Observatory Historic District** and lead to its focal point, the Cincinnati Observatory. The residences on either side of Observatory Place evolved from 1874 to 1916, and the result is a lovely streetscape that has several different styles, including French Second Empire and Classical Revival. Designated a National Historic Landmark, the oldest professional observatory in the United States, and one of the most important buildings in Cincinnati, the ❽ **Cincinnati Observatory** consists of two buildings, with the larger one housing an aperture refracting telescope. The observatory originally sat on 4 acres at the top of Mount Ida, which Nicholas Longworth donated. President

Like other neighborhood theaters, Mount Lookout Theater outlived its original use, but it remains a vital part of its surroundings as The Redmoor.

John Quincy Adams presided over the dedication on November 9, 1843, before a crowd of thousands. It was here that Adams gave his last public speech. Mount Ida was renamed Mount Adams shortly afterward. To get away from the pollution of the basin, the telescope moved to this new location 5 miles east of the city in 1873. The area was renamed Mount Lookout in honor of the new observatory. Board member John Kilgour donated the land and underwrote much of the construction with a $10,000 donation. Cincinnati architect Samuel Hannaford designed the larger Greek Revival–style building. The smaller Mitchel Building holds the original telescope taken from the Mount Adams Observatory.

The second observatory director, Cleveland Abbe, published the nation's first weather forecasts, and he later assisted in the founding of the National Weather Service. Today, there is a ton of programming, including regular stargazing, and the landscaping has an integrated solar system feature. Astronomer Dean Regas is the cohost of *Star Gazers,* which airs on more than 100 PBS stations.

The rest of this walk is a series of twists and turns, and ups and downs, with few notable landmarks along the way. Simply enjoy the exertion of discovering this fascinating residential hilly section of Cincinnati.

After taking in the Observatory Historic District, turn left on gaslit Avery Lane, which becomes Avery Lane Steps midblock. Turn left on Wellston Place. Walk to the end of this short block of adorable bungalows and cross Observatory Avenue.

Follow Park Ridge Place, similar in scale to Suncrest Drive, to Griest Avenue. Turn right on Griest Avenue and follow it several blocks to Delta Avenue. On the northeast corner is the two-story ⑨ **East Exchange Building,** which Cincinnati and Suburban Bell Telephone Company built from handmade brick and stone trim in 1935. Cincinnati architects Harry Hake Sr. and Harry Hake Jr. are responsible for the design.

Cross at the traffic signal and pass brick-paved Corbett Street and Halpin Avenue on the left. Turn left on Inglenook Place and walk downward to the cul-de-sac. Look for the Inglenook Place Steps on the left at 1120 Inglenook Pl. and descend to Halpin Avenue. Turn right on Halpin and walk to Linwood Avenue. Cross Linwood with caution and turn left. Turn right on Kinmont Street and veer left. Look closely for the steep Fawn Alley Steps on the left, descend to Mount Lookout Square, and seek a place to eat and drink.

(continued on next page)

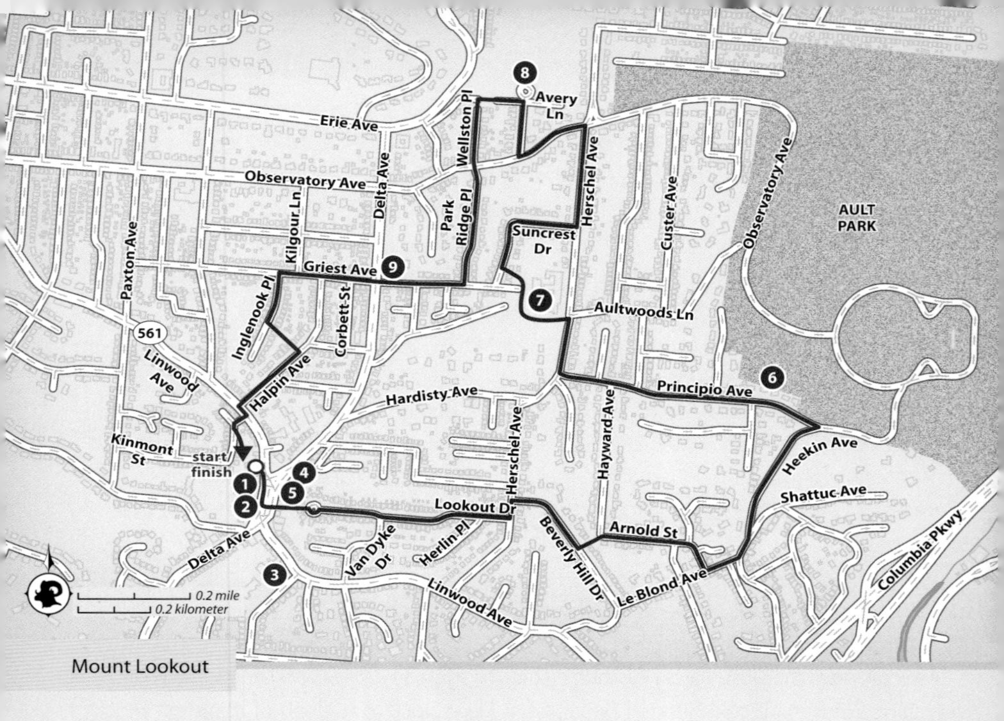

Points of Interest

1. **Lookout Joe** 3181 Linwood Ave., 513-871-8626, lookoutjoe.com
2. **The Redmoor** 3187 Linwood Ave., 513-871-6789, theredmoor.com
3. **Christ the King Church** 3223 Linwood Ave., 513-321-4121, ourlordchristtheking.org
4. **Zip's Cafe** 1036 Delta Ave., 513-871-9876, zipscafe.com
5. **Ichiban Restaurant** 1020 Delta Ave., 513-321-8686, ichibancinci.com
6. **Ault Park** 5090 Observatory Cir., 513-357-2604, aultparkac.org
7. **Kilgour School** 1339 Herschel Ave., 513-363-3000, kilgour.cps-k12.org
8. **Cincinnati Observatory** 3489 Observatory Pl., 513-321-5186, cincinnatiobservatory.org
9. **East Exchange Building** Greist and Delta Aves.

18 Columbia-Tusculum

San Francisco on the Ohio

Above: Columbia-Tusculum's painted ladies

BOUNDARIES: Columbia Pkwy., Eastern Ave., Stites Ave., Alms Park
DISTANCE: 2.5 miles
DIFFICULTY: Flat and then dramatically hilly, with some delightfully steep areas
PARKING: Columbia Square
PUBLIC TRANSIT: Take route 28 to Eastern Ave.

Located about 4.5 miles east of downtown, along Columbia Parkway, rests the oldest neighborhood in Cincinnati, Columbia-Tusculum. Founded as Columbia near the Little Miami River in 1788, it was established just one month prior to Cincinnati. Many of the early settlers are buried in the former Columbia Baptist Cemetery, founded in 1790, which is now Pioneer Memorial Cemetery. Cincinnati annexed the area in 1873. The community owes its compound name, Columbia-Tusculum, to the subdivision of Nicholas Longworth's property in Columbia in 1866.

His heirs created a large subdivision on the steepest part of the hillside and called it Mount Tusculum, for people seeking a rural setting with quick access to downtown.

This picturesque neighborhood is known for clusters of colorful Victorian-era homes decorated as painted ladies. The most significant sections are in a local historic district, which allows the city to perform design review for exterior work and discourage demolition. It is also home to popular local restaurants, such as Allyn's Cafe and the Precinct, which is housed in restored Police Station No. 6 (1896), designed by Samuel Hannaford & Sons. Several performing arts groups are housed in restored buildings along Eastern Avenue. While there are no historic squares or open spaces like those found in nearby Hyde Park and Mount Lookout, the neighborhood is home to 85 acres of lush parkland at Alms Park at the top of Mount Tusculum. It has stunning views of Lunken Airport and the Ohio River stretching west toward downtown.

Take note of the painted ladies' artistic detailing as you walk through Columbia-Tusculum.

Walk Description

Park your bike or car in the Columbia Square parking lot at Hoge Street on the south side of Columbia Parkway. Turn right on Columbia Parkway, which is not for the faint of heart, to embark on this flat-to-vertical hike. While there's rarely a person walking along here, you'll see a great deal of car traffic and maybe even a darting Lazarus lizard.

Turn right on Stanley Avenue and walk past ❶ **Stanley's Pub,** a longtime neighborhood gathering spot.

Turn left on Eastern Avenue for a tour of some of the oldest surviving buildings in Cincinnati. This is the oldest and flattest section of Columbia-Tusculum, platted in 1834. What is believed to be the oldest continuously occupied home in Hamilton County stands at 3644 Eastern Avenue. James Morris reportedly built it as a log cabin in 1805 and later updated it to the Gothic Revival style. Across Eastern is a railroad tunnel that leads to Congress Avenue.

On your left, the historic ❷ **Langdon House**'s architectural style stands out as one of the only remaining Steamboat Gothic houses in Cincinnati. This house was built in 1855 and purchased in 1865 by Dr. Henry Archer Langdon. It sat vacant for many years, but in 1976 it was purchased and has been restored over time.

Farther along Eastern, past Tusculum Avenue, is the original business district. ❸ **Columbia Baptist Church** has the oldest congregation in Hamilton County. It currently houses the Riley School of Irish Music. Andrew Carnegie gifted 3738 Eastern Ave. as a public library to the community in 1906 under the specifications of noted architectural firm Samuel Hannaford & Sons. It was reopened as an events space, the ❹ **Carnegie Center,** in the mid-1990s.

Across the street are 3 of 17 Columbia-Tusculum properties collectively listed on the National Register of Historic Places. ❺ **Kellogg House** was constructed circa 1835 in the Federal style with distinctive, divided windows. ❻ **The Bates Building** is a simple frame building constructed in 1865. Former ❼ **Spencer Township Hall** was built in 1860 in the Greek Revival style.

At the northeast corner of Stites Avenue and Eastern Avenue is the former Columbia Methodist Episcopal Church, built in 1894 and designed by Charles Crapsey.

Walk briefly up Stites Avenue to the ❽ **Hezekiah Stites Jr. House,** also listed on the National Register of Historic Places. This Federal-style house was built facing the Ohio River in 1835 by the family of Benjamin Stites, one of Columbia's founders.

Return to Eastern Avenue and turn right. Turn right again onto Donham Avenue. Next to St. Stephen Church are the Donham Avenue Steps, which once led to Columbia Parkway but are now closed. Continue northwest along Morris Place to Tusculum Avenue.

Turn right onto Tusculum Avenue, cross Columbia Parkway, and then walk up, up, up to Sachem Avenue.

Turn right on Sachem and continue your ascent of Mount Tusculum. Once you reach the top, you will see the ❾ **Alms Park Steps** leading into the woods. Follow the path to the left toward the clearing with the bronze statue of Stephen Foster. An accompanying plaque explains Foster's connection to Cincinnati, where he wrote most of his songs about Kentucky.

Turn right and follow the drive to the overlook. Here, you'll see Lunken Airport and connecting Otto Armleder Park.

Continue down the drive past the Longworth wine cellar back to Tusculum Avenue.

Turn left on Tusculum and continue down, down, down. This area north of Columbia Parkway was settled in the 1880s and laid out in a modified grid pattern because of the steep terrain. Upcoming are two more properties listed on the National Register of Historic Places. ❿ **Stephen Decker Rowhouse** is the only one of its kind in Cincinnati, with robust Victorian detailing. Eight other nearby houses were patterned after the ⓫ **Norwell Residence**, at 506 Tusculum Ave., because of its architectural significance.

Cross Columbia Parkway and turn right on Morris Place. Turn right on Stanley Avenue and retrace your steps to your parked bike or car.

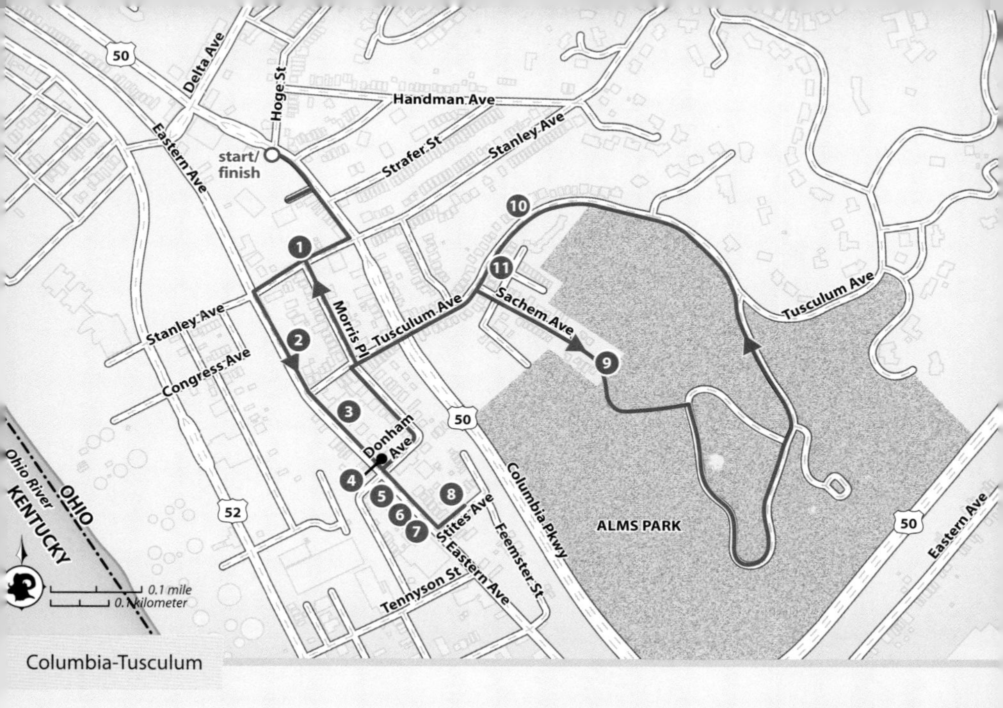

Columbia-Tusculum

Points of Interest

1. **Stanley's Pub** 323 Stanley Ave., 513-871-6249
2. **Langdon House** 3626 Eastern Ave.
3. **Columbia Baptist Church/Riley School of Irish Music** 3718 Eastern Ave., rileyirishmusic.com
4. **Carnegie Center** 3738 Eastern Ave., 513-473-5745, thecarnegiecenter.org
5. **Kellogg House** 3807 Eastern Ave.
6. **Bates Building** 3819 Eastern Ave.
7. **Spencer Township Hall/Ballet Theater** Midwest 3833 Eastern Ave.
8. **Hezekiah Stites Jr. House** 315 Stites Ave.
9. **Alms Park** 711 Alms Park Ln., 513-352-4080, cincinnatiparks.com/alms-park
10. **Stephen Decker Rowhouse** 531–541 Tusculum Ave.
11. **Norwell Residence** 506 Tusculum Ave.

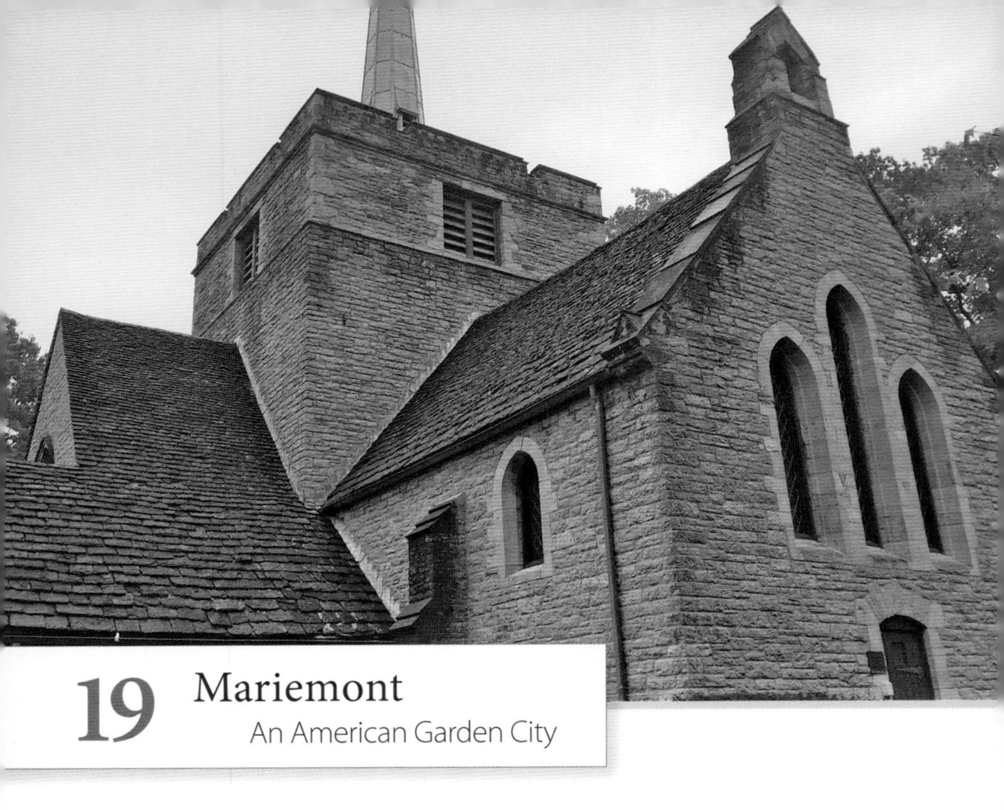

19 Mariemont

An American Garden City

Above: The first building completed in Mariemont, Mariemont Community Church illustrates 1920s English town-planning ideals. *Photo by Warren LeMay*

BOUNDARIES: Miami Bluff Dr., Murray Ave., Beech St., Madisonville Rd., Crystal Springs Rd.
DISTANCE: 2.4 miles
DIFFICULTY: Easy
PARKING: Park on Chestnut St. in front of Mariemont Community Church.
PUBLIC TRANSIT: Metro (go-metro.com) buses serve this area. Take route 28 or 29X to Milford.

For one of Cincinnati's great walking experiences, head to Mariemont. Located about 10 miles east of downtown Cincinnati, Mariemont is one of America's most picturesque communities. It is like no other place in Cincinnati, with its linear street grid, lush gardens and parks, stucco-and-Tudor architecture, and undeniable sense of place.

Mary Emery was the visionary who funded the village, named after her estate in Rhode Island. Emery (1844–1927) moved from Brooklyn, New York, with her family to Cincinnati in 1862. Upon the death of her husband, Thomas Emery, in 1906, she embarked on generously supporting the Cincinnati Zoo, Children's Hospital, and Cincinnati Art Museum.

Mary Emery and Charles Livingood, her business manager and right-hand man, hired John Nolen, a renowned landscape architect and community planner, to design Mariemont as an English garden suburb. In 1923, Mrs. Emery formed the Mariemont Company to supervise design and construction. In all, 27 architects contributed to the appearance of Mariemont. It took a mere two years, from 1924 until 1926, to build the village. Initially intended to include all economic classes, construction costs drove rents higher than planned, and Mariemont developed as a middle-income enclave. Unlike the northern suburb of Glendale, Mariemont was planned as a relatively self-sufficient community, with proximity to the job-producing industrial sections of Oakley and Norwood.

Mariemont Preservation Foundation, which has programs and events that promote the community's planning principles and history, helped secure National Historic Landmark designation in 2007. The American Planning Association named Mariemont a Top 10 Great Neighborhood in America in 2008 for its important role in town planning in the 1920s.

Walk Description

Start your walk adjacent to the old town square at the Norman-style ❶ **Mariemont Community Church,** which sits at the southeast corner of Oak and Chestnut Streets. The first building to be completed in the village, the limestone church features a stone-tile roof and a wooden spire. Walk toward the fountain and look across the street at two corner buildings that make up Ripley apartments and town houses. Built in 1924, these buildings, along with the church and nearby **Dale Park School** (now Cincinnati Waldorf School), make up the original town center. Dale Park Fire Station (3914 Oak Street) is tucked away just north of the eastern apartment building and now houses offices.

Cross Oak Street and walk to three single-family houses at 3875, 3885, and 3895 Oak Street known as the Short Group, built in 1924. Designed by Charles W. Short Jr., these half-timbered stucco houses were intended to reflect Mariemont Community Church. Turn left on Chestnut Street. On the left is the Ziegler Group (6617–6635 Chestnut St.), eight stucco-and-frame houses with massive chimneys. Ahead are three flats that comprise the Cellarius Group (3893–3905 Beech St.). Off Beech Street to the left is Linden Place, a row of 12 single-family frame cottages with communal garages designed by Elzner & Anderson, the prominent Cincinnati architectural firm known for designing the Ingalls Building (1903) downtown.

Turn right on Beech Street and walk to Murray Road. On the right are the three-story McKenzie Apartments. Clinton McKenzie of New York designed apartments and town houses that extend along the block to 6639 Murray Avenue. The streetcar line to Cincinnati ran along the center of Murray Avenue until 1942. Turn right on Murray and cross Oak Street, walking in front of the Gilchrist Group (6703–6725 Murray Rd.), a series of Georgian Revival town houses with varying setbacks reminiscent of 18th-century Philadelphia. Nick's Hardware once occupied the quaint wooden storefront set back from the street at 6705 Murray Avenue.

Turn right on Plainville Road. Keep an eye out on your right for an archway with a honeymoon apartment overhead. Maple Street, running through the arch, was designed with decreasing setbacks. It gradually narrows by 6 feet from east to west, giving the impression that the street is longer than it is. Set back from the street at 3919 Plainfield Road is Mariemont Preservation Foundation. Next door, at 3915 Plainfield, is the **Ferris House,** one of the oldest brick buildings (built 1812–13) in Hamilton County and adjacent to the site of ground-breaking for Mariemont on April 23, 1923.

Dale Park features a statuary group named Les Enfants *that depicts a Normandy peasant family.*

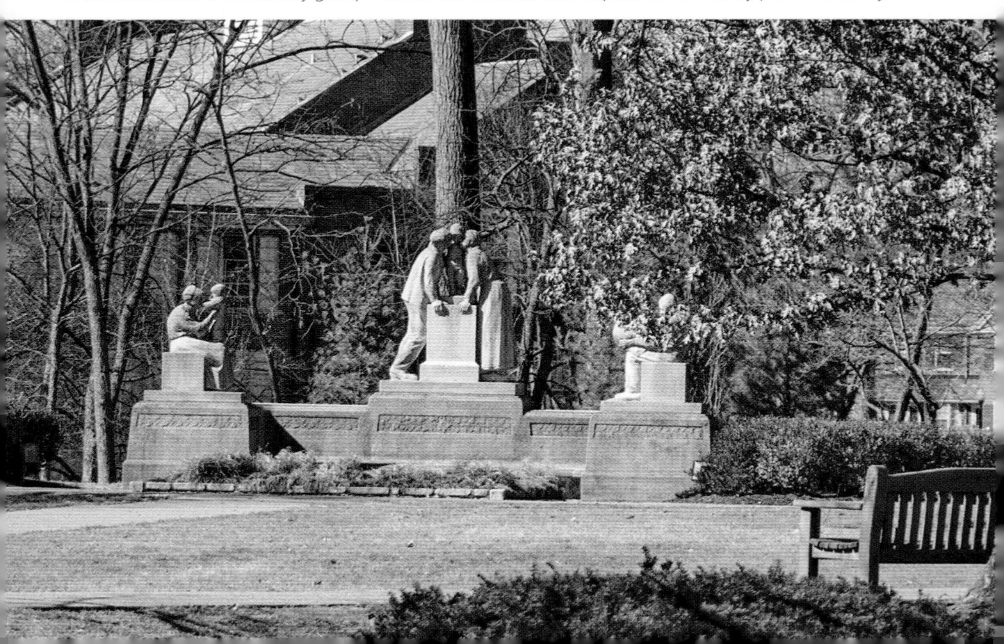

Backstory: American Indian Artifacts

University of Cincinnati students unearthed 9,000 American Indian artifacts from the Mariemont flood plain in early 2013. They believe they found a long-house, where Fort Ancient people ate and socialized. Radiocarbon tests dated the site at AD 1610 to 1670, just at the period of contact with European explorers. It sits directly below an embankment on the bluff that is believed to be the world's largest serpent mound. The head surrounds an American Indian cemetery at the Madisonville site, widely considered one of the most famous archaeological sites in eastern North America. Many of these sites were home to the Fort Ancient people, ancestors of the Shawnee, Delaware, and Miami tribes. There's talk of recognizing the entire area as a National Registered Archaeological District.

Cross Chestnut Street and look right toward Georgian Revival–style Dale Park School, which now houses the Cincinnati Waldorf School. Dana Apartments and Town Houses on the north side of Chestnut Street was the first group of houses to be completed in 1924–25. The large building across the street on your left, complete with clock tower, is the ❷ **Parish Center for Mariemont Community Church,** completed in 1929.

Continue walking south along Plainville Road past **Dale Park,** which sits east of Pioneer Cemetery and War Memorial. On the right is a statuary group named *Les Enfants* by French sculptor Lucien Alliot. It depicts a Normandy peasant family—parents, with boy in center, and grandmother and grandfather with grandchildren at either side. Turn left on Wooster Pike and walk past the former Mariemont High School (built in 1939 with an addition in 1957), now Mariemont Elementary School, with a pedimented portico and a cupola.

Continue walking on Wooster toward the Village Square, which is noted for its half-timbered commercial buildings and broad streets that radiate axially from the center. **Mariemont Strand** (6800–6834 Wooster Pike) is a modern interpretation of architectural roots in Mariemont. It houses an impressive row of shops and eateries, including ❸ **The Wardrobe** women's apparel store, ❹ **Jules & Bing** monograms and embroidery store, ❺ Dilly bistro and wine shop, ❻ **Sara Benjamin's** gift shop, ❼ **Pomegranate & Lime** gift shop, and ❽ **Rooted Juicery & Kitchen.** Designed by Zettel & Rapp of Cincinnati and built in 1929, ❾ **Mariemont Inn** (now a Best Western Premier) is one of the most recognizable buildings in Mariemont. It houses **The National Exemplar,** which has served Hungarian mushroom soup and other dishes for more than three decades. A Verdin clock stands out front.

Cross Madisonville Road and walk past ❿ **Mariemont Theatre** (one of the few remaining neighborhood movie houses in the region) to ⓫ **Graeter's Ice Cream,** part of a small local chain that started in 1870. After enjoying some of Graeter's famous French Pot–method ice cream, cross Wooster Pike through the south parking plaza to Crystal Springs Road. Mariemont Municipal Building is on the left. Turn right on Sheldon Close. The **Atterbury Group,** a collection of 10 impressive half-timber-and-stucco houses, named for the older son of Mr. and Mrs. Thomas J. Emery, faces a common green. At the end of the street is a roofed gate that leads to a service courtyard for garages.

Return to Crystal Springs Road and turn left. Turn left on E. Center Street, and then left again on Center Street (the sidewalk is on the west side of the street). Follow Center two blocks south, where it ends at the landscaped **Mariemont Concourse** along Miami Bluff Drive. Built in 1925, the stone and wooden pergola holds wisteria vines above a concourse that overlooks the Little Miami River valley, Mariemont Gardens, and South 80 Park below. Deer, coyotes, mink, wild turkeys, freshwater mussels, bats, and migrating waterbirds all live here. The lower Little Miami River valley is compared to Egypt's Valley of the Kings because it is so rich in American Indian embankments, mounds, and ancient sites. If Ohio Department of Transportation officials proceed with the Eastern Corridor Project, it would impact all of this.

Continue back along Center Street, turning left on W. Center Street and left again on Miami Road. On the left is **Albert Place,** a cute cul-de-sac named after Emery's younger son. It is lined with charming English cottage–style houses painted white. A serene service lane meanders behind the houses. Continue left on Miami Road, and then turn right on West Street. Turn left on Fieldhouse Way and left again on **Denny Place,** where gabled cottages of rough-cut stone face an oval-shaped green. Two women architects, Lois Lilley Howe and Eleanor Manning, are responsible for the design.

Turn right on Pleasant Street and walk past ⓬ **Dogwood Park,** which houses the largest public area in Mariemont and impressive Emery Carillon, built in 1929. Constructed with a full range of 49 bells, it was a gift from Mrs. Emery's sister, Isabella Hopkins. Turn left on Wooster Pike. On your left is a rustic stone building that once served as a boathouse and faced a lagoon that was filled in the 1940s.

Continue along Wooster Pike and cross at Oak Street. Cross to the east side of Oak, walk through the small lych-gate along the stone pathway past Pioneer Cemetery, and eventually call it a day at the church.

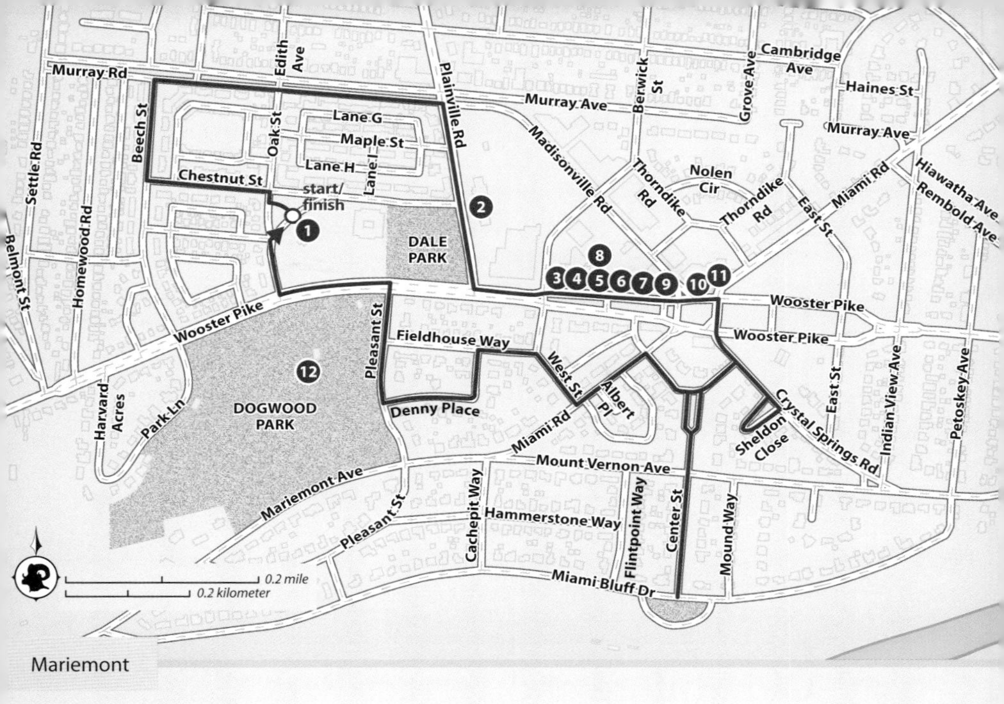

Mariemont

Points of Interest

1. **Mariemont Community Church** 6713 Cherry Ln., mariemontchurch.org
2. **Parish Center for Mariemont Community Church** 3908 Plainville Rd., 513-271-4376, mariemontchurch.org
3. **The Wardrobe Cincinnati** 6816 Wooster Pike, 513-271-4800, thewardrobecincinnati.com
4. **Jules & Bing** 6814 Wooster Pike, 513-271-5853, julesandbing.com
5. **Dilly** 6818 Wooster Pike, 513-561-5233, dillybistro.com
6. **Sara Benjamin's** 6810 Wooster Pike, 513-272-2280, sarabenjamins.com
7. **Pomegranate & Lime** 6804 Wooster Pike, 513-271-1012
8. **Rooted Juicery & Kitchen** 6844 Wooster Pike, 513-271-0432, rootedjuicery.com
9. **Mariemont Inn/The National Exemplar** 6880 Wooster Pike, 513-271-2103, nationalexemplar.com
10. **Mariemont Theatre** 6906 Wooster Pike, 513-272-0222, mariemonttheatre.com
11. **Graeter's Ice Cream** 6918 Wooster Pike, 513-272-0859, graeters.com
12. **Dogwood Park** 3721 Pleasant St., mariemont.org

20 Old Milford and Terrace Park

Early Settlements to Suburban Villages

Above: Enjoy this popular view from adirondack chairs along the Little Miami River.

BOUNDARIES: Mill St., Garfield Ave., Main St., Water St., Miami Ave., Harvard Ave., Elm Ave., Wooster Pike
DISTANCE: 3.75 miles
DIFFICULTY: Easy
PARKING: Free parking is available in public lots along Main Street.
PUBLIC TRANSIT: Metro (go-metro.com) buses serve this area. Take route 28 or 29X to Milford.

Milford was incorporated as a village in 1836, although the settlement dates back earlier. Revolutionary War veteran John Nancarrow arrived from Virginia in 1796 and surveyed the area near where two rivers—the Little Miami River and East Fork—come together. Milford is named after a series of mills located nearby along the river and the "ford," a shallow place on the river where one could cross. This ford was the first safe place to cross the river north of the Ohio River. It was here, too, that an old American Indian trail and later US 50 crossed the Little Miami River. Early growth of Milford was due to its river location. Later development was the result of rail traffic spurred in the late 19th and early 20th centuries.

Terrace Park was incorporated as a village in 1893, but settlement dates back to the late 1700s when Abraham Covalt purchased land from John Cleves Symmes. Most of what is now Terrace Park was developed as summer residences for wealthy Cincinnatians looking to escape the bad air trapped in the Cincinnati basin. The first subdivision was developed by two men from Milford (including future governor John Pattison) in 1886. Additional subdivisions were added until final incorporation in 1893.

This walk is essentially two parts, Milford and then Terrace Park, travelling in a large figure-eight. If you don't have time to walk the entire route, you could divide the walk into two shorter outings.

Walk Description

Start in front of ❶ **Little Miami Brewing Co.**, offering different ales, lagers, porters, and stouts along with seasonal food pairings on the site of a series of mills along the Little Miami River and millrace. It has quickly become a hub of activity along with the rest of downtown Milford, once a sleepy historic strip that is now home to an impressive collection of restaurants, specialty shops, condos, and town houses. A bridge has stood here over the Little Miami River since 1818, when a wooden covered bridge with a toll spurred the growth of Milford, followed by a series of iron bridges until the completion of the current one. Part of the old bridge approach is still visible in front of what was an old gas station across the street (5 Water St.).

Across the street, the building widely known as the ❷ **Millcroft Inn** was initially built as a residence. Mathias Kugler purchased it along with an attached mill and the millrace in 1828. Mathias and his son John were influential in the development of Milford. The Millcroft Inn dominates the entrance to town from Wooster Pike. John Kugler built the beautiful stone buildings along Mill Street. The small structure at the rear of the Millcroft Inn was a stable and barn. The building at 224 Mill Street was built circa 1840 as a corn warehouse. The long stone building at 2–6 Main Street, where Mill and Main Streets intersect, was built about 1862 and served as the whiskey warehouse and had a cooperage on the second floor.

Continue up Mill Street another block for a view of what is known as South Milford. Historic South Milford includes some great homes. It is the location for the town's initial settlement and includes sites associated with early Milford families. Turn left on High Street and follow it to Garfield Avenue. The house at the northeast corner of Garfield is now the ❸ **Old Milford Inn Bed &**

Breakfast. The building at the northwest corner at 101 High Street held the old passenger station for the C & C traction line on the first floor. The structure at the southwest corner at 29 High Street was built as the exchange building for Cincinnati & Suburban Telephone Co.

Turn left on Garfield Avenue and walk down the slope to Main Street, the spine of downtown Milford. To the left is ❹ **May Cafe,** where the sandwich reigns supreme in a classic Italian deli–style space, and coffee is king at ❺ **The Main Cup.** The building on the northwest corner of Main Street and Garfield Avenue houses the restaurant ❻ **20 Brix,** which specializes in local and seasonal fare. Constructed in 1846 as a masonic lodge, the building has been greatly altered from its original appearance.

Turn right and walk along a mostly intact streetscape of charming historic buildings. Along with a few antiques stores, Main Street features a resilient group of small businesses that attract locals and visitors alike. ❼ **Padrino** is a reliable stop for specialty pizzas, hoagies, pasta dishes, and salads with a casual dining area and shaded patio. ❽ **Old Milford Parlor** is a Creamy Whip with a full espresso menu in what was originally a barber shop. A framed photo of the shop from the 1940s hangs over a vintage barber chair. Across the street is ❾ **Roads Rivers and Trails,** where dreams of outdoor adventure do come true. There is a wall of colorful kayaks, plenty of resource books (including *Walking Cincinnati*), camping gear galore, and a schedule of events to motivate you to get outside and stay there as long as possible. Across the street is ❿ **Scintilla on Main** (look for the purple awnings), a good destination for all sorts of gifts.

Cross Elm Street. On the left, at 211 Main Street, is ⓫ **Row House Gallery** in the brick row house, appropriately enough, that John Kugler built in 1840. A few doors down, ⓬ **Chappy's Bar and Grill** is a requisite stop for bourbon and the occasional band. Laurent and Catherine Degois left the west coast of France for Milford to open ⓭ **Chez Renée French Bistrot,** which features traditional French dishes and good desserts. Cross Locust Street for ⓮ **Harvest Market,** a small convenience store that specializes in fresh, local foods and other goods. The highlight is the food counter, where owners Ben and Maureen Redman prepare a lunch special and soup of the day (Tuesday–Saturday), and tap local kombucha. Across the street is ⓯ **Bishop's Bicycles,** established in 1890, which claims to be the oldest bicycle shop in the United States. It is an easy walk to ⓰ **Tickled Sweet Artisan Chocolates and Candies,** where most everything is made in-house.

Continue east on Main Street, and start the gradual incline out of the river valley. Just before Maple Street, the large Italianate house with decorative brackets and cupola on your left is **Craver-Riggs Funeral Home & Crematory.** D. K. Harvey constructed the building in 1870 on land where there was a school from 1833, which relocated farther east to a larger building. It has remained a funeral home since Charles Johnson purchased it in 1913 and relocated his funeral home business from along the river due to damage sustained in the 1913 flood.

Across Maple Street from the funeral home is the ⓱ **Milford First United Methodist Church.** The simple, English Gothic Revival–style church was originally built in 1836 with the central bell tower and rear Sunday school rooms added in 1870. Founded in 1797, it was the first Methodist congregation in the Northwest Territory. Next door is ⓲ **St. Andrew Catholic Church and School,** which was originally at Elm and Water Streets. After repeated flood damage, the parish moved up the hill to this Tudor Gothic Revival–style church, completed in 1923. The original rectory next door was completed in 1919. The Art Deco school was completed in 1948. On this side of the street the convent building (now a rectory) was built in 1956, and the Parish Center was completed in 1991.

Proceed to the crosswalk just past the school and cross Main Street. Turn around on Main Street and head back toward downtown to see the two oldest brick houses in Milford. Turn right on Maple Street and then left on Beech Street. The first and oldest house is 504 Beech Street, completed circa 1805. The second-oldest house is around the corner to the left at 512 High Street, facing what is now Riverside Park. Higher ground has protected both houses from intermittent flooding.

Return to Main Street via High Street. Turn right on Main and continue back into the business district. Turn right into Memorial Park at Sycamore Street, and follow it until turning left when the road becomes Polk Street. Turn right on Locust Street, and then left on Cash Street. There is a series of small framed wood-and-brick houses in this section. This low area was exceptionally susceptible to flooding and historically just outside the original plat of the town. At the end of Cash Street, follow the public sidewalk through Riverwalk Park in front of **Riverwalk Flats & Rowhouses** (built in 2014) to Water Street. Across the street is **Milford Lodge #54** (built in 1926). Turn right and proceed to the corner to see another project of John Kugler, the ⓳ **Milford Public Library.** Completed around 1860, the first floor was used as a warehouse with the second floor set aside as a public meeting room.

Cross the street back to Little Miami Brewing, and walk across the bridge on the south side. Across US 50 is the **Milford Trailhead** and the former Milford train station for the Little Miami Railroad, which became the first railroad to link Cincinnati to the rest of the United States in 1847. Tracks were removed in the 1980s in anticipation of the Little Miami Scenic Trail, the final stop on this walk. The Little Miami Scenic Trail, which connects Newtown and Springfield, is one of several major trails that converge in Milford.

Turn left on Wooster Pike. The small collection of buildings here used to be part of the community of Montauk. Prominent Cincinnatians laid it out in 1840 with the hope of capitalizing on

The Gothic Revival–style Milford First United Methodist Church was the first Methodist congregation in the Northwest Territory, the predecessor to the state of Ohio.

its proximity to Wooster Pike, the Little Miami River, and the railroad. Frequent flooding washed away those hopes, and Montauk became part of Milford in 1888. A few historic buildings remain, including the brick Cincinnati, Milford & Blanchester Traction Company Power Station (now Alma Granite, 110 Wooster Pike) and the Miami Baptist Church (130 Longworth St.) built in 1847.

Just before The Olde Garden Shack at 222 Wooster Pike, turn left on Miami Avenue and enter Terrace Park. At what is now east of the corner of Miami Avenue and Terrace Place, across from the church, Abraham Covalt and others established Covalt Station in January 1789. This station was essentially a small fort and served as protection from American Indians. A plaque commemorating Covalt Station sits in front of ⑳ **St. Thomas Episcopal Church,** which was founded in 1876. John G. Robinson of Robinson Circus fame lived in Terrace Park and was instrumental in the development of the church. Robinson's grandfather founded the circus in 1842.

Walk down Miami Avenue to Oxford Avenue and turn right. Continue on Oxford Avenue and turn left on Yale Avenue. The two blocks from Oxford to Harvard Avenue are James Sibley's original subdivision where a few houses built prior to 1893 remain. Continue to Harvard Avenue and turn right. The **James Sibley House** (311 Harvard Ave.), on the left, was constructed around 1887. On your left as you approach Terrace Place is Village Green and a small collection of buildings that once served as a village center. The Green was dedicated in 1930, and the gazebo is a relatively new addition from 1989. The buildings along Terrace Place just north of the Village Green include a former market (415 Terrace Pl.) built in 1903 and the post office (409 Terrace Pl.).

Turn left on Terrace Place and make an immediate right on Elm Avenue. You will cross over the former Little Miami Railroad, now the Little Miami Scenic Trail. Among some nice homes on Elm Avenue is the ㉑ **Terrace Park Community House,** originally a church completed in 1891 and sold to the town in 1922. Its construction is poured concrete, early for its time. The **District #9 Schoolhouse** (702 Indian Hill Rd.) was built in 1853 and was used until 1870, when a larger school was built on the site of the current elementary school in 1913. Next door to District #9 is ㉒ **The Birch,** a casual neighborhood spot to enjoy creative soups, salads, and sandwiches alongside a glass of wine or a craft brew inside or on the patio.

Turn right on US 50, then right again on New Street. At this intersection, look up the driveway to your right and see the second-oldest home in Terrace Park. A beautiful stone structure, the **Covalt-Traber-Boone House** (601 Wooster Pike) was built about 1810. (The oldest home in Terrace Park is outside this walk; find it on the south side of Elm Ave. just east of the Terrace Park Swim Club.)

Before New Street joins Terrace Place, turn left on the Little Miami Scenic Trail, taking you northeast along the old railroad to the former train station and the Milford Trailhead. Back at the trailhead, cross back over the Little Miami River into Milford and return to your starting point.

Points of Interest

1. **Little Miami Brewing Co.** 208 Mill St., 513-713-1121, littlemiamibrewing.com
2. **Millcroft Inn** 200 Mill St.
3. **Old Milford Inn Bed & Breakfast** 405 Garfield Ave., 513-239-5805, oldmilfordinn.com
4. **May Cafe** 5 Main St., 513-831-2233, maycafemilford.com
5. **The Main Cup** 18 Main St., 513-248-2089, themaincupmilford.com
6. **20 Brix** 101 Main St., 513-831-2749, 20brix.com
7. **Padrino** 111 Main St., 513-965-0100, padrinoitalian.com
8. **Old Milford Parlor** 119 Main St., 513-239-5704, cincinnatiparlor.com

(continued on next page)

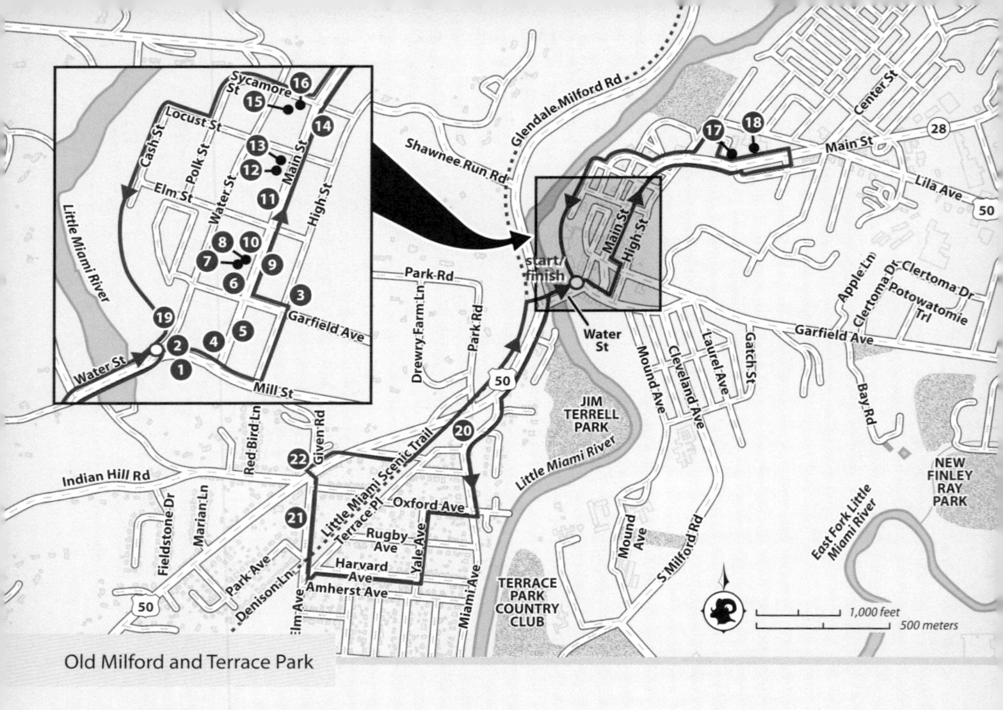

Old Milford and Terrace Park

(continued from previous page)

9. **Roads Rivers and Trails** 118 Main St., 513-248-7787, roadsriversandtrails.com
10. **Scintilla on Main** 127 Main St., 513-781-4912, scintillaonmain.com
11. **Row House Gallery** 211 Main St., 513-831-7230, rowhouse.com
12. **Chappy's Bar and Grill** 227 Main St., 513-239-8530
13. **Chez Renée French Bistrot** 233 Main St., 513-248-0454, chezreneefrenchbistrot.com
14. **Harvest Market** 308 Main St., 513-239-5400
15. **Bishop's Bicycles** 313 Main St., 513-831-2521, bishopsbicycles.net
16. **Tickled Sweet Artisan Chocolates and Candies** 317 Main St., 513-880-4169, tickledsweet.net
17. **Milford First United Methodist Church** 541 Main St., 513-831-5500, milfordfirstumc.org
18. **St. Andrew Catholic Church and School** 552 Main St., 513-831-3353, standrew-milford.org
19. **Milford Public Library** 19 Water St., 513-248-1256
20. **St. Thomas Episcopal Church** 100 Miami Ave., 513-831-2052, stthomasepiscopal.org
21. **Terrace Park Community House** 428 Elm Ave., 513-831-2138
22. **The Birch** 702 Indian Hill Rd., 513-831-5678, thebirchtp.com

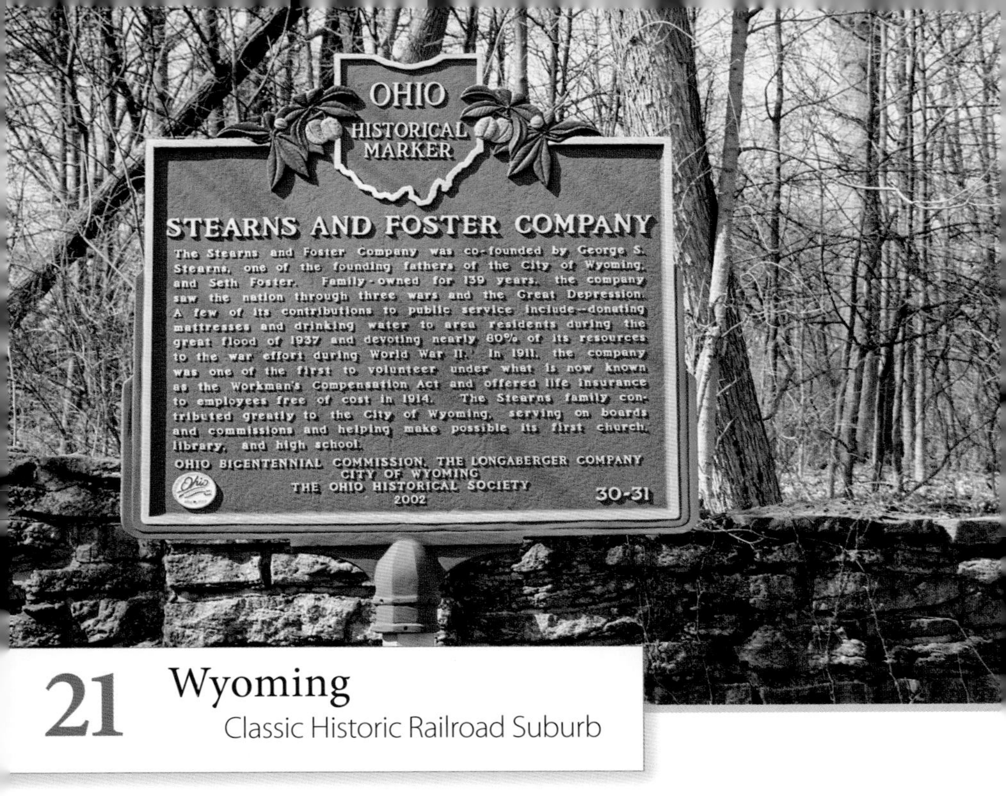

21 Wyoming

Classic Historic Railroad Suburb

Above: Stearns Woods is a cherished nature preserve in suburban Wyoming.

BOUNDARIES: Glenway Ave., Oliver Rd., Pendry Ave., Grove Ave., Elm Ave., Walnut Ave.
DISTANCE: 3 miles
DIFFICULTY: Easy, with some hills on streets west of Springfield Pike
PARKING: On-street parking along Wyoming Ave. between Springfield Pike and Grove Ave.
PUBLIC TRANSIT: Metro buses (go-metro.com) serve this area. Take route 78 to Springfield Pike and Wyoming Ave.

A pilgrimage to Wyoming, 14 miles north of downtown Cincinnati, is worthy of several hours of your day. This beautiful historic suburb, known for its exemplary school system along Mill Creek, was first settled around 1806. Significant growth started when the Cincinnati, Hamilton, and Dayton Railway was put into service in 1851. While this commuter lifestyle is now mostly in the hands of the automobile, historic houses and a commitment to progressive community life remain.

Backstory: Lockland

In the 1820s, rich farmland west of Mill Creek caught the eye of Cincinnati investors like Nicholas Longworth, who were in-the-know about plans to build the Miami and Erie Canal, connecting the state's interior farmland with the Ohio River. Cincinnatians encouraged a canal design that would harness water flow through four locks, which lowered the waterway by 48 feet and created a manufacturing hub there named "Lockland." Throughout the 1800s, raw materials arrived at Lockland's mills by canal boat and were processed into lumber, paper, starch, cotton, and other products. But the railroad eventually upstaged the quiet canal in transportation efficiency. By the mid-1900s, the canal's right-of-way was used to create the I-75 interstate corridor. Today, most of the architecture from that booming industrial era has disappeared, but if you stand on the overpass bridge on Wyoming Avenue and squint at the highway, you can follow the slope of the original locks as they lowered the waterway, creating what was once the largest industrial center in the Mill Creek valley.

In 1979, a local historic preservation group identified Wyoming's historic buildings, resulting in a multiple property submission of 18 houses, Wyoming Presbyterian Church, and one large historic district to the National Register of Historic Places in 1985. Wyoming's most historic section is situated between Wentworth Avenue, the former Baltimore & Ohio Railroad tracks, E. Mills Avenue, and Springfield Pike, and comprises more than 275 contributing buildings. Many of these late Victorian, Revival-style, and Craftsman houses fall within the boundaries of this walk.

Walk Description

Start your walk with breakfast or lunch at ❶ **Half Day Cafe** or the newer ❷ **Wyoming Community Coffee**, which serves La Terza Coffee, gelato, pastries, bagels, sandwiches, and sides. Out front is a plaque (with some errors) commemorating Robert Reily, who named (not founded) Wyoming. The town was first settled around 1806 and Reily arrived in the 1850s. He hosted a house party to name the little hamlet in 1861 and then died in the Civil War.

Across the street is a view that will get your brain fixated on the historic eye candy you're about to encounter for 3 leisurely miles. The ❸ **Riddle-Friend House** was built in 1835 and listed on the National Register of Historic Places. Cross Springfield Pike, walk north to Reily Road, and turn left. The first house on the right is the ❹ **Luethstrom-Hurin House**, also listed on the National Register.

Continue walking along Reily Road past the intersection with Larchmont Drive, which features a winding creek underneath. On the right is the ❺ **John C. Pollack House**, another National Register property. Built in the 1870s, it is an early Italianate cottage featuring a weatherboard exterior, stone foundation, and pressed metal roof. Reily Road features more impressive houses as it winds upward another half mile or so to Hillcrest Drive. For now, turn right on sloping Glenway Avenue. Walk north along winding Glenway Avenue to the ❻ **Stearns Woods** entrance on the left. This was once the property of Roderick Barney, a well-regarded Cincinnati publisher and mayor of Wyoming. The Stearns family (of the Stearns and Foster Company) eventually purchased this land and donated it for Wyoming green space. Enter the woodland and follow the uphill trail to Oliver Road.

Turn right on Oliver Road and look for the ❼ **Josiah Kirby House** on the right. Built in 1890 and listed on the National Register, this Queen Anne house was the primary residence for Josiah Kirby, one of Cincinnati's leading industrialists in the late 19th century. Kirby got his big break when he invented a "bung-making machine": bungs are those holes in whiskey, bourbon, and beer barrels. This little invention made him one of the richest men in Cincinnati. He held executive positions at two different railroad companies, served as president of the Cincinnati Board of Trade, and was in the Ohio Senate from 1880 to 1881.

Continue along Oliver Road to Springfield Pike. Turn left and then make a quick right on Pendery Avenue. On the left is ❽ **Wyoming High School,** which is one of the highest-ranking high schools in the country, per the annual U.S. News Best High Schools survey. On the right, at 749 Stout Avenue, is the ❾ **Charles H. Moore House.** Built in 1910, this large Colonial Revival house is listed on the National Register.

Turn right on Stout Avenue and continue south to Wentworth Avenue. Look for the entrance to a walkway that extends three blocks to Worthington Avenue. Walk two blocks to Wyoming Avenue and turn left. The first house on the left is the ❿ **John Wilmuth Hill House,** built in 1870. Next door, at 212 Wyoming, is an excellent Queen Anne house. Across the street, at 217 Wyoming, is a Gothic-style house that served as a parsonage for more than 100 years. Next up is the Romanesque Revival ⓫ **Wyoming Presbyterian Church.** Wyoming Presbyterian Church was the first church built in Wyoming in the 1870s. It was a frame structure and was later replaced with the far more magnificent Samuel Hannaford & Sons church built in 1890. Like many buildings on this route, the church is listed on the National Register of Historic Places.

Walk past Burns Avenue to Grove Avenue. Before turning right, take a quick loop through Wyoming's charming historic commercial heart. Small in scale, it features ⓬ **Wyoming Fine Arts Center,** ⓭ **Village Green Park,** and a block of locally owned businesses. Longtime merchants, such as ⓮ **Williams Jewelers** and ⓯ **Wyoming Pastry Shop,** sit across the street from younger establishments like ⓰ **Patina at Home.** At 400 Wyoming Avenue, the Wyoming Art

Show committee commissioned *Windows of Wyoming,* painted windows on the building with notable residents looking out.

Turn right on Grove Avenue and walk three blocks to S. Cooper Avenue. The 300 block of Grove Avenue features a lively group of late Victorian houses dating from the 1890s. Turn right on S. Cooper Avenue. Before turning left on Burns Avenue, look past Stearns Avenue on the right to the ⓱ **Gideon-Palmer House.** Perched on a hillside, this Italianate beauty was built in the 1860s and has changed little since.

Turn left on Burns Avenue. The house at 233 Burns dates from 1865. Look south for a view of ⓲ **Wyoming Baptist Church.** Built in 1882, this frame building has a pretty shingled steeple.

Turn right on Elm Avenue, right again on Walnut Avenue, and eventually right on Beech Avenue. Walk to Worthington Avenue. To the right, at 200 Worthington, is a fine example of an Italianate house built after the Civil War. The three frame houses on the north side of the street closest to Burns Avenue are "sister houses" from the 1860s. Where Beech Avenue intersects with Worthington Avenue, look for a walkway on the north side of Worthington just before Wyoming Middle School. Walk one block north to Wyoming Avenue and turn left. This takes you back to Springfield Pike and the end of this walk.

Points of Interest

❶ **Half Day Cafe** 1 Wyoming Ave., 513-821-2323, halfdaycafe.org

❷ **Wyoming Community Coffee** 434 Springfield Pike, 513-510-4765, wyomingcommunitycoffee.com

❸ **Riddle-Friend House** 507 Springfield Pike

❹ **Luethstrom-Hurin House** 30 Reily Rd.

❺ **John C. Pollack House** 88 Reily Rd.

❻ **Stearns Woods** Glenway Ave. and Oliver Rd., wyomingohio.gov

❼ **Josiah Kirby House** 65 Oliver Rd.

❽ **Wyoming High School** 106 Pendery Ave., 513-206-7050, wyomingcityschools.org

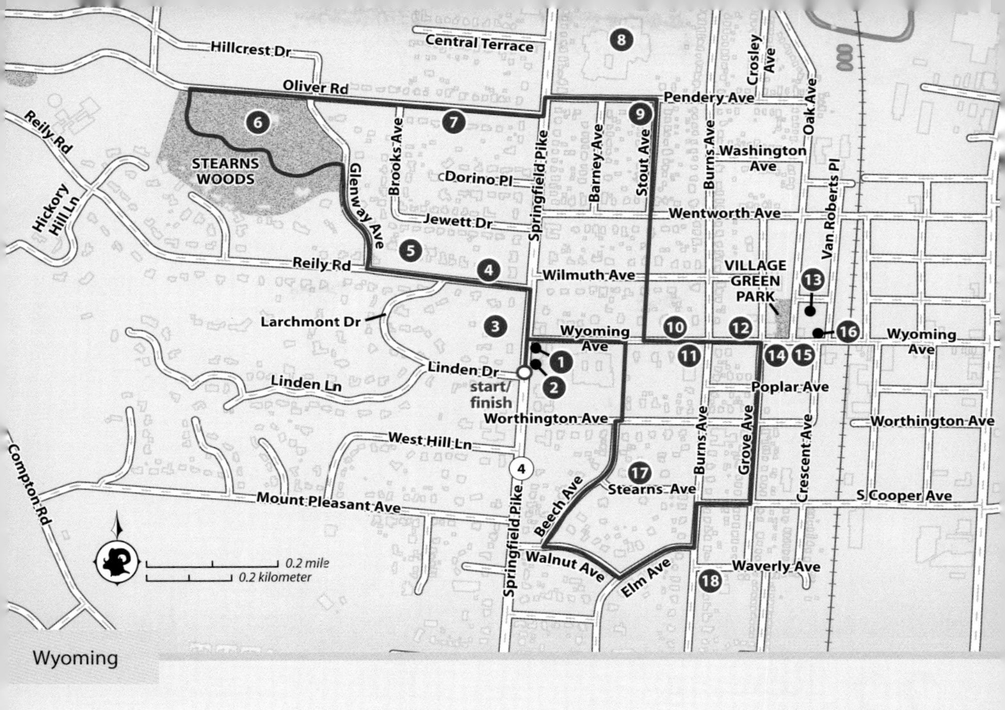

9 **Charles H. Moore House** 749 Stout Ave.

10 **John Wilmuth Hill House** 132 Wyoming Ave.

11 **Wyoming Presbyterian Church** 225 Wyoming Ave., 513-821-8735, pcwyoming.org

12 **Wyoming Fine Arts Center** 322 Wyoming Ave., 513-948-1900, musicartdance.org

13 **Village Green Park** 400 Wyoming Ave., wyomingohio.gov

14 **Williams Jewelers** 415 Wyoming Ave., 513-761-4367, williamsjewelersinc.com

15 **Wyoming Pastry Shop** 505 Wyoming Ave., 513-821-0742, wyomingpastryshop.com

16 **Patina at Home** 504 W. Wyoming Ave., 513-353-8991

17 **Gideon-Palmer House** 124 Stearns Ave.

18 **Wyoming Baptist Church** 170 Burns Ave., 513-821-8430, wyomingbaptistchurch.org

22 Reading

More Than a Bridal District

Above: The Gahl Building welcomes you to the Reading Bridal District. *Photo by Jody Johnson*

BOUNDARIES: Reading Rd., Mill St., Columbia Ave., Market St.
DISTANCE: 1.7 miles
DIFFICULTY: Easy
PARKING: Public lot on corner of Market and Benson Streets
PUBLIC TRANSIT: Metro (go-metro.com) buses serve this area.

Founded by Revolutionary War veteran Abraham Voorhees in 1794, Reading was one of the first established settlements north of Cincinnati. Its historic architecture and modest homes belie the community's embrace of state-of-the-art life-science industries, educational excellence, and wedding fashions. Located 10 miles north of downtown Cincinnati, Reading features five life-science firms that employ 1,500 workers and generate $78 million in payroll; a Reading Branch Library (8740 Reading Rd.); and the Reading Bridal District, which attracts people from all over looking for the latest in wedding fashion. In all, Reading has a varied mix of old and new.

Walk Description

Start your tour at the ❶ **Reading Historical Society Museum,** housed in a 1905 brick Colonial Revival home with concrete block porch columns and a palladium window on the gable. It was the home of George Hausser, a local roofer, plumber, and sheet metal contractor, as well as Reading fire chief from 1938 to 1947. On the northeast corner of W. Benson and Market Streets is the billboard highlighting the Bridal District's business roster. Next to this is a display of Reading history provided by the Cincinnati Bicentennial Commission.

Turn right on Market Street and walk toward ❷ **Reading City Hall** on the northeast corner of Pike Street. It appears to be a 1950s building, although the bell tower is evidence of the original 1902 building underneath. Established in 1886, the Reading Fire Department is currently housed here.

Turn right at Pike Street and walk toward Reading Road. Known as the Great Road, Reading Road began as a buffalo trace and then an Indian path. Later it became a major stagecoach/mail artery to Dayton, Springfield, and Detroit. Reading Road is part of US 42, an east–west federal highway that runs southwest–northeast for about 350 miles from Louisville, Kentucky, through Cincinnati to Cleveland. It is a busy thoroughfare and requires caution when crossing.

Turn right on Reading. On the right is ❸ **Tres Belle Cakes,** a small cafe and coffeehouse. Past the parking lot on the right is ❹ **Lucy's Diner,** another eatery and community gathering spot. Walk south to Benson Street. On the corner is the ❺ **Gahl Building,** an imposing Queen Anne–style building from circa 1890 that anchors the eastern edge of Benson Street with its decorative corner tower. For many years this was a pharmacy and a shoe store (with an X-ray machine to get the perfect fit). Today, it is **White Wisteria Bridal Boutique** and the first sign that you have reached the **Reading Bridal District** (readingbridaldistrict.com), which stretches along W. Benson Street from Reading Road to Mill Street and is the largest bridal district in North America.

Turn right on W. Benson Street. Across the street is the *Love Blooms* mural. One of more than 130 murals from Cincinnati ArtWorks, this mural marks the eastern entrance of the Bridal District. Designer Elizabeth Hatchett blends traditional handcrafted wedding lace patterns with a simple black-and-white graphic style. The letters L-O-V-E provide an uplifting message for passersby. Back across the street is the former Lyric Theater (10 W. Benson St.), which featured silent movies and The Charleston dance contests in the 1920s. A look inside reveals an intact tin ceiling. A couple more doors down is ❻ **Redwine & Co.** (another place to grab a bite to eat) near our starting point.

Continue west on Benson Street, crossing Market Street. As you walk along Benson Street, you will notice that, while storefronts have changed over the years, late-19th-century Italianate details remain throughout the district. At 200 W. Benson is ❼ **Foley's Irish Pub,** an unpretentious destination for happy hour deals and late-night grub.

At the corner of 300 Benson Street and Jefferson Avenue is ❽ **Bridal and Formal,** the first bridal shop in Reading. Opened in 1979, it has grown to become one of the largest bridal shops in the country, with more than 50 employees. A few doors down and across the street, **Molly Grosse Photography** (341 Benson St.) is one of numerous photography studios found here. It is housed in a one-story commercial building with a fantastic false front featuring square dentils in the cornice. A trap door leads to the basement, which some believe was a speakeasy during Prohibition.

On the northwest corner of Church and W. Benson Street you will see ❾ **O. G. Gallery & Studio,** a bright and airy art gallery that specializes in gifts from regional artists. The gallery is housed in a well-preserved building that was originally Koehler Hardware Store, built in 1910.

Pop into ❿ **Benson's Tavern** for a cold drink if you passed on the other two taverns earlier on this walk. At the end of the block at Mill Street, ⓫ **Every Now and Then Antique Furniture Mall** occupies a 1920s storefront inside a brick building from the 1880s.

Look west before turning right onto Mill Street to see the **Benson Street Bridge** (locals refer to it as Rainbow Arch Bridge), built in 1910. In 1989, the Army Corps of Engineers proposed to build a new bridge. The communities of Reading and Lockland opted to rehabilitate the bridge, honoring its original design. The project was completed in 1992.

Turn right on Mill Street, right again on Pearl Street, and then left on Church Street to view the soaring ⓬ **Sts. Peter & Paul Church,** built in 1860 after a tornado damaged the original church.

Turn right on Vine Street. On the corner at Jefferson Avenue is **Veterans Memorial Plaza,** which was rededicated in 1992 with markers honoring all military services. The World War I doughboy statue was dedicated on June 8, 1919. The names of 231 soldiers from Reading and neighboring communities are featured on the monument.

Take a left on Jefferson Avenue. The unassuming Cape Cod house on the left between Walnut Street and Halker Avenue is the headquarters of the **Mill Creek Alliance** (themillcreekalliance.org), a multi-community nonprofit organization working to improve water quality along this important waterway. A rain garden illustrates one of the methods that is used to improve Mill Creek water quality while putting the work of the organization on full view.

Turn left on Halker Avenue and enjoy some peace and quiet in the aptly named **Quiet Park** on the left. Continue on Halker Avenue as it becomes Koenig Street, and turn right on Columbia Avenue. Stroll through ⓭ **Reading Cemetery,** where 85 Civil War veterans are buried. It is the oldest of four cemeteries in the city and served as the churchyard for the Reading Presbyterian Church, the city's first religious group, founded in 1823. Buried here are Abraham Voorhees and Henry Redinbo, who suggested the name change from Voorhees Town to Reading. Turn left on Market Street for an ice-cream stop (during the season) at ⓮ **Don's Creamy Whip** before returning to the start (southbound on Market Street) at Reading Historical Society Museum.

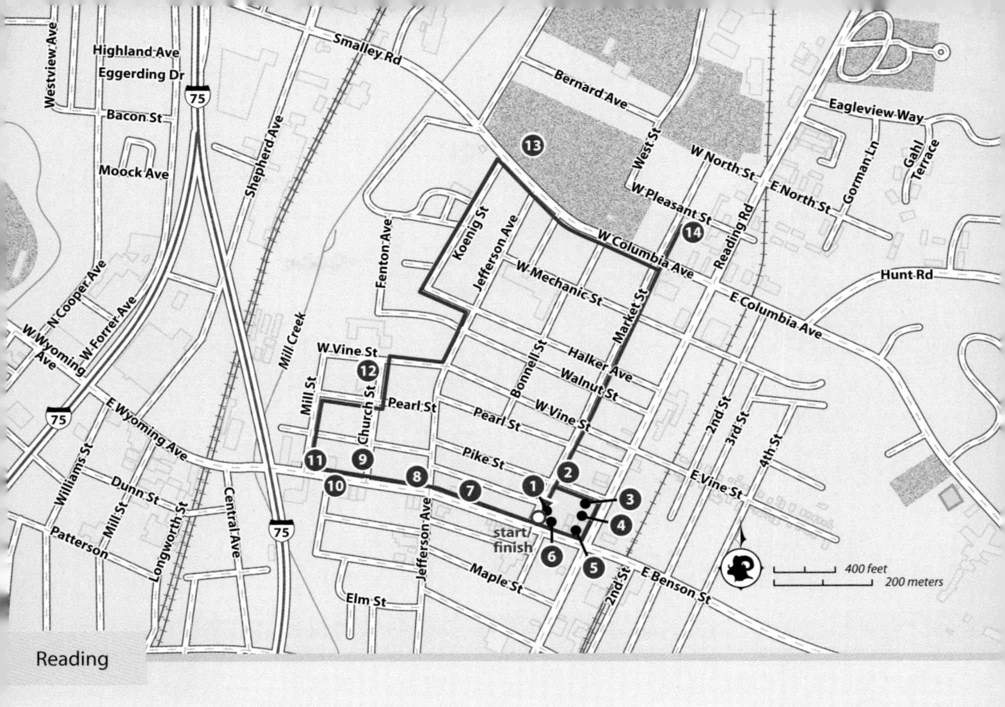

Points of Interest

1. **Reading Historical Society Museum** 22 W. Benson St., 513-733-2787 by appointment, readingohio.org
2. **Reading City Hall** 1000 Market St., 513-733-3725, readingohio.org
3. **Tres Belle Cakes** 8921 Reading Rd., tresbellecakes.com
4. **Lucy's Diner** 8907 Reading Rd., 513-821-5900
5. **Gahl Building/White Wisteria Bridal Boutique** 6 W. Benson St., 513-761-4696, whitewisteriabridalboutique.com
6. **Redwine & Co.** 20 W. Benson St., 513-975-0440, redwineandco.com
7. **Foley's Irish Pub** 200 W. Benson St., 513-948-9163
8. **Bridal and Formal** 300 W. Benson St., 513-821-6622, bridalandformalinc.com
9. **O.G. Gallery & Studio** 400 W. Benson St., 513-570-6070, oggallery.com
10. **Benson's Tavern** 419 W. Benson St., 513-918-5310, bensons-tavern.com
11. **Every Now and Then Antique Furniture Mall** 430 W. Benson St., 513-821-1497, cincinnatiantiquefurnituremall.com
12. **Sts. Peter & Paul Church** 330 W. Vine St., 513-554-1010, ssppcatholic.church
13. **Reading Cemetery** 200 W. Columbia Ave., 513-554-1027
14. **Don's Creamy Whip** 1522 Market St., 513-554-1969

23 Glendale

One of America's Earliest Planned Suburbs

Above: Glendale showcases impressive architecture from multiple eras.

BOUNDARIES: Greenville Ave., Fountain Ave., Church Ave., Washington Ave.
DISTANCE: 2.2 miles; 0.5-mile detour
DIFFICULTY: Moderate, with rolling terrain
PARKING: On-street 2-hour (or less) parking in Village Square west of railroad tracks, or follow signs with directions to park in the lot east of the tracks.
PUBLIC TRANSIT: Metro buses (go-metro.com) serve this area. Take route 78 (Springdale–Vine/Lincoln Heights) to Springfield Pike and Fountain Ave.

Founded in 1851, Glendale is one of the earliest planned suburbs in America and the oldest in Ohio. It may well be the first with a curvilinear plan—most often used in subdivisions intended for wealthier communities—and is considered the first planned railroad commuter town in the United States. Some historians claim that Glendale is America's earliest planned suburb. It predates Riverside (1869) and Lake Forest (1856) near Chicago, Llewellyn Park (1853) in New Jersey, and little Evergreen Hamlet (1851) outside Pittsburgh with only four houses.

Like Woodlawn and Wyoming to the south, Glendale became a residential retreat for some of Cincinnati's early industrialists because it was easily accessible via the Cincinnati-Hamilton-Dayton Railroad. Noting these distinctions, Glendale Historic District was added to the National Register of Historic Places in 1976. The following year, it was declared a National Historic Landmark. Glendale remains a remarkably intact and beloved community. Its gas-lit and curving streets, and vast collection of early Victorian-era homes and civic buildings, are all set in a naturalistic arrangement. To appreciate picturesque Glendale even more, travel 2 miles north to the mid-20th-century suburban sprawl that spreads from OH 747 and Kemper Road in Springdale or east toward I-75 in Sharonville. Glendale's founders had ample opportunity to incorporate the surrounding areas made up of farmland. Instead, they chose to keep Glendale the quiet residential village it is today.

Note: If you're interested in planned communities, check out Walk 19: Mariemont. To get a perspective of American planning principles in the 1860s and 1920s, all one has to do is visit Glendale and Mariemont, respectively.

Walk Description

Begin your walk at ❶ **Bluebird Bakery.** Open for breakfast and lunch Monday through Saturday, the bakery is known for its seasonal pies and scones. It's housed in the **Willis-Dooley Building,** which has changed little since it was built in 1880. At one time, the third story portion to the south served as the Masonic Lodge. Walk north along Village Square to Greenville Avenue. On the left is ❷ **Meritage,** which encourages you to stay for a leisurely evening of good food and a fantastic wine list. Turn around and head to ❸ **Railroad Depot** across from Bluebird Bakery. Built in 1880, it currently houses the Glendale Preservation Museum.

From here, head west on Willow Avenue, making a left on E. Fountain Avenue. The road splits around **Van Cleve Park.** On the right side of the park is a pre-Civil War house (160 E. Fountain Ave.), and on the left side is the ❹ **First Presbyterian Church** complex. The smaller building was Glendale's first church, a Gothic Revival–style structure built in 1860. To its left was the manse for the pastor. The larger church, designed by A. C. Nash, was built in 1873.

Cross through **Floral Park,** which was set aside as open space when Glendale was platted in 1851. The fountain in the center was installed in memory of Charles Sawyer. Unusual for this part of the country, black squirrels scramble across the grounds here and throughout the village. Architect James McLaughlin designed the lampposts that surround Floral Park and line most Glendale streets. At the Sawyer fountain, take the path to the right and head up the north side of the park toward Glendale's highest point. The house that sits here (70 E. Fountain Ave.) dates from the early 1850s and looks incomplete because a fire after World War II destroyed the second floor. Continue on E. Fountain Avenue until you reach Congress Avenue, without crossing. The **Robert House** (780 Congress Ave.) was built 1855–57 and reportedly served as a hiding place for escaped slaves before and during the Civil War. Diagonally across Congress is the **Samuel Allen House** (25 W. Fountain Ave.). Built in 1859, this massive Gothic Revival mansion has incredible south-facing views.

Turn right and proceed north on Congress. On the left is ❺ **Glendale New Church,** built in 1861. It is a superb example of vernacular Gothic architecture and houses the only Swedenborgian congregation in Cincinnati. Apparently Johnny Appleseed, the American pioneer who introduced apple trees to large parts of the Midwest, spent time here. Next to the church is ❻ **Glendale Lyceum,** a social and recreational center since 1891. Up a bit is **Glendale Elementary School,** a Spanish Revival building from 1900 that makes you feel like you are in southern California. Across from the school is the **McLean-Johnston House** (20 Erie Ave.), retrofitted with geothermal energy. Over its long life, the large brick house was previously a summer hotel and boys' school.

Continue on Congress to Glendale's main intersection at Sharon Road. On the southeast corner is ❼ **Grand Finale Restaurant,** originally J. J. Kelley's Saloon. It is known throughout the region for its desserts and Sunday brunch. The same folks own and operate the ❽ **Friendly Stop Bar and Grill,** across the street. Cross to the north side of Sharon Road and turn left. Walk west past St. Gabriel Consolidated School and St. Gabriel Parish (built in 1866) to get to ❾ **St. Gabriel Church.** This Richardsonian Romanesque church was built in 1907.

Turn right on Church Avenue and then right on Washington Avenue to the former **Eckstein School,** which served as a grade school for African American children from 1915 to 1958. Continue walking east along Washington Avenue, crossing Congress Avenue and turning right.

Walk south on Congress and turn left on Lake Avenue. You will pass **Caruthers Park,** originally a lake. At the stop sign, continue on Lake Avenue to the left on your way back to Sharon Road. On your right is the back side of the ❿ **Glendale Town Hall,** designed by Samuel Hannaford and built in 1875. The first floor houses council chambers and the volunteer fire department. Upstairs is an auditorium that fits about one-quarter of the town's population of 2,100. Across from town hall is Glendale's War Memorial, backed by a stone, cylindrical water tower built in 1892. Only the stone base remains, as its top exploded in 1927. Anderson & Hannaford designed the Gothic-style ⓫ **Christ Church Glendale,** built in 1869.

Turn left on Sharon Road and follow it east. On the left, at 100 and 110 E. Sharon Road, are twin houses dating from the early 1850s. On the opposite corner is **Glen Gables** (985 Laurel

Ave.), which started as a log cabin in 1807 and has undergone at least five renovations, possibly a record for Glendale. Cross Laurel Avenue to reach 160 E. Sharon Road, home of Robert Crawford, one of two men responsible for Glendale's subdivision plan and its first mayor in 1855. Built in 1853, this five-bay Greek Revival house is lovingly occupied.

For a semi-rural diversion, turn left on Willow Avenue and follow it to Coral Avenue, then back down Greenville Avenue to Sharon Road. Cross the road and look to the left past the railroad tracks toward the **Glendale Police Department,** built in 1871, before turning right. On the left is **12 Cock & Bull Public House,** which opened here in 2008 and is the second of four locations in the regional chain known for their British-inspired fish and chips. Walk a few hundred more feet and you have arrived at **13 Harry Whiting Brown Community Center,** Glendale's community gathering spot. It hosts a community library, seasonal farmers market, annual Glendale Street Fair in September, and arts and music programming. Return to Village Square for something to eat or drink before heading home.

A real black squirrel poses behind one of several fiberglass squirrel statues in Glendale.

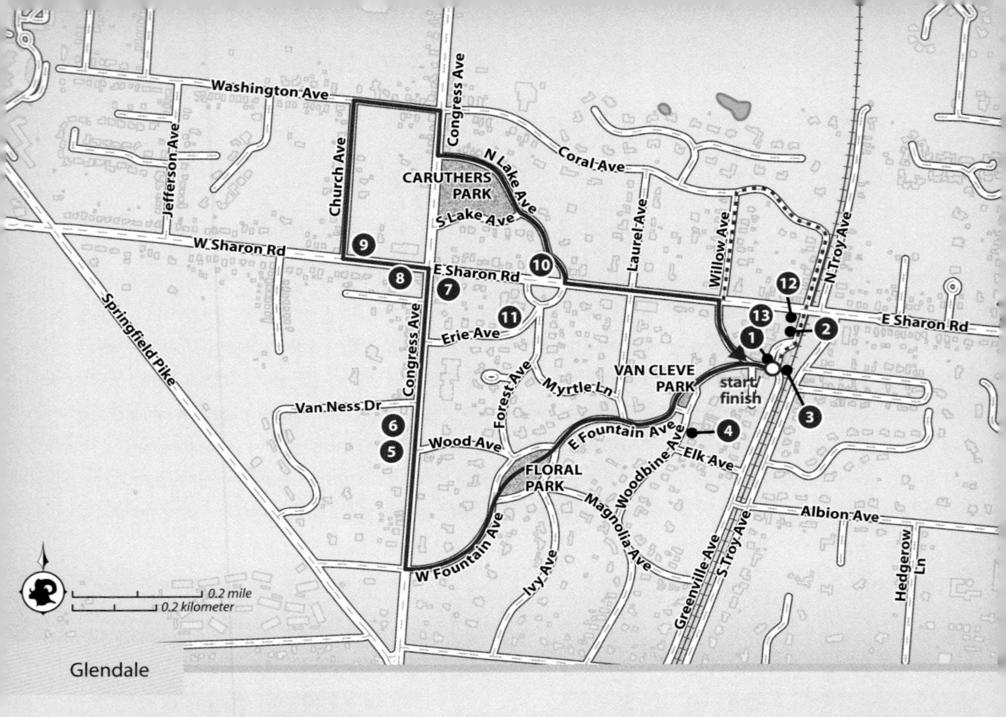

Points of Interest

1. **Bluebird Bakery** 29 Village Square, 513-772-5633, bluebirdbakery.com
2. **Meritage** 40 Village Square, 513-376-8134, meritagecincy.com
3. **Railroad Depot** 44 Village Square, 513-771-8722, glendaleheritage.org
4. **First Presbyterian Church** 155 E. Fountain Ave., 513-771-6195, firstpresbyterianglendale.org
5. **Glendale New Church** 845 Congress Ave., 513-772-1478
6. **Glendale Lyceum** 865 Congress Ave., 513-771-8383, glendalelyceum.com
7. **Grand Finale Restaurant** 3 E. Sharon Rd., 513-771-5925, grandfinale.info
8. **Friendly Stop Bar and Grill** 985 Congress Ave., 513-771-7427, friendlystop.com
9. **St. Gabriel Church** 48 W. Sharon Rd., 513-771-4700, gabrielglendale.org
10. **Glendale Town Hall** 80 E. Sharon Rd., 513-771-7200, glendaleohio.org
11. **Christ Church Glendale** 965 Forest Ave., 513-771-1544, christchurchglendale.org
12. **Cock & Bull Public House** Glendale Village, 275 E Sharon Rd., 513-771-4253, cockandbullcincinnati.com
13. **Harry Whiting Brown Community Center** 205 E. Sharon Rd., 513-771-0333, hwbcommunitycenter.org

24 East Price Hill
Catch a Sunrise

Above: Olden View Park offers incredible views of downtown Cincinnati, especially under a blue sky.

BOUNDARIES: Hawthorne Ave., Warsaw Ave., Purcell Ave., W. Eighth St., Mt. Hope Ave., Bodley Ave., Murdock Ave., Elberon Ave., Crestline Ave., Considine Ave.
DISTANCE: 3.2 miles
DIFFICULTY: Strenuous
PARKING: Park along Hawthorne Ave. or Price Ave.
PUBLIC TRANSIT: Metro buses (go-metro.com) serve this area. Take route 32 Delhi–Price Hill–Downtown to Grand and Price Aves., and walk one block west on Price Ave. to Hawthorne Ave.

Cincinnati's second-largest neighborhood, Price Hill covers more than 6 square miles, is home to more than 31,000 residents, and encompasses Lower Price Hill, East Price Hill, and West Price Hill. While each community deserves its own walk, this book focuses on the Incline District in East Price Hill. Price Hill's growth started in the mid-19th century as the original settlements in Cincinnati became more populated and wealthy residents looked to surrounding hillsides to escape

Backstory: Enright Ecovillage

Just 5 miles from Fountain Square is Price Hill's Enright Ecovillage (enrightecovillage.org), a place for people who live with goats and chickens. It is an intentional community with goals to become more socially, economically, and ecologically sustainable. Located south and east of Old St. Joseph's Cemetery (3819 W. Eighth St.), Enright Ridge Urban Ecovillage encompasses some 130 houses on five parallel streets—Enright Avenue, Enright Avenue, Terry Street, McPherson Place, and Wells Street—south of W. Eighth Street. The village shares land for organic gardening, youth groups, community dinners, and Imago Earth Center, a 16-acre nature preserve with hiking trails and educational programs. Homes here are reasonably priced and energy efficient.

pollution and overcrowding. After the construction of the Price Hill Incline at the base of Eighth Street and Warsaw Avenue in 1874, thousands of residents of Irish and German descent settled here and established a thriving suburb with commercial districts along Warsaw and Glenway Avenues. Merchant Evans Price and his son, Rees, owned and developed the land originally called Bold Face Hill (reportedly for an American Indian who lived in the area).

Price Hill is a tight-knit and diverse community of immigrants, longtime residents, and first-time home buyers, with hundreds of historic houses, impressive Catholic churches, and at least 17 schools, including three large high schools. Price Hill was home to the first Skyline Chili, which operated on Glenway Avenue from the mid-1940s to 2002. Parts of Price Hill boast of themselves as green neighborhoods, with seven parks, one prominent eco-village (see backstory), Imago Earth Center, Cincinnati Zen Center, and initiatives that encourage recycling. Neighborhood traditions include Price Hill Creative Community Festival, Music in the Woods, and the granddaddy of all local events, Price Hill Thanksgiving Day Parade. Price Hill Will, a nonprofit community development corporation, is leading the renovation of key historic properties, cleaning neighborhood streets, and promoting commercial interests.

Walk Description

Start your walk at the center of the emerging entertainment district envisioned along Price Avenue that is moving eastward toward Olden View Park. If you arrive late afternoon and want to linger a bit, begin with a glass of wine at ❶ **Somm Wine Bar,** and then add a charcuterie/cheese plate or smoky baba ghanoush. If tacos feel like a better start, cross Price Avenue and head to

❷ **Veracruz Mexican Grill.** On the northeast corner of Price and Hawthorne Avenues is ❸ **Flats Art Gallery,** in a renovated apartment building.

Walk north along Hawthorne Avenue. About one-quarter mile up on the left is ❹ **Price Hill Recreation Center.** Continue north and turn left on Warsaw Avenue, stopping in the middle of the block. Price Hill's finest collection of civic buildings is gathered here. Across the street at the northeast corner of Considine and Warsaw Avenues is the former Fire Company No. 24, built in 1889. Now ❺ **Warsaw Avenue Firehouse,** it is the home of MYCincinnati Firehouse Performing Arts Center, a youth orchestra program of Price Hill Will and producer of the Price Hill Creative Community Festival. In partnership with the Contemporary Arts Center, the free performing arts and neighborhood festival occurs over two days.

On the northwest corner is one of the first ArtWorks murals in Price Hill. *Natural Migration* draws inspiration from the neighborhood's dedication to growth and abundant green spaces, while welcoming everyone. There are many public art murals throughout Price Hill. Most recently, ArtWorks collaborated with Price Hill Will to add a series of five new murals designed by resident Lizzie DuQuette.

Back on the south side of the street and on your left is the former **Cincinnati Police District 3,** a magnificent Classical Revival building listed on the National Register of Historic Places. Built in 1908, it was originally a combined station house and patrol house. To the right and propped up from the street is the French Renaissance–style ❻ **Price Hill Library.** Opened in 1909, it is one of nine libraries in Hamilton County built with funds from the Andrew Carnegie Foundation. Notable features include a roof with tin deck and slate slopes, bird-head door handles, and interior cherry wood shelves. (The ceiling collapsed in 2018, and officials are unsure if the library will reopen, as the building has structural and accessibility issues.)

Before turning left on Purcell Avenue, look ahead to ❼ **St. Lawrence Church,** the first Catholic church in Price Hill. Designed by Adolphus Druiding and built in 1894, this soaring Gothic Revival structure with front towers can be seen from miles away. Turn left on Purcell Avenue. Behind the library on your left, you will pass **Price Hill Community Garden** (turnerfarm.org), a 0.5-acre site that provides space for residents to grow food in a collectively managed market-style garden with individual plots. Walk to **Dempsey Playground.** It features the first soccer and futsal facility—a partnership of FC Cincinnati's community fund and the recreation commission—in Cincinnati with an aim to grow soccer's popularity at underutilized recreational sites.

Cross Price Avenue. On the right is the first of two masonic lodges in this part of Price Hill. Designed by Samuel Hannaford and Sons and built in 1912, Price Hill Masonic Lodge No. 524 served the largest fraternal organization in the neighborhood for 77 years. Once threatened with demolition, the three-story Neoclassical Revival building was designated a local landmark to protect it from insensitive alterations and demolition. It is being converted into a venue called the ❽ **Incline Arts and Event Center.**

Continue walking south to 805 Purcell Avenue, the oldest house on this block and likely built for two families. According to *Digging Cincinnati History,* it was part of farmer and gardener John Stryker's property in 1869. His son, John P. Stryker, was an architect. The Strykers (originally spelled Stroeker) were early settlers of this part of Cincinnati, where J. P. Stryker designed other residences, as well as the St. Lawrence Roman Catholic Church School. John Stryker Sr. lived at the southwest corner of Price and Purcell Avenues.

Turn left on W. Eighth Street and walk to Hawthorne Avenue. On the right, at 3101 W. Eighth Street, is a remarkably intact American Foursquare house associated with Holy Family Church, coming up across the street. Walk around the corner to 741 Hawthorne Avenue, featured on the national television series *Rowhouse Showdown* in July 2014, along with row houses at 775 and 783 Summit Avenue. Return to W. Eighth Street. On the opposite corner is the Beaux Arts–style ❾ **Holy Family Church,** completed in 1884 to accommodate the growing Catholic population.

Continue eastward along W. Eighth Street for three blocks to Mt. Hope Avenue. On the left, at 801 Mt. Hope, is the redeveloped Price Hill Lodge, a mix of residential, office, and retail space. ❿ **BLOC Coffee Company** reopened here, just a few blocks away from their original location, in fall 2018. The shop serves locally roasted coffee and offers an all-day breakfast menu. Cross Mt. Hope Avenue. On the left is ⓫ **Warsaw Federal Incline Theater,** a 229-seat performing arts venue. This is the second venue for Cincinnati Landmark Productions, which operates Covedale Center for the Performing Arts in West Price Hill.

At the end of W. Eighth Street is **Olden View Park,** an overlook offering incredible views. The park marks the top of the Price Hill Incline, which was built in 1874 and operated until 1943. Mr. and Mrs. William H. Whiting donated the land for the park. Mrs. Whiting was the daughter of Harry L. Olden, a Cincinnati industrialist and the founder and 20-year president of the Boys Club of Cincinnati. The park features bronze plaques mounted in a parapet wall of granite blocks salvaged from multiple streets downtown.

Ahead are two of Price Hill's most popular dining spots. On the right is ⓬ **Incline Public House,** which derives its name from the old incline and features a 1,400-square-foot outdoor deck ideal for taking in vistas, food, and cocktails. To the left is ⓭ **Primavista,** one of the city's best dining experiences, offering classic Italian dishes and wine amid spectacular views (especially at night) of the city below.

Return to Mt. Hope Avenue and turn left. On the left, at 716 Mount Hope and almost impossible to see from the street, is the historic **Moore-Knight House,** built in the mid 1800s. On a cliff overlooking downtown, this Italianate gem was home to Cincinnati Mayor Robert Moore before it became the home of the Knights, a prominent African American family who owned it for more than 80 years.

Turn right on Bodley Avenue and walk past **Wilson Common,** one of many parks on Cincinnati's west side. Its overlook is its best feature, with a trail that connects to a lower terrace. Follow the edge of the park and turn left on Wilsonia Drive, and then right on Nonaly, a quiet paved alley. Turn left on Grand Avenue and walk south along this shady stretch. 430 Grand Avenue is the first in a group of houses on large lots with stunning views of the city.

Walk to Murdock Avenue and turn right, crossing Hawthorne, Considine, and Purcell Avenues. Walk down the Murdock Avenue Steps (between 397 and 403 Purcell Ave.) to Elberon Avenue.

Cross Elberon Avenue at the crosswalk and walk up the Mount Echo Park Steps, built with funding from President Franklin D. Roosevelt's Works Progress Administration in 1939. Follow the sidewalk into **Mt. Echo Park,** an 84-acre park established in 1908 that features wooded hillsides, hiking trails, picnic areas, and an overlook (adjacent to a historic pavilion) with a dramatic view. Walk through the play area to the rear of the park to Crestline Avenue. Head to 408 Crestline Avenue and note the top of the disheveled and increasingly forgotten Pica Street Steps, which lead back down to Elberon Avenue.

Continue north on Crestline to Bassett Road and turn right. Cross Elberon Avenue and walk to Purcell Avenue. Turn left onto one of the finest residential blocks in Price Hill, where lovingly maintained houses range from Victorian era and Tudor Revival to American Craftsman. The most significant property is the **George Scott House** (565 Purcell Ave.), a private residence listed on the National Register of Historic Places. Built in 1887, Samuel Hannaford designed this large two-and-a-half-story brick house with Queen Anne details. Scott was one of the executives at George Scott's Sons Pottery, which was prosperous due to its production of potteries, including yellowware, an earthenware named after its yellow appearance.

Turn right on Phillips Avenue and then left on Considine Avenue. On the left is the former **Price Hill Methodist Church** (707 Considine Ave.), built from 1889 to 1891. Designed by church architects Crapsey & Brown in the Shingle style, this was the original Methodist Episcopal church in Price Hill. Continue north on Considine Avenue and cross W. Eighth Street to return to Price Avenue and the end of this walk.

East Price Hill

Points of Interest

1. **Somm Wine Bar** 3105 Price Ave., 513-244-5843, sommwinebarcincinnati.com
2. **Veracruz Mexican Grill** 3108 Price Ave., 513-244-1757
3. **Flats Art Gallery** 3028 Price Ave., 513-244-8044, theflatsartgallery.com
4. **Price Hill Recreation Center** 959 Hawthorne Ave., 513-251-0279, eastpricehill.org
5. **Warsaw Avenue Firehouse** 3120 Warsaw Ave., 513-251-3800, mycincinnatiorchestra.org
6. **Price Hill Library** 3215 Warsaw Ave., 513-369-4490, cincinnatilibrary.org/branches/pricehill.html
7. **St. Lawrence Church** 3680 Warsaw Ave., 513-921-0328, stlawrenceparish.org
8. **Incline Arts and Event Center** 3301 Price Ave.
9. **Holy Family Church** 3006 W. Eighth St., 513-921-7527, holyfamilycincinnati.org
10. **BLOC Coffee Company** 801 Mt. Hope Ave., 513-429-4548
11. **Warsaw Federal Incline Theater** 801 Matson Pl., 513-241-6550, clpshows.org
12. **Incline Public House** 2601 W. Eighth St., 513-251-3000, inclinepublichouse.com
13. **Primavista** 810 Matson Pl., 513-251-6467, pvista.com

25 Westwood

Cincinnati's Biggest Neighborhood

Above: Neighborhood residents Phillip Longworth and James Gamble appear in the Westwood Story *mural outside Henke Winery.*

BOUNDARIES: Epworth Ave., Werk Rd., Harrison Ave., Urwiler Ave.
DISTANCE: 2.9 miles
DIFFICULTY: Moderate
PARKING: Park for free along Epworth Ave., south of Harrison Ave.
PUBLIC TRANSIT: Metro buses (go-metro.com) serve this area. Take route 21, 40x, or 41 to Harrison Ave. at Epworth Ave.

Originally established as a residential enclave for many of Cincinnati's wealthy mid-19th-century industrialists, Westwood has evolved into a socioeconomically and culturally diverse neighborhood with a lot of heart and a commitment to family life. Incorporated as a village in 1868, Westwood was annexed into the City of Cincinnati in 1896. It is the city's largest neighborhood and the most populous in Hamilton County. Located about 7 miles west of downtown Cincinnati, its main thoroughfares and side streets feature many decorative houses, with a cluster of remarkable civic buildings surrounding Westwood Town Hall. Immediately to the west is Cheviot, one of the oldest suburban communities in Hamilton County. Where these two communities begin and end is ambiguous and confounds even longtime residents. Mt. Airy Forest, immediately to the north, is Cincinnati's largest forest and one of the largest municipal parks in the United States at 1,470 acres.

Walk Description

Start your walk with a glass of wine and a bite to eat at ❶ **Henke Winery,** which started in 1996 in Winton Place and moved here several years later. The winery is closed on Sunday, so plan accordingly. Proceed south on Epworth Avenue. On the left is the magnificent ❷ **Westwood Town Hall.** Designed by architects Charles Crapsey and William Brown in the Shingle style and completed in 1889, the building originally served as town hall for the village of Westwood. The YMCA was housed here from the late 1800s until the Gamble Nippert branch was built farther west, at 3159 Montana Avenue, in 1966. The Cincinnati Recreation Commission operates the building and offers a variety of programs, while the Cincinnati Park Board controls the surrounding property.

Turn right on Junietta Avenue. The first building on the right is former Firehouse Engine Co. No. 35, also known as Junietta Firehouse. Built in the Beaux Arts style, this single-bay building served Westwood for generations. Harry Hake was responsible for the design of this firehouse and many others, as well as the eclectic Cincinnati and Suburban Bell Telephone building across Harrison Avenue. The city's Department of Community and Economic Development chose the bid from Over-the-Rhine's ❸ **Nation Kitchen & Bar** to open their second location (in 2019) here.

Walk past the wonderful collection of houses on Junietta Avenue and then turn left on Stathem Avenue, named after David Stathem, who was the father-in-law of architect Samuel Hannaford. Turn left on Montana Avenue and cross at the Epworth Avenue traffic signal. On your way, look across the street at 3025 Montana,

Westwood boasts an impressive collection of civic buildings, including Westwood Elementary School.

a house built in the 1880s that features a front room with an octagonal shape. The first building on the right is ❹ **Westwood Branch Library,** part of the Westwood Town Center Historic District, which contains a range of buildings representing architectural types of the late 19th and early 20th centuries. The festive library building was completed in 1931 to replace a small branch located inside Westwood Elementary School. Interior elements include a stone fireplace, a balcony above the circulation desk, and solid oak shelving. Across the street is the aforementioned **Westwood Elementary School.** Designed by prominent Cincinnati architect Frederick W. Garber, original floor plans were published in *Modern School Houses* in 1915. This impressive building escaped demolition after lengthy community discussion.

Continue south on Epworth Avenue, crossing Daytona Avenue. Epworth Avenue is an early Westwood street, and many homes here were built from the early 1900s to the 1920s. They reflect a variety of architectural styles and sizes. Some early farmhouses and other homes from the 1800s are tucked in between. This mile-long residential street, which extends north from Wardall Avenue to Werk Road on the south, is one of Cincinnati's most pleasant.

The house at 3265 Epworth is an early farmhouse, likely dating from the Civil War era. Lillian Werk Price, granddaughter of businessman Michael Werk, built the 1928 English Tudor residence at 3249 Epworth. The small house at 3217 Epworth and Lischer Avenue is another farmhouse from the 1800s. Originally built in 1866 and then rebuilt in 1868 after a fire in 1867, the Italian villa John M. Miller built at 3217 Epworth once sat on property that extended north to Daytona Avenue. Miller maintained diaries from the age of 15, which were later published to give a glimpse into life in Westwood in the mid-to-late 1800s. Clarence Heidrich, founder of Miami Margarine Co., which made Nu-Maid Margarine, built the 1925 Colonial Revival house at 3181 Epworth Avenue.

Walk one more block to the former **Mother of Mercy High School,** designed by Samuel Hannaford and Sons and completed in 1923. Formerly a Roman Catholic girls' high school, it once housed a kindergarten and grade school for both girls and boys. Cincinnati Public Schools purchased the property and is repurposing it for another West Side public school.

Turn left on Werk Road, named for Michael Werk, who owned large tracts of land in Westwood. Werk was the owner of M. Werk Company, which manufactured candles and soap and was active in the farming of grapes and winemaking. The stretch of Werk Road from Ferguson Road to Harrison Avenue was once home to three soap magnates: James N. Gamble (Ivory Soap inventor), Michael Werk (Tag Soap maker), and Dr. Charles McCarty (Biz Stain & Odor Remover developer).

Walking east on Werk Road, the house at the southwest corner of Ferguson Road and 2981 Werk is the 1897 residence of Alfred K. Nippert. Nippert married Maud Gamble, daughter of James N. Gamble. The Geyer family, early Westwood residents, built the house at 2972 Werk Road in the

1870s. It is said to have been a rooming house for people who wanted to escape the heat and smells of the city in summer. (The address is difficult to see. It is diagonally opposite 2981 Werk Rd.)

Back on the north side of the street—along the first poured concrete sidewalk in Westwood—is where Cincinnati lost part of its soul. After a brave fight involving residents and elected officials, the **James N. and Margaret Penrose Gamble House** (2918 Werk Rd.) was torn down April 1, 2013. (The entrance to the drive and the front stairs remain, but there is no evidence of a house number or a foundation.) It was originally the farmhouse of an early Westwood settler, Richard Gaines, possibly as early as 1840. His son John Gaines, who inherited it, became the first mayor of the village of Westwood. Gamble and his wife, Margaret Penrose Gamble, bought the house in 1870 and greatly expanded it. He lived there until his death at the age of 95 in 1932. Gamble was active in governing the village of Westwood and served as its last mayor before it was annexed into the City of Cincinnati. Architect Solon Spencer Beman designed the surviving barn. He is also responsible for the P&G Ivorydale plant in St. Bernard and the renowned planned Pullman community in South Chicago.

On the opposite side of the street, at 2921 Werk Road, is the Norman-style residence where William Zimmer, former CEO of Cincinnati Gas & Electric Company, and Dr. Charles McCarty, P&G researcher who developed color-safe Biz bleach, both lived at different times.

Turn left on McKinley Avenue. Just past 2882 McKinley, on the left, is the rear entrance to the Gamble estate. Continue following McKinley to Harrison Avenue. The Cincinnati & Westwood Railroad originally crossed at 2852 McKinley Avenue. Turn left on Harrison Avenue, originally known as Harrison Pike, a major route connecting the central city with parts west. Many large estates and other significant homes were demolished here in the 1970s and 1980s to make way for apartment buildings. Although currently empty, The Paramount (2883 Harrison Ave.) is a remarkably intact example of an earlier apartment building common along other city thoroughfares, such as Reading Road in North Avondale and Madison Road in Hyde Park. The Eggers homestead (2949 Harrison Ave.) is a rare survivor that dates back to the 1800s.

Continue on Harrison to ❺ **Westwood First Presbyterian Church** on the left. This impressive church, with its window designed by G. C. Riordan Co., was built in 1926, with extensions added later. Return to the Westwood business district, passing Westwood Elementary School on the left. Cross Harrison Avenue at Montana Avenue. The first building, on the northeast corner, is the three-story Ruehlman Building (3020–3036 Harrison Ave.), built in 1937. Jerry Springer, former Cincinnati mayor and talk show host, once lived in an apartment upstairs. Storefronts along Harrison Avenue include a recent influx of new businesses, including late-night comfort food spot ❻ **Muse Café**, ❼ **Fuzzybutts Dry Goods** pet supply store, ❽ **Treasure Alley** antiques store, and ❾ **Wooden Hill** art gallery.

Continue north on Harrison Avenue, crossing Ruehlman Place. Cincinnati's communal love for beer extends to Westwood, like most city neighborhoods. ⑩ **West Side Brewing** opened here in the former Wullenweber car dealership in 2017, with views of Westwood Town Hall across the street. The lively brewery offers 30 taps' worth of beers, wines, and ciders. It's family-friendly and community-oriented, featuring cornhole and a regular rotation of food trucks.

Walk north, and turn right on Epworth Avenue. The impressive Bell Telephone Exchange Building, and its endearing terra-cotta cherubs, is wedged inside the intersection of Epworth and Harrison Avenues. Architect Harry Hake designed this 1928 Classic Revival building with Italian Renaissance influence for the utilitarian purpose of accommodating large telephone-switching equipment and the workers who operated it. This is an early version of a "big box" building. Unlike its current equivalents, it was intentionally designed to complement and enhance the surrounding neighborhood. When modern switching equipment made the building obsolete, the Public Library of Cincinnati and Hamilton County acquired the building for use as a book repository. The City of Cincinnati gave $500,000 to ⑪ **Madcap Puppets** for its plan to remodel the historic building into a performance space, which opened in late 2018.

After soaking in all sides of the Bell Telephone Exchange Building, turn right on Urwiler Avenue. On the left is ⑫ **Westwood United Methodist Church,** designed by Samuel Hannaford and built in 1897. A combination of Indiana limestone, Ohio River cut stone, slate, and glass, this church played a large role in the Gamble family. James N. Gamble's wife donated the original organ, and Alfred Nippert and Maude Gamble were the first couple to be married here in 1898.

Continue walking east to 2943 Urwiler Avenue, one of the original homes of Westwood. Likely built around the time of the Civil War, this simple frame farmhouse was once home to the Urwiler family for whom the street is named. On the other side of the street, at 2924 Urwiler, is the second-largest sweet gum tree in Ohio. Turn left on Hazelwood Avenue and then left on Montclair Avenue, continuing toward Epworth Avenue. At the northeast corner of 2946 Montclair (on the right) and Epworth Avenues is the former parsonage (built in 1900) of Westwood United Methodist Church. Across Epworth from the former parsonage is a Civil War–era house, at 3004 Montclair Avenue, on a larger piece of property that originally faced Harrison Avenue. James N. Gamble owned this house at one time on behalf of Westwood United Methodist Church.

Cross Epworth, turning right, then turn left on Temple Avenue. Turn left on Harrison Avenue to return to the business district. On the left, at 3150 Harrison Avenue, is a former Masonic Lodge, designed by Hannaford and Sons. Built in 1900, it is now owned by Westwood United Methodist Church. Continue walking along Harrison Avenue to return to Henke Winery.

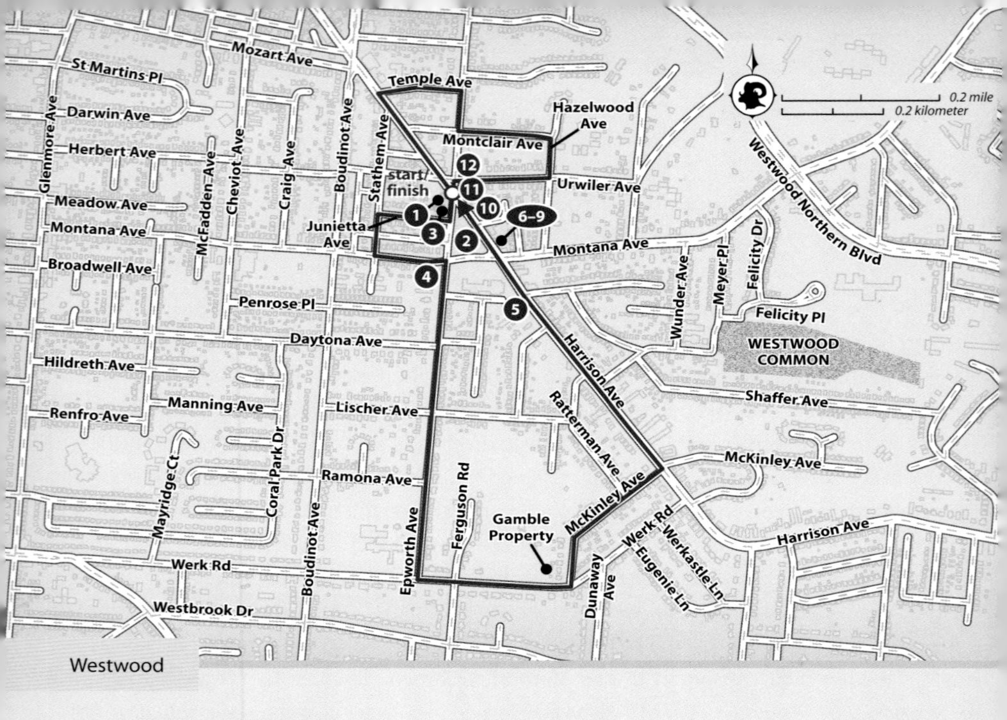

Points of Interest

1. **Henke Winery** 3077 Harrison Ave., 513-662-9463, henkewine.com
2. **Westwood Town Hall** 3017 Harrison Ave., 513-662-9109, cincyrec.org
3. **Nation Kitchen & Bar** 3002 Junietta Ave., nationkitchenandbar.com
4. **Westwood Branch Library** 3345 Epworth Ave., 513-369-4474, cincinnatilibrary.org
5. **Westwood First Presbyterian Church** 3011 Harrison Ave., 513-661-6846, wfpc.org
6. **Muse Café** 3018 Harrison Ave., 513-906-7743
7. **Fuzzybutts Dry Goods** 3022 Harrison Ave., 513-906-7115, american-canine.com
8. **Treasure Alley** 3034 Harrison Ave., 513-728-0244
9. **Wooden Hill** 3036 Harrison Ave., 513-405-4013
10. **West Side Brewing** 3044 Harrison Ave., 513-661-2337, westsidebrewing.com
11. **Madcap Puppets** 3064 Harrison Ave., 513-921-5965, madcappuppets.com
12. **Westwood United Methodist Church** 3460 Epworth Ave., 513-661-3139, westwoodunitedmethodist.org

26 Sayler Park

A Tale of Cincinnati's Western Tail

Above: Colorfully painted Victorian homes line Gracely Drive.

BOUNDARIES: Gracely Dr., Revere Ave., Home City Ave., River Rd.
DISTANCE: 4.9 miles
DIFFICULTY: Moderate, with some rolling terrain
PARKING: Enter Sayler Park from River Rd. via Gracely Dr. at traffic signal, past St. Aloysius On the Ohio (134 Whipple St.), and find parking on Gracely Dr. between Meridian St. and Revere Ave.
PUBLIC TRANSIT: Metro buses (go-metro.com) serve this area. Take route 50 (Sayler Park) to Gracely Dr. and Revere Ave.

Approximately 2 miles long and 1 mile wide, Sayler Park is as far west as you can travel and still be in Cincinnati. First settled in the early 1800s as Home City, this unassuming riverside neighborhood was incorporated in 1879. Its name changed to Sayler Park, honoring Nelson Sayler, the village's first mayor, when it was annexed into the City of Cincinnati in 1911. Sayler Park sits curvaceously on the Ohio River, 10.5 miles west of downtown—about the same distance Mariemont

Backstory: Western Wildlife Corridor

University of Cincinnati Geologist Richard Durrell realized that the portion of the Ohio River corridor extending from Price Hill to Rapid Run Creek was a very special natural area. Durrell noted that the extremely narrow valley here stemmed from a glacier damming the river 350,000 years ago. The resulting lake finally found a low spot about where the Anderson Ferry crosses the Ohio River. The sudden massive erosion that occurred as the water rushed out of this lake created an unusually narrow river valley with steep slopes. Stream channels cutting into the region's bedrock expose the marine fossils that have caused Cincinnati's name to be appropriated for one of North America's geologic time spans, the Cincinnatian Epoch of the Ordovician Period. With a mission to preserve the scenic beauty and natural resources of the Ohio River corridor from Mill Creek to the Great Miami River near Indiana, the Western Wildlife Corridor (westernwildlifecorridor.org) is a go-to resource for environmental stewardship for this part of town. Buckeye Trace in Sayler Park is one example of the efforts of Western Wildlife Corridor volunteers. This property has a beautiful mature forest and a ready-made trail leading to the meadow on top, while other WWC trails provide magnificent views of the Ohio River.

lies to the east. Sayler Park is a close-knit, genteel Midwestern town that works undercover as a city neighborhood. City trash cans and recycling bins and a public elementary school give clues that you're in Cincinnati. Dotted with Victorian-era frame houses and brick ranches on rolling hills, many parks and recreation centers, and hidden walking steps, Sayler Park makes for a relaxing morning or afternoon getaway.

Walk Description

Start your walk in front of the ArtWorks mural, ❶ **A Day in the Life of Sayler Park** at Gracely Drive and Revere Avenue, the easternmost boundary of the business district. Painted in partnership with Sayler Park Village Council, this mural is designed like a scrapbook honoring past and present life in Sayler Park. A Kroger grocery store once occupied the storefront (now a residence) when the supermarket chain was common in traditional neighborhood business districts around the city.

Standing in front of the mural facing northwest, walk along Gracely Drive. The house at 6380 Gracely Dr. was home to Gibson Greeting Cards founder Robert H. Gibson. He purchased the house around 1875 and died there in 1895. His wife stayed in the house until at least 1910. The Colonial Revival house at 6432 Gracely Drive features a two-story portico angled to claim its corner plot.

Turn right on Zinn Place and walk to vinyl-clad Revere Dance Studio (6435 Revere Ave.), formerly a Methodist church from 1869. Turn left on sloping Revere Avenue. The twin houses with hip roofs on the right, at 6458–60 Revere, were originally used to store blocks of ice cut from the Ohio River. After 6504 Revere Avenue, there is no sidewalk, so proceed with caution or switch to the other side. Just past the First Baptist Church of Delhi (6515 Revere Ave.), on the left, take the Ivanhoe Avenue Steps, which descend into a ravine and come up the other side onto Parkland Avenue.

Turn right at the top of the steps. O'Shaughnessy grocery store, a popular after-school stop for neighborhood kids, once occupied the first house on the right at 6528 Parkland Avenue. Continue northwest to ❷ **Parkland Theatre & Entertainment Centre,** which runs films that mostly attract West Side residents. Opposite is the Sayler Park Firehouse (6558 Parkland Ave.).

Turn left on Twain Avenue and return to Gracely Drive. On the left is the former First Presbyterian Church (6558 Gracely Dr.), built in 1867. Turn right on Gracely Drive and walk to Monitor Avenue. Turn right on Monitor Avenue and cross through **Nelson Sayler Memorial Park,** which hosts a weekly farmers market May through October and other special events. Just as you start on the diagonal path, there is an interpretive sign that covers a bit of neighborhood history. The McQuitty family donated land for the park. (The McQuitty family home at 206 Twain Ave. is one of Sayler Park's oldest properties.) The 2-acre park became city property when the Village of Sayler Park was annexed to Cincinnati in 1911. A tornado on April 3, 1974, caused great damage to the neighborhood. Fifty-two trees were lost, as well as stone benches, lawn areas, and concrete paths. In October of that year, Cincinnati Parks planted more than 90 flowering and shade trees as the first step in restoring the tornado-ravaged park. The large sycamore tree in the park's center survived the tornado.

Once you walk through the park, turn right on Parkland Avenue and walk to Monitor Avenue. The group of homes between Monitor and Thelma Avenues is commonly called Doctors' Row because of the number of doctors who lived here from the 1920s through the 1950s. Built in 1880, the large frame home at 6624 Parkland Avenue was originally planned as a hospital. Instead it became the residence of Dr. Benjamin Lehman and his family. Retrace your steps back to Thelma Avenue past the small barber shop at 6648 Parkland Avenue, and turn right on Elco Street.

Ahead is the impressive ❸ **Sayler Park Elementary School,** which resembles McMicken Hall at the University of Cincinnati on a smaller scale. As we enjoy the shade from the tree canopy along Elco Street, it's as though we're walking through a small college town. The school, which instructs grades K through 8, opened in 1929.

Turn left on Home City Avenue and continue northwest, past ❹ **Sayler Park Community Center.** Homes along this stretch of Home City Avenue were built after the tornado of 1974. Turn left on Cherokee Avenue and walk two blocks to Parkland Avenue. Turn right on Parkland Avenue. On what is now an empty lot between the church and 6818 Parkland, there was once an

American Indian mound. In the 1800s, the mound was used as a racetrack for horses. Excavated in the mid-1950s, relics are stored at the Museum of Natural History & Science at Union Terminal. American Indian mounds were common throughout Cincinnati until the early 20th century, when they were nearly all demolished.

Turn right on Parkland Avenue and then left on Laura Lane, named for Nelson Sayler's wife. Walk past the Lodwick estate (6900 Gracely Dr.) on the right. Turn right on Gracely Drive. Houses on the right sit on hilltops with sweeping river views, while houses on the left sit just above River Road. Continue along Gracely Drive, and cross Wilkins Short Road. On the right, at 7128 Gracely, is the **Rudolph Siegel House,** which dates from 1903. Dr. Siegel was a pioneer in the field of endodontics, the study and treatment of dental pulp.

Turn right on Catalpa Road and continue to Fernbank Avenue. The house on the right (7141 Fernbank Ave.) is an outstanding example of an American Craftsman–style bungalow, which represents the middle-class roots of Sayler Park with its use of local natural and handcrafted materials.

For a semi-rural diversion, cross Fernbank and continue on Catalpa Road to Overcliff Road to see Fernbank Golf Course (7036 Fernbank Ave.) and the Muddy Creek ravine below. At the end of the street are two well-preserved early-20th-century houses (7250 Catalpa and 161 Overcliff Rd.).

Return to—and turn right at—Fernbank Avenue, a boulevard with a divided median in the middle, and walk to the end, turning left on Overcliff Road. Note that there is no sidewalk in this direction. Ahead is the Drewry House (121 Overcliff), with an impressive stone wall that extends to Gracely Drive and surrounds the neighboring March estate at 7302 Gracely.

Turn right on Gracely Drive and then right again on Kirkwood Lane. Up the hill on the right is former ❺ **St. Luke Episcopal Church.** Charles Short, who platted Fernbank in 1875, and his brother John Cleves Short donated money to erect a church building in honor of their deceased parents. An English Gothic–influenced design was chosen, and Samuel Hannaford was hired as the architect. St. Luke's is typical of Hannaford's churches from the period, most of which were stone Gothic Revival structures. The building is listed on the National Register of Historic Places and is the current meeting place for the Sayler Park Historical Society.

Continue on Kirkwood Lane past the midcentury modern house at 7376, built on stilts in 1957. Turn left on Lowland Road, and then left again on Gracely Drive. Follow Gracely Drive to **Thornton Triangle,** a tiny park centered on the J. Fitzhugh Thornton Memorial at the intersection of Gracely Drive and Thornton Avenue. Eliza Thornton, whose home sits in the background, at 95 Thornton Avenue, dedicated the zinc statue of an eastern Woodlands Indian to her husband in 1912. The statue acquired the name Tecumseh, after the Shawnee intertribal leader who led resistance against white expansion into the region. Cincinnati's tiniest park, with a total area of .01 acre, Thornton Triangle was partially submerged in the great flood of 1937. Three years later, a car struck the statue and the city sold it to an antiques dealer in Indiana. Sayler Park residents organized to find and return the Indian to its cast-iron pedestal several months later. Today, it's a protected local historic landmark under the care of Cincinnati Parks.

Opposite the park, at 7342 Gracely Drive, is an outstanding example of a Swiss Chalet–style house. Continue walking along Gracely Drive past Kirkwood Lane and then Overcliff Road. Turn right on Topinabee Road for a view of four brick houses that are very similar in style with impressive brickwork. Follow the curving street back to Gracely Drive, past 82 Topinabee, 7222 Catalpa, and 7223 Gracely Road. Turn right on Gracely Drive, passing Catalpa Road on the left. 7151 and 7141 Gracely are nice examples of Queen Anne architecture.

Walk to Wilkins Shortcut Road, which is missing a street sign, and look to your right. Just beyond the railroad crossing is **Fernbank Park,** a 58-acre riverfront park with a 1.2-mile paved trail, 1-mile nature trail, and playground that buffers river-related industries. It is made possible through a partnership between the Cincinnati Park Board and Great Parks of Hamilton County. (For more information, visit greatparks.org.)

Cross Wilkins Shortcut Road and pass 7033 Gracely Drive, a former school building. Walk to Laura Lane. On the right is the site of the former Sayler mansion, which was heavily damaged in the tornado of 1974 and demolished. The carriage house barely survives as a laundry room in a courtyard of town houses. The pair of columns at Laura Lane and Gracely Drive (and at the western entrance to the parking lot) are part of the original Sayler mansion. Stuart Park, across the street, was once home to Fernbank Sunoco, where drivers and crew members worked on many different kinds of race cars.

Walk three blocks to Thelma Avenue. On the right is ❻ **Buddha Barn,** a Thai restaurant housed in an old building that survived the 1974 tornado. At the end of the block is ❼ **Bizy Bees Bakery,** a local bakery known for its glazed doughnuts.

Cross Twain Avenue. On the right is an old masonic lodge (6557 Gracely Dr.), which is now a real estate office and apartments. In the middle of the block, also on the right, is the **Twitchell House** (6533 Gracely Dr.), built in 1860. Its namesake owner, Ernest Twitchell, invented the process of saponification, which is used to make vegetable oil.

Cross Ivanhoe Avenue. The 6400 block of Gracely Drive has some lovely older homes on the north side of the street. Return to the start of the walk, in front of the *A Day in the Life of Sayler Park* mural.

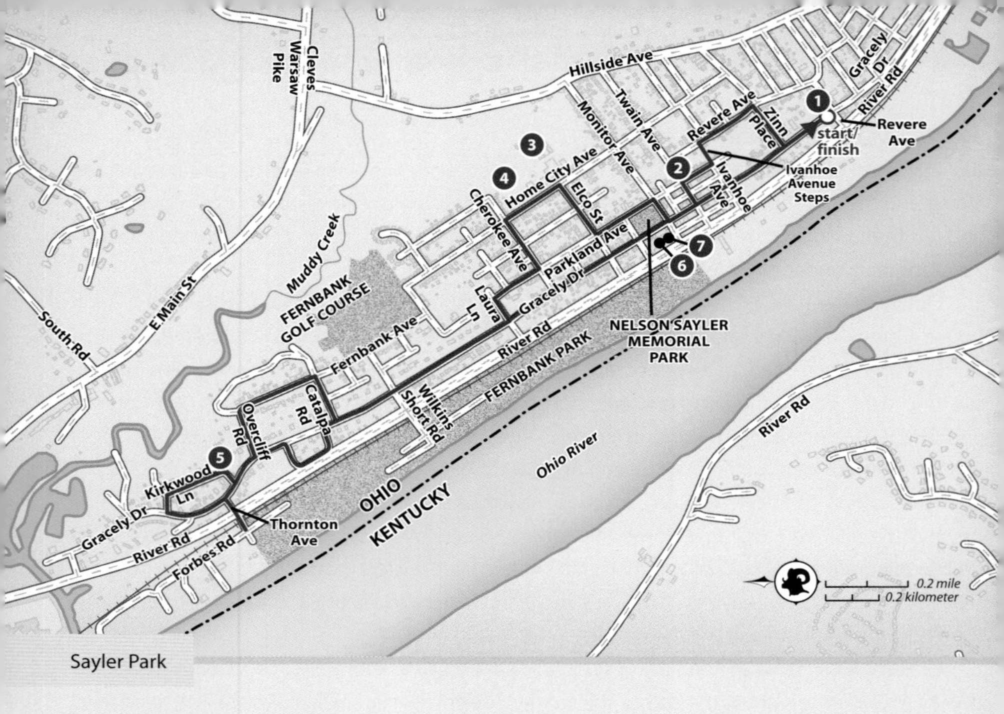

Sayler Park

Points of Interest

1. *A Day in the Life of Sayler Park* 6356 Gracely Dr., artworkscincinnati.org
2. Parkland Theatre & Entertainment Centre 6550 Parkland Ave., 513-600-7900, parklandtheatre.com
3. Sayler Park Elementary School 6700 Home City Ave., 513-363-5100, saylerpark.cps-k12.org
4. Sayler Park Community Center 6720 Home City Ave., 513-941-0102, saylerpark.org
5. St. Luke Episcopal Church 7340 Kirkwood Ln., 513-941-3650, episcopalchurch.org
6. Buddha Barn 6625 Gracely Dr., 513-442-2010, buddhabarnthai.com
7. Bizy Bees Bakery 6601 Gracely Dr., 513-941-2930

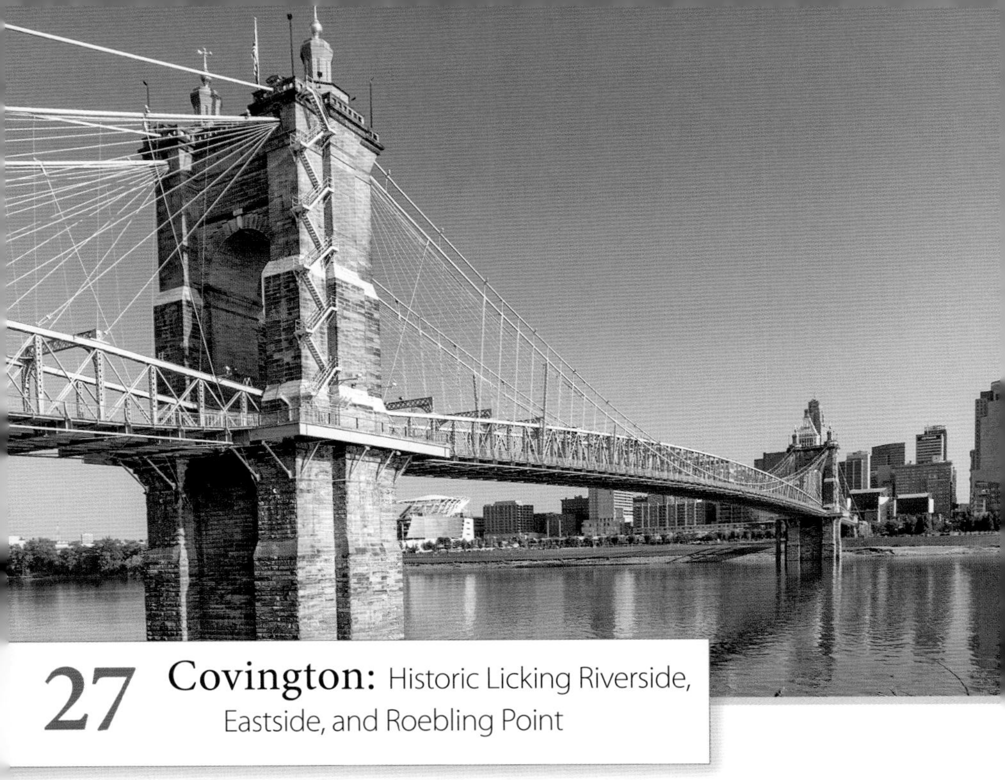

27 Covington: Historic Licking Riverside, Eastside, and Roebling Point

Above: The Roebling Suspension Bridge crosses the Ohio River to connect Covington and Cincinnati.

BOUNDARIES: Riverfront, Shelby St., Martin Luther King Blvd., Madison Ave.
DISTANCE: 2.9 miles
DIFFICULTY: Moderate
PARKING: On-street parking, pay lot at RiverCenter and Madison
PUBLIC TRANSIT: TANK transit station at 220 Madison Ave. or Southbank Shuttle at Third and Greenup. Red Bike at Madison Ave/RiverCenter Blvd. or Third and Greenup.

Historic Licking Riverside is home to some of the most well-maintained and significant historic homes in the region. The area includes beautiful views of the Ohio River, John A. Roebling Suspension Bridge, and Cincinnati skyline. This walk starts in the Historic Licking Riverside neighborhood and travels south to visit portions of the Eastside neighborhood and finishes in the Roebling Point business district. These neighborhoods are brimming with historic significance and still function as cultural destinations.

The northeast corner of Covington, which is now the Historic Licking Riverside neighborhood, was the original five-by-six-block plat of Covington. In 1814, John Gano, Richard Gano, and Thomas Carneal invested $50,000 to buy the 150 acres that was originally established, called Covington Company. The north–south streets lined up with streets in downtown Cincinnati and were named east to west after the first five governors of Kentucky: Shelby, Kennedy, Garrard, Greenup, and Scott. Later, Madison Avenue was named for George Madison, the sixth governor.

Before Gano, Gano, and Carneal purchased and established the Covington Company, the area that is now Riverside Drive was once the training ground for a cavalry brigade under the leadership of Lieutenant Leonard W. Covington. At the Battle of Fallen Timbers, in 1794, Europeans first fought with cavalry against the American Indians, resulting in a decisive victory. For this, General Covington was revered and later became the namesake of the city.

The Eastside neighborhood is located between the Licking River and Madison Avenue and from Eighth Street to 16th Street. It is home to the Carnegie Visual and Performing Arts Center; the Lincoln-Grant School building, which provided education to African American children before desegregation; Covington Latin School; and the world-renowned St. Mary's Cathedral Basilica of the Assumption.

Walk Description

Start at Covington Landing, where Madison Avenue meets the Ohio River. From here, walk east toward the Roebling Suspension Bridge, along the **floodwall murals.** These murals depict a timeline of the history of Covington. Led by artist Robert Dafford, a team of artists created this series in 2002. For in-depth insights on the murals, visit nkyarttours.com. You can follow the murals closely, but to continue the walk, take the lower path under the ❶ **Roebling Suspension Bridge.**

Stay east on Riverside Drive under the bridge to begin your walk in the Historic Licking Riverside neighborhood. As you pass the bridge, you can hear the humming of the cars passing, which is why it is sometimes referred to as The Singing Bridge. At the time of completion, in 1865, the Roebling Suspension Bridge was the world's longest suspension bridge. Today, it is a regional icon for its beauty, history, engineering, and role in opening access between the North and South. This bridge was the prototype for the Brooklyn Bridge. Just past the bridge you'll find a statue of John A. Roebling, which is the first of seven statues recognizing iconic Covington figures.

Continue east along Riverside Drive. You'll pass seven lifelike bronze statues of historical figures, including John A. Roebling, Chief Little Turtle, Simon Kenton, John James Audubon, James Bradley, Mary B. Greene, and Daniel Carter Beard. You will also pass **George Rogers Clark Park,** a great place to have a picnic and enjoy the serenity of the Ohio River. It's worth exploring some of the statues and landmarks, including an original bench from the Greene Line Steamboats.

At the end of the road, you'll arrive at The Point, where the Licking River and Ohio River come together. This confluence became an iconic point for early pioneers due to the uniqueness of the north-flowing waters. The Shawnee called the Licking River the Nepernine River, and it is one of three preglacial streams that flow north in eastern North America.

Turn right on Shelby Street, and then take another right on E. Second Street. To your right you'll see a beautifully restored mansion known as the **Carneal House.** Aaron Gano, son of John Gano, lived in the house until 1825. Although it is called the Carneal House, there isn't much evidence that Thomas Carneal had anything to do with it. The house was built in 1815 and is the oldest brick house in Covington.

Turn Left onto the pedestrian alley at Park Place. As you walk down the road, you'll pass Governors' Point Condominiums to your left. Originally the site of the Amos Shinkle mansion, it became the William Booth Memorial Hospital in 1914 and was torn down in 1920.

Turn right on E. Third Street. At the corner of Park Place and E. Third Street, you'll find the **Daniel Carter Beard House.** This Victorian was the boyhood home of Daniel Carter Beard, the first National Commissioner of the Boy Scouts of America. It wasn't until "Uncle Dan" was in his 50s that he would found a couple of organizations—Sons of Daniel Boone and Boy Pioneers. These then merged with a couple of other organizations to become Boy Scouts of America. His program for young boys was based on his youthful experiences in Covington—canoeing the Licking River, camping along its banks, and learning survival skills from the Union troops who occupied the town during the Civil War. The home is still a private residence but bears markers commemorating it as a National Historic Landmark.

Turn left on Garrard Street and continue through the tree-lined residential streets until you reach **Randolph Park** at E. Eighth Street. Turn Right on E. Eighth Street. This 6.5-acre park is named after Dr. James E. Randolph. Between 1922 and 1958, Dr. Randolph delivered nearly all African American babies born in Covington. He was the first African American physician to be on staff at St. Elizabeth Hospital. He charged only $7 for a visit, but if a patient was unable to pay, Dr. Randolph did not turn them away. He died in 1981 at the age of 93.

Turn left on Scott Boulevard and continue for three blocks, past the fire station for Company One of the Covington Fire Department.

Next, you'll reach the ❷ **Carnegie Visual and Performing Arts Center.** Like 1,700 other communities in the United States, Covington benefited from a grant from Andrew Carnegie. In 1904, the City of Covington constructed the magnificent Carnegie Library and Auditorium, an example of Beaux Arts architecture with a rotunda modeled after the Library of Congress. For decades, Carnegie Library and Auditorium was the center of the cultural scene, with numerous play productions, speakers, and community activities. Today, the building has been reborn as the Carnegie Visual and Performing Arts Center and hosts a variety of exhibits, performances, classes, and community projects. The Carnegie is open to the public Monday–Friday, 10 a.m.–5 p.m. and Saturday, noon–3 p.m.

At 11th and Scott stands the midcentury modern–style Kentucky Federal Savings and Loan building. This building was constructed in 1958 for $100,000 as a demonstration of a forward-thinking institution. This savings and loan association was originally formed as a collective organization for the purpose of providing financial assistance, allowing citizens who were not wealthy to develop a plan and path for homeownership.

Continue on Scott Boulevard and in the next block you'll reach the back sides of Covington Latin School and St. Mary's Cathedral. **Covington Latin School** is a small coed Catholic school that was founded in 1923 by Bishop Howard. The school's curriculum is based on the German Gymnasium Model, offering an accelerated academic program, graduating many students at 16 years old.

Turn right on Martin Luther King Jr. Boulevard, a major east–west connector that provides convenient access from Interstate 71/75 to Covington, Newport, and other cities in Campbell County. You'll notice the redbrick streetscape and bold, black street furnishings. The 12th Street expansion project took nearly two decades to complete, including relocations of four historic buildings, and was finished in 2013.

Turn right on Madison Avenue to face the front of ❸ **St. Mary's Cathedral Basilica of the Assumption.** You may consider walking across the street to St. Mary's Park, where you can sit down and take in a wider view of the cathedral.

St. Mary's Cathedral is an architectural landmark and home to an active congregation. The project began in 1894 and ended in 1915, incomplete. Twenty-six sinister gargoyles overlook the cathedral. They're said to personify human qualities antithetical to the behavior of virtuous Christians. The tympanum above the entrance was carved from Bedford limestone and depicts the Assumption of Mary into Heaven. Interior features include 82 hand-poured stained glass windows crafted in Germany, including a 24- by 67-foot window in the North Transept (one of the largest in the world) and two rose windows (each one 26 feet in diameter) above the organ galleries. St. Mary's Cathedral is open to the public Monday–Saturday, 9:30 a.m.–4 p.m.

Turn right on E. 11th Street and walk one block to stroll through **Howard Park.** Named after Bishop Francis Howard, the founder of Covington Latin School, this little park is a nice spot to take a seat and enjoy the shade of an urban parklet.

Turn left on Greenup Street, which you'll follow for the next 10 blocks. At 11th and Greenup, you will see the newly constructed River's Edge at Eastside Point, a HOPE VI project that consists of nine (three-story) apartment buildings and two (one-story) buildings housing senior cottages. From 1939 until 2012, this was the location of Jacob Price Homes, which were 23 bunker-style buildings containing 163 rent-subsidized units.

You are currently walking in the northern portion of the Eastside neighborhood. Formed in the early 1900s, this neighborhood has a rich cultural heritage and continues to be the most diverse neighborhood in Northern Kentucky. Historically, Eastside has produced a large number of talented leaders, including doctors, politicians, teachers, social workers, and business leaders, many of whom helped advocate for civil rights in the area.

Once you pass E. Ninth Street, to your right you will see the **Lincoln-Grant Scholar House,** formerly the Lincoln-Grant School. This school played a pivotal role in the history of Covington. In the 1870s, William Grant promised Covington's African American community a school in return for their support of John Stevenson for governor. In 1880, Grant deeded land to the Covington Board of Education for Grant High School and Lincoln Elementary. In 1930, the new Lincoln-Grant School combined both schools. Through the 1960s, the school provided high-quality education. Members of the faculty held advanced degrees from national universities. Parents from as far away as Indiana sent their children to attend Lincoln-Grant. In the 1960s and '70s, integration spelled the end of Lincoln-Grant as a school. Today, Lincoln-Grant offers housing opportunities for single parents who are actively pursuing higher education.

At Seventh and Greenup you'll find ❹ **Left Bank Coffee House,** a community gathering spot. This quaint Franco-inspired independent coffee shop serves up great drinks and locally sourced snacks.

Next, you'll see the campus of ❺ **Baker Hunt Art and Cultural Center,** which includes two mansions, an auditorium, and studio space. The beautiful gardens are maintained with help from local volunteers and are open to the public to enjoy. Named for Margaretta Baker Hunt, the Center was established in 1922 to encourage the study of art, education, and science. Today, the mission continues with a vast number of arts-based classes and programs.

As you pass over E. Fourth Street, you'll enter the Roebling Point business district, home to several restaurants, bars, law offices, and other small businesses.

❻ **Molly Malone's** (112 E. Fourth St.) is a three-story Irish pub and restaurant that has a great beer selection and authentic pub food. Molly's is also your go-to in Cincinnati for watching soccer matches in the company of real soccer fans.

❼ **Blinker's Tavern** (318 Greenup St.) is a locally owned steakhouse that is regularly voted the Best Steak of Northern Kentucky.

❽ **Smoke Justis** (302 Court St.) is a relatively new food and beverage addition to Roebling Point with smoked meats, a vast bourbon supply, plenty of screens for game day, and an arcade in the basement. The historic building elements combine well with the Covington Blue Sox interior design themes. Smoke Justis was the name of the original pitcher for Covington's short-lived baseball team.

❾ **Keystone Bar & Grill** (313 Greenup St.) is famous for its mac and cheese but also has a nice selection of local and draft beer.

❿ **Lil's Bagels** (308 Greenup St.) opened their walk-up window in 2017 and has been a regional favorite for handmade bagels ever since. Owner Julia Keister combines a mastery of bagel baking with creative spreads, sandwiches, and always fresh bagel-inspired puns.

Next door, at the corner of Third and Greenup is ⓫ **Roebling Point Books & Coffee,** a locally owned coffee shop and independent bookstore. It is also home to the Ohio office of AdventureKEEN, the parent company of the most excellent publisher Wilderness Press. The bookstore has become a hub of community meetings and local gatherings and is a great place to stop in for shopping or a drink. If you happen to be strolling through on a Saturday between May and October, the Covington Famers Market sets up here on E. Third Street between Scott and Greenup from 9 a.m. to 1 p.m. The Covington Farmers Market hosts about 20 weekly vendors, as well as live music, programming, and special guest vendors.

Continuing down toward the Ohio River, ⓬ **The Gruff** (129 E. Second St.) is a deli, restaurant, and micro-grocery with plenty of locally sourced options for dining in or taking home.

Turn left onto E. Second Street. As you pass under the entry to the Roebling Suspension Bridge, you'll find **Piazza at RiverCenter** to your right. This office tower complex is home to several more food and beverage destinations, including ⓭ **Biscuits to Burgers,** ⓮ **Butler's Pantry,** and ⓯ **Fire.**

Continue to Madison Avenue and turn right to finish the walk at the starting point.

Points of Interest

❶ **John A. Roebling Suspension Bridge** 1 Roebling Way, roeblingbridge.org

❷ **Carnegie Visual and Performing Arts Center** 1028 Scott Blvd., 859-491-2030, thecarnegie.com

❸ **St. Mary's Cathedral Basilica of the Assumption** 1101 Madison Ave., 859-431-2060, covcathedral.com

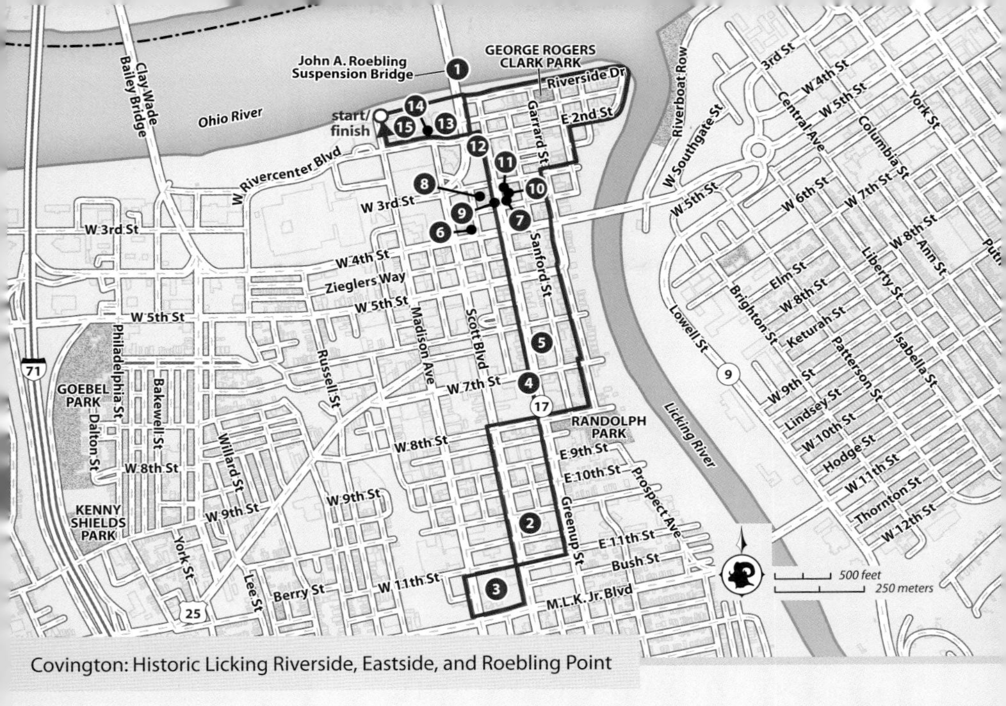

Covington: Historic Licking Riverside, Eastside, and Roebling Point

4. Left Bank Coffee House 701 Greenup St., 859-431-4655, leftbankcoffeehouse.com
5. Baker Hunt Art and Cultural Center 620 Greenup St., 859-431-0020, bakerhunt.org
6. Molly Malone's Irish Pub 112 E. Fourth St., 859-491-6659, covington.mollymalonesirishpub.com
7. Blinker's Tavern 318 Greenup St., 859-360-0840, blinkerstavern.com
8. Smoke Justis 302 Court St., 859-814-8858, smokejustis.com
9. Keystone Bar & Grill 313 Greenup St., 859-261-6777, keystonebar.com
10. Lil's Bagels 308 Greenup St., lilsbagels.com
11. Roebling Point Books & Coffee 306 Greenup St., 859-815-7204, facebook.com/roeblingpointbooksandcoffee
12. The Gruff 129 East Second St., 859-581-0040, atthegruff.com
13. Biscuits to Burgers 50 E. RiverCenter Blvd., 859-292-5034, biscuitstoburgers.com
14. Butler's Pantry 50 E. RiverCenter Blvd., 859-292-1699, butlerspantrymarket.com
15. Fire 50 E. RiverCenter Blvd., 859-392-2850, fireatrivercenter.com

28 Downtown Covington

A Great American Main Street

Above: The grand Hotel Covington sits at the corner of Seventh Street and Madison Avenue.
Photo courtesy of Hotel Covington

BOUNDARIES: Riverfront, Scott Blvd., E. Eighth St., Russell St.
DISTANCE: 1.8 miles
DIFFICULTY: Easy
PARKING: RiverCenter Parking Lot (pay) or on-street
PUBLIC TRANSIT: TANK transit station at 220 Madison, Red Bike at RiverCenter Blvd.

Covington's downtown is lined with historic buildings dating back to the 19th century. As many cities were undergoing urban renewal, Covington was suffering economically, and as a result, the buildings survived the era and still stand today. For years, efforts were undertaken to bring these buildings back and revitalize downtown. Over the past five years, those efforts have shown significant results, including signature projects such as The Mutual Building, Hotel Covington, The Boone

Block, and The Bradford Building. In 2017, downtown Covington was recognized with the Great American Main Street Award by Main Street America for its preservation-based revitalization efforts and successes. Today, downtown is a combination of those historic building-lined streets alongside some spectacular murals and a variety of hip, fun dining, drinking, and shopping businesses.

Historically, Madison Avenue emerged in the mid-19th century as the John A. Roebling Suspension Bridge was constructed and rail connected Pike Street to Cincinnati as well as Lexington and Louisville. Several of the earliest buildings, such as Oddfellows Hall (1857) and Marx Brothers Furniture (1888), can be found on this walk. At its peak in the 1920s, Madison Avenue was a cultural epicenter, with premier shopping, banking, theaters, and downtown celebrations.

In addition to visiting Madison Avenue, this tour takes you down Pike Street and W. Seventh, home to many unique local businesses, including Braxton Brewing, Co. To the east, this tour travels along Scott Boulevard, passing such places as the award-winning Kenton County Public Library, the U.S. Post Office, and several newly rehabilitated large historic buildings.

Walk Description

Start at **Covington Landing,** where Madison Avenue begins at the Ohio River. Here you can find a striking view of the Cincinnati skyline and the Roebling Suspension Bridge.

Walk south on Madison to E. Third Street. You will pass the Northern Kentucky Convention Center and the Kenton County District Courthouse. The 204,000-square-foot multipurpose convention center was built in 1998.

Turn left on E. Third Street. Look up and you can't miss **The Ascent.** This modern architectural icon, designed by Daniel Libeskind, was completed in 2008. Libeskind is the same architect who was chosen for the reconstruction of the World Trade Building in New York. The swooping design and iconic blue were designed to honor and highlight the historic Roebling Suspension Bridge. Within the 70 high-end condominiums reside some of Covington's most affluent and influential residents.

Walk one block and turn right (south) on Scott Boulevard. To the east you will pass the Roebling Point business district. To find out more about this area, see Walk 27.

The Bradford Building (326 Scott Blvd.) is under redevelopment and poised for completion in 2019 as a mixed-use property with available storefronts and upper-floor condos. Originally named after Bradford Shinkle (son of Amos Shinkle, famous financier of the Roebling Suspension Bridge) but later home to places like Viva La Foxx strip club, this transformation is long awaited.

Continue south on Scott Boulevard. As you cross Fourth Street, look up to your right to see the beautiful windows and architectural styles of the Old Masonic Building. On your left is the

Boone Block (406–422 Scott Blvd.), which recently underwent a major rehabilitation, transitioning from primarily vacant/storage to nine single-family town houses. The north side of the property is home to a large mural by internationally renowned street artists The London Police.

A little farther down Scott on the right is the Kentucky Natural History ArtWorks mural, created in partnership with Kerry Collision Center and the City of Covington. This mural features symbols of Kentucky's diverse wildlife and rich natural history. From right to left: a mastodon skeleton, a viceroy butterfly, a spotted bass, goldenrod blossoms with a honeybee, a male cardinal, a Kentucky tulip poplar blossom, and a brachiopod fossil.

Cross Fifth Street. On the other side of the street is the ❶ **Kenton County Public Library.** Opened in 1974, this library continues to win awards for its great service, collections, and genealogy department. In 2013, branch manager Julia Allegrini was one of 10 in the United States to win the Carnegie Corporation of New York/*New York Times* I Love My Librarian Award. For three consecutive years, Hennen's American Public Library Ratings (HAPLR) Index has ranked the Covington branch the top library in Kentucky.

Continue south until you reach Pike Street. At the corner of Scott Boulevard and Pike sits an old Covington Brewery Building. Built in 1870, this building housed The Covington Lager Beer Brewery beginning in 1837 and operated under various owners until it closed at the start of Prohibition.

Turn right on Pike Street and cross Madison Avenue. As you approach Madison Avenue, you'll notice the unique angles at the intersection of Pike and Madison. On the corner stands The Mutual Building, another newly rehabilitated building in the heart of downtown Covington. Apartments fill the top floor, and you'll notice ❷ **The Hannaford** on the corner. This cocktail bar is named after Samuel Hannaford, architect of the Mutual Building, and is a popular spot for local politicians and community folks. Continue west on what is commonly referred to as Short Pike.

A few doors down from The Hannaford, you'll find ❸ **Handzy,** a shop with an array of cute cards and paper items designed by owners Suzy and Brittany, as well as clothes and other gifts.

In the 1970s, this area of Pike Street was paved into a pedestrian mall called Old Town Plaza. In 1993, it was returned to allow vehicular traffic. You'll see remnants of that history in the names of two businesses: ❹ **Old Town Cafe** and ❺ **Olde Towne Tavern.** Old Town Cafe is a family-owned diner since 1988. You'll find longtime customers at the counter or in the booths beginning at 6 a.m. They are there for breakfast just as much as they are to talk politics, family, and local issues with owners Frank and Debbie Bonfilio.

On the north side of the street is Covington City Hall. Just past City Hall is ❻ **BLDG,** a branding and design firm/creativity hub with a gallery, studio, and loft. BLDG's influence can be seen throughout Covington, having hosted such renowned street artists as Vhils, Faile, and The London Police. In 2013, The London Police installed 11 new murals throughout Covington, bringing the total to 12 (the original you passed at Fourth Street and Scott Boulevard).

Next door, ❼ **Franks on Pike,** previously Frank's Men's Shop, is now an urban men's apparel store. This shop was opened in 1918 by the grandfather of the current owner, Edward Frank, as Covington Cap Company.

❽ **Grainwell Market** is another great independent shop on this block. Owned by three sisters, this business features custom wood products and home décor and is a must visit.

Turn left on Washington Avenue. At the median you'll see a statue of Frank Duveneck, one of Covington's most celebrated artists, holding a portrait of his wife, Elizabeth.

Turn left on W. Seventh Street to circle back toward Madison Avenue. To your right is the newly constructed Duveneck Square, part of a multiphase development with 108 residential units. Just beyond Duveneck Square is ❾ **Braxton Brewing, Co.,** which hit the scene in 2013 and has been a community hub and transformational addition to the neighborhood ever since. Stop in to try their popular golden cream ale, Storm, or something more daring like one of their experimental variations from Braxton Labs, which is featured in the Bellevue walk.

To your left is ❿ **Klingenberg's,** an independent neighborhood hardware store that has served the neighborhood for decades. To your right is ⓫ **Rich's Proper Food and Drink,** a new modern restaurant with southern culinary influences and a vast selection of bourbon.

Continue on Seventh to cross over Madison Avenue. At the northeast corner of Seventh and Madison is ⓬ **Hotel Covington.** This beautiful boutique hotel opened in 2016 and has 114 rooms, as well as event spaces, Coppin's restaurant, a retail shop, a coffee stand, a walk-up window, and an outdoor atrium. Originally home to Coppin's Department Store, the hotel features many references to the building's history, as well as locally sourced products in the shop, on the menu, and throughout the guestrooms. The bar and restaurant have been developed as a place for the local community to gather, and the interior design is gorgeous and worth seeing, so you may want to walk in the front door, through the restaurant, and out the back door on the right to capture the grandeur of this Covington icon.

Turn right on Scott Boulevard. As you turn the corner, you'll pass ⓭ **Garden Grove Organics,** a must-visit for the agriculture and hydroponic enthusiast. Across the street is the expansive US Post Office building, still operating as a post office.

Turn right on E. Eighth Street, and then right again on Madison Avenue. You'll continue straight on Madison all the way until you reach the starting location. Madison Avenue is home to a variety of small and independent businesses, housed in some of the region's premier architectural and historic buildings.

14 **Madison Theater** (730 Madison Ave.) was originally The Lyric; the Madison Theater opened on September 9, 1912. In the 1910s, The Lyric offered daily Vaudeville acts, for which the tickets cost 5¢. During the 1920s, motion picture shows replaced live performers. Each week two different movies were shown; admission was 30¢. In 1942 the theater was renamed The Madison. Today, The Madison Theater is an independently owned and operated music venue and entertainment space.

15 **Motch Jewelers** (613 Madison Ave.) is a family owned and operated business that has been in the same location since 1857, when Michael C. Motch, a French immigrant, first opened the jewelry store. The current building was designed by James W. McLaughlin and built in 1871. The Boston E. Howard and Co. cast-iron clock, located on the sidewalk, is an icon of Madison Avenue and visible in many historic photographs.

Formerly the Marx Furniture building, built in 1888, the **TIE Building** (522 Madison Ave.) is home of the Gateway Technology, Innovation, and Entrepreneurship programs.

16 **KungFood Chu's AmerAsia** (521 Madison Ave.) is an eccentric restaurant where soul food meets Kung Food. Stop in for some delicious Chinese/Taiwanese fare and a huge beer selection. Peek around the corner to find another mural from The London Police.

On the corner of W. Seventh Street and Madison Avenue, the You Belong Here! Millennium Mosaic *consists of 25 panels and more than 100,000 mosaic tiles.*

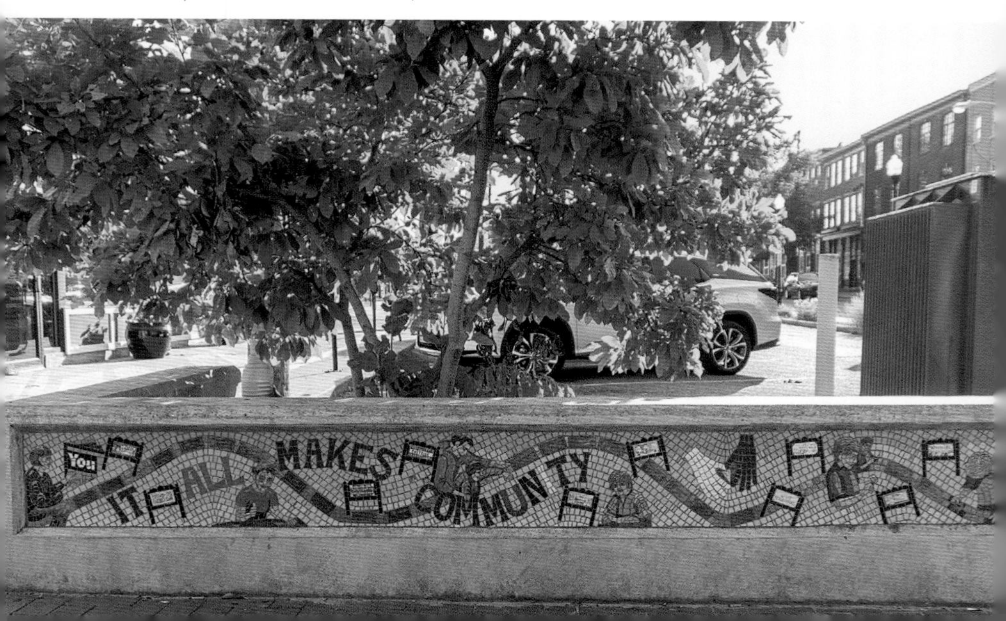

⑰ **Riverside Korean** (512 Madison Ave.) offers authentic Korean dishes. You can sit at a booth or on the floor, the traditional Korean style.

⑱ **Odd Fellows Hall** (440 Madison Ave.) is one of the most historic buildings in Covington and was once the center of civic and political happenings in the city. It was constructed in 1856 by the Independent Order of Odd Fellows Lodge. During the Civil War it served as a holding center and military court for Confederate soldiers, and at the conclusion of the Civil War, a reception was held to honor Union General Ulysses S. Grant. In the 1950s, the second-floor ballroom was converted into a popular roller skating rink. In 2002, while the building was being restored by the current owners, a fire destroyed all but the facade and back wall of the landmark building. The restoration was completed by 2007, and the current building is home to The Grand, a special-events space with a 460-seat ballroom with two levels.

⑲ **LaRosa's** (417 Madison Ave.) is a Cincinnati classic. With a host of hard-core regulars, this LaRosa's continues to prosper on Madison Avenue. If you stop in, ask for owner Jon Meyer. He can tell you anything you want to know about Covington.

The last featured point on this walk is ⑳ **Trinity Episcopal Church**, founded in 1842. The current building was constructed between 1857 and 1859 and is an excellent example of the Gothic Revival style, showing the influence of medieval designs on Anglican Church buildings during that period. The church is home to three tranquil gardens, which are maintained by church members and provide a welcome respite to all visitors. The congregation and current Reverend Peter D'Angio are committed to local community service.

Finish your walk by continuing north to return to the Ohio River.

Points of Interest

1. **Kenton County Public Library** 502 Scott Blvd., 859-962-4060, kentonlibrary.org
2. **The Hannaford** 619 Madison Ave., 859-261-2178, thehannaford.com
3. **Old Town Cafe** 9 W. Pike St., 859-291-0664
4. **Olde Towne Tavern** 35 W. Pike St., 859-581-3509
5. **Handzy** 15 W. Pike St., hellohandzy.com
6. **BLDG** 30 W. Pike St., 859-491-4228, bldgrefuge.com

(continued on next page)

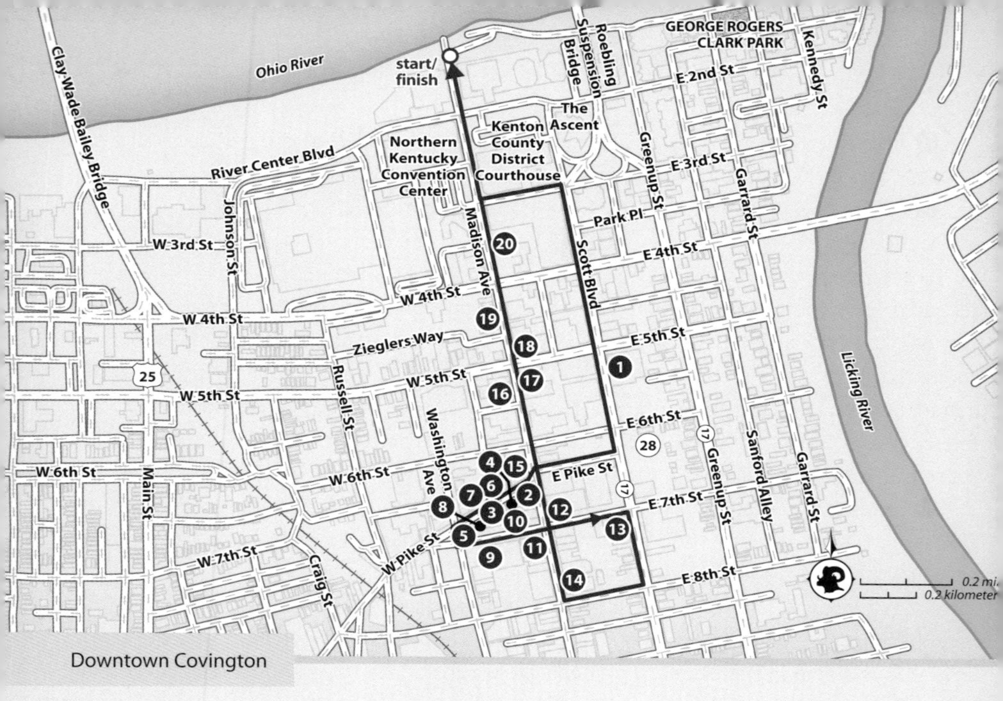

Downtown Covington

(continued from previous page)

- 7 **Franks on Pike** 32 W. Pike St., 859-431-0667, franksonpike.com
- 8 **Grainwell Market** 33 W. Pike St., 859-415-4955, grainwell.com
- 9 **Braxton Brewing Co.** 27 W. Seventh St., 859-261-5600, braxtonbrewing.com
- 10 **Klingenberg's** 26 W. Seventh St., 859-431-0922, klingenberg.doitbest.com/home.aspx
- 11 **Rich's Proper Food and Drink** 701 Madison Ave., 859-415-0069, richsproper.com
- 12 **Hotel Covington** 638 Madison Ave., 859-905-6600, hotelcovington.com
- 13 **Garden Grove Organics** 701 Scott Blvd., 859-360-1843
- 14 **Madison Theater** 730 Madison Ave., 859-491-2444, madisontheateronline.com
- 15 **Motch Jewelers** 613 Madison Ave., 859-431-1745
- 16 **KungFood Chu's AmerAsia** 521 Madison Ave., 859-261-6121
- 17 **Riverside Korean** 512 Madison Ave., 859-291-1484, riversidekoreanrestaurant.com
- 18 **Odd Fellows Hall** 440 Madison Ave.
- 19 **LaRosa's** 417 Madison Ave., 513-347-1111, larosas.com
- 20 **Trinity Episcopal Church** 326 Madison Ave., 859-431-1786, trinitychurchcovky.com

29 Covington: MainStrasse Village and Old Seminary Square

Above: Farny Art Park honors Henry Farny, who was a Covington resident and well-known artist.

BOUNDARIES: W. Sixth St., Goebel Park, Russell St., West Robbins St.
DISTANCE: 1.95 miles
DIFFICULTY: Easy
PARKING: Fifth Street parking lot, on-street
PUBLIC TRANSIT: 1x, 2x, 17x, 28x, 30x; Southbank Shuttle at Fifth St. parking lot between Philadelphia and Main; Red Bike at Sixth/Main

MainStrasse, also known as Mainstrasse Village, or by locals as simply The Village, is a tight-knit community of businesses and residents, with plenty of restaurants, bars, parks, shopping, and entertainment to spend a full day exploring. Most of the homes were built by 1880 and feature architectural styles ranging from Greek Revival to Queen Anne. A national historic district, MainStrasse was modeled after German Village in Columbus, Ohio, and has several unique German Village landmarks nestled among the parks and promenades.

The commercial entertainment district is famous for festivals and public events such as Maifest and Oktoberfest. These events and others are curated by an independent nonprofit, MainStrasse Village Association (MSVA). To find out what's going on during your visit, check out mainstrasse.org.

West of the commercial district is Goebel Park, which has been undergoing a community-led transformation since 2015, including arts and placemaking work, new play equipment, and the Goebel Goats. The Goebel Goats live in the park from May through October. They are locally loved and became world famous when they got loose in the city during The Running of the Goats in May of 2016.

This walk also includes Old Seminary Square, an adjacent historic neighborhood with beautifully restored Victorian homes. In 1845, this tree-lined neighborhood was home to The Western Baptist Theological Institute. Their campus was divided by the Covington and Lexington (C&L) Railroad tracks, but many of the buildings remain. In the 1970s, the neighborhood revitalization began with the impetus of a few local champions, several of whom still live in the neighborhood today.

Walk Description

Start on Sixth and Philadelphia Streets at the perimeter of **Goebel Park.** To get situated, look up for the Carroll Chimes Bell Tower, a 1970s faux German glockenspiel. The park is named after Kentucky Governor William Goebel, a Covingtonian and the only Kentucky governor to be assassinated. You'll explore the park in more depth at the end of this walk.

Turn left on Sixth Street. To your left is ❶ **Piper's Café,** a great walk-up restaurant with locally sourced menu items and soft-serve ice cream.

If you walk down the central promenade, you're walking down Steinford Park. A small plaque on the right recognizes neighborhood residents George and Rose Steinford, who generously provided toys for children at Christmas for 50 years, beginning in 1900.

If it's the time of day when a cocktail may be in order, MainStrasse is a great place to be. In fact, you might even turn this walk into a pub crawl, if you're up for it. To start, on your left are two bars—❷ **Zazou** (502 W. Sixth St.) and ❸ **Pachinko** (424 W. Sixth St.)—just don't try to hit them all, it's humanly impossible.

As you approach Main Street, you'll encounter the Goose Girl Fountain. This fountain is inspired by the Brothers Grimm Goose Girl fairy tale to commemorate the many goose farms that used to be in Covington.

The intersection of Sixth and Main Streets has long been a vibrant restaurant and commercial area. On the northwest corner is ❹ **Dee Felice,** a Cajun and Creole restaurant opened by a longtime jazz drummer in 1984. Just north of Dee Felice are two newer restaurants, ❺ **Otto's** and ❻ **Bouquet**, both of which have received many accolades for their food and drink.

On the northeast corner is ❼ **Lisse**, an upscale Dutch-inspired steakhouse that has a great rooftop for drinks and dining. Across the street is ❽ **Frida 602**, which opened in 2015 and features Latin street cuisine and a tequila and mezcal bar. Finally, located on the southwest corner is ❾ **Cock & Bull Public House**, an English pub with a house brew and great outdoor seating. On a nice night, these restaurants and many others in the village offer great outdoor dining options, filling the promenade with additional seating and live music.

Continue along Sixth Street and you'll pass a great shop, ❿ **Stoney's Gift and Toy Shoppe.** You'll usually find owner Sandi Stonebraker at home in the shop—her contagious, creative, and wondrous energy alone are worth the visit.

Follow Sixth Street through the CSX Underpass. It's very recognizable by the brilliant geometric art installation and hanging chandeliers, which were installed by local business owner Emily Wolff and her family to enhance the walkability of the neighborhood. (Thanks, Emily!)

Walk past the little library and continue on Sixth for one block.

Turn right on Russell Street at Greenline Salon. This full-service Aveda salon was named after the historic Green Line streetcar, which greatly influenced the economic growth of Covington and Newport in the first half of the 20th century.

Continue along Russell Street, where you'll pass Hub + Weber Architects, which is located in the historic train depot called Covington Station. The architects at Hub + Weber have been instrumental in many of the major historic rehabilitation projects that have transformed Covington over the past five years, including Hotel Covington, Mutual Building, Boone Block, and Road ID.

Continue straight through the underpass to stay on Russell Street. You'll have to cross the street, or you'll end up on Pike Street.

As you continue along Russell Street for the next three blocks, you'll enter the Old Seminary Square neighborhood. Old Seminary Square is one of Covington's smaller neighborhoods, but it is dense with beautiful homes and landscaping. In the 1850s, this area was built up around the Baptist Theological Institute, but today only the president's home remains, now known as the **Sanford House** (1026 Russell St.). Owned since 1988 by some of the modern-day neighborhood pioneers, Linda and Dan Carter, this building is one of the oldest in Kenton County. It was built by Alfred Sanford, another US congressman from Covington, in the 1820s.

Turn right on West Robbins Street and you'll find the **Henry Farny Art Park** on your left. The Farny Art Park was designed and created by members of the Westside Action Coalition and the Old Seminary Square Neighborhood Group to honor Henry Farny, a former resident and well-known painter of western landscapes and American Indian culture. Farny was a colorful figure and prolific artist. Local artist David Rice created the sculptures in the park.

Continue past John G. Elementary School. The school is named for John G. Carlisle, who was re-elected to the U.S. Senate seven times starting in 1877 and also served as lieutenant governor of Kentucky.

Turn right on Holman Avenue. If the weather's warm, you'll likely pass neighborhood kids playing basketball or baseball on the school's grounds.

Cross Pike Street and continue straight onto Greer Street. On the right, you'll pass Blank's Pharmacy, which has been there since 1933. Now you have re-entered the MainStrasse neighborhood.

Turn left on W. Eighth Street to return to Main Street. Turn right on Main Street at Leapin' Lizard, a former church turned private event space. Main Street is full of locally owned shops, bars, and restaurants. This is a great place to spend time exploring. Some stops for food and drink include ⓫ **Crafts and Vines** (642 Main) for a broad wine selection, charceuterie, and cool clientele; ⓬ **Gypsy's** (641 Main St.) for good drink specials, funky décor, and a great outdoor patio; ⓭ **Strasse Haus** (630 Main St.), a neighborhood staple with a streetside front patio, perfect for a nice day; ⓮ **OKBB/Old Kentucky Bourbon Bar** (629 Main St.), which has more than 50 bourbons to choose from; ⓯ **Zola** (626 Main St.), another laid-back bar known for its burgers; and ⓰ **The Up Over** (624 Main St.), a self-proclaimed dive bar that attracts an eclectic and creative crowd. You're in luck if you catch longtime Covington bar owner Amy Kummler in the house—she has some stories. Also check out ⓱ **Commonwealth Bistro** (621 Main St.) for farm-to-table dining; ⓲ **Mainstrasse Village Pub** (619 Main St.), a local hangout where time passes unnoticed, thanks to the pool tables, darts, and jukebox; and ⓳ **Goodfella's Pizzeria**

Begin this walk near the Carroll Chimes Bell Tower.

(603 Main St.), where you can find upstairs Wiseguy Lounge, a speakeasy-inspired bar with talented bartenders and craft cocktails.

In addition to all the food and drink options, this stretch is home to several funky independent small retail businesses such as ⓴ **Village Gifts** (613 Main St.) for all your Kentucky-proud items; ㉑ **Julie's Inspiration Consignment Shoppe** (608 Main St.) for quality thrift shopping; ㉒ **Blume** (607 Main St.) for flowers and floral design; and ㉓ **Strasse Dog** (605 Main St.) for toys, treats, and outfits for the pups.

Turn left onto W. Sixth Street and walk toward the park where you began. This walk continues with a half-mile circle through Goebel Park. Cross Philadelphia Street and continue along the path that meanders to the back of the park. Here you will notice fencing and signage on your left. Continue along the path around the fencing. This is where you'll find the Goebel Goats. These goats are a trial land management practice led by Wolf Tree Farms, The Center for Great Neighborhoods, and many other local sponsors. They're cute and provide service clearing the invasive species on the hillside. Follow this trail until you pass Goebel Pool, a Covington public pool that is open June–August, daily, noon–6 p.m. Goebel Pool is free to Covington residents but requires registration through the City's Parks and Rec Department.

Turn left to walk through the parking lot and out to Philadelphia Street. Turn left on Philadelphia Street and continue along these residential blocks to return to your starting location.

Points of Interest

1. Piper's Café 520 W. Sixth St., 859-291-7287, piperscafe.biz
2. Zazou 502 W. Sixth St., 859-261-9111, zazougrillandpub.com
3. Pachinko 424 W. Sixth St., 859-431-6400
4. Dee Felice 529 Main St., 859-261-2365, deefelicecafe.com
5. Otto's 521 Main St., 859-491-6678, ottosonmain.com
6. Bouquet 519 Main St., 859-491-7777, bouquetrestaurant.com
7. Lisse 530 Main St., 859-360-7008, lisse.restaurant
8. Frida 602 602 Main St., 859-815-8736, fridaonmain.com
9. Cock & Bull Public House 601 Main St., 859-581-4253, cockandbullcincinnati.com
10. Stoney's Gift and Toy Shoppe 323 W. Sixth St., 859-655-9571, stoneystoys.com

(continued on next page)

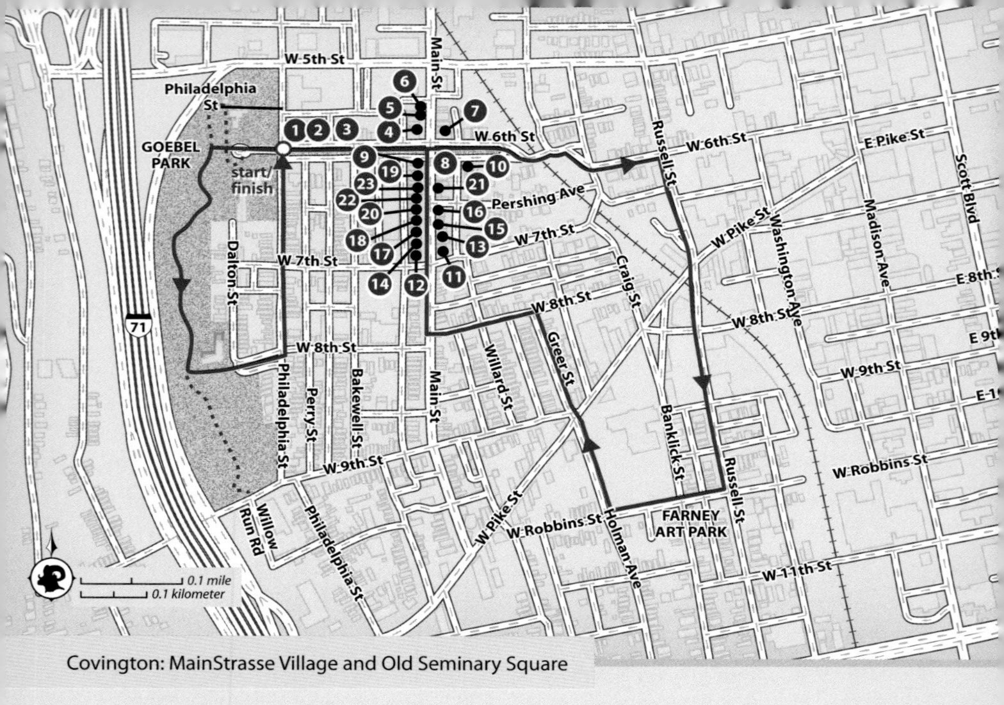

Covington: MainStrasse Village and Old Seminary Square

(continued from previous page)

11. Crafts and Vines 642 Main St., 859-360-0476, craftsandvines.com
12. Gypsy's 641 Main St., 859-261-5111
13. Strasse Haus 630 Main St., 859-261-1199
14. Old Kentucky Bourbon Bar 629 Main St., 859-581-1777
15. Zola 626 Main St., 859-261-7510, zolapubandgrill.com
16. The Up Over 624 Main St., 859-581-1300
17. Commonwealth Bistro 621 Main St., 859-916-6719, commonwealthbistro.com
18. Mainstrasse Village Pub 619 Main St., 859-431-5552, mainstrassevillagepub.com
19. Goodfellas Pizzeria/Wiseguy Lounge 603 Main St., 859-916-5209, goodfellaspizzeria.com
20. Village Gifts 613 Main St., 859-878-2858, www.villagegiftsky.com
21. Julie's Inspiration Consignment Shoppe 608 Main St., 859-291-8200, juliesinspiration.com
22. Blume 607 Main St., 859-360-6064, blumemainstrasse.com
23. Strasse Dog 605 Main St., 859-431-7387

30 Covington:
Devou Park and Kenton Hills

Above: Prisoner's Lake at Devou Park was once a stone quarry.

BOUNDARIES: Drees Pavilion, Park Ln., Edgehill Rd., Montague Rd.
DISTANCE: 2 miles
DIFFICULTY: Strenuous
PARKING: Drees Pavilion
PUBLIC TRANSIT: None

This walk will give you a glimpse of Devou Park and the adjacent Kenton Hills neighborhood. The 704-acre park is a beautiful oasis just minutes from urban Covington and is known for beautiful views of downtown Cincinnati. On this walk you will visit or pass the park's 18-hole golf course, multiple playgrounds and picnic shelters, more than 8 miles of mountain bike trails, an amphitheater, and a fishing lake. You may also want to stop for a visit at the Behringer-Crawford Museum, which features Northern Kentucky history and culture as viewed through the lens of transportation.

Devou Park truly reflects a history of citizens dedicated to high-quality recreation space in Covington. In 1910, William P. and Charles P. Devou donated 500 acres of land to the city on the condition it become a park named in memory of their parents. The Devou Family Trust provided assets for continued growth of the park over the next almost-100 years. In February 2003, The Drees Company announced the donation of a new reception and banquet facility, the Drees Pavilion, to replace the Memorial Building. The $2 million donation was made to commemorate the home-building company's 75th anniversary. All proceeds of the facility are contributed to the Devou Park Fund, more than $3,500,000 to date. Then, in 2008, another enthusiastic Devou Park supporter, Chad Irey, initiated the process of developing the now nationally recognized bike trail system and cyclocross course.

Walk Description

Start at the lot at ❶ **Drees Pavilion.** This 10,000-square-foot pavilion opened its doors to the public in January 2004. At the dedication ceremony on February 3, 2004, a time capsule was sealed in the brick facade of the pavilion, to be opened in 2053.

The Band Shell at Devou Park has hosted many concerts over the years.

If you walk out to the bottom lot overlooking Covington and Cincinnati, you'll find a beautiful view and photo opportunity. These picnic tables present a perfect spot for a serene lunch above the city.

Cross through the parking lot and out to Park Lane. To your right, you'll catch a glimpse of the **Devou Park Golf Course** (devouparkgolf.com). The course originally opened in 1922, with nine holes designed by John Brophy, golf professional at Ft. Mitchell Country Club. In 1995, the inward nine opened, designed by renowned golf course architect Gene Bates.

Follow Park Lane to W. Park Road to meet the Devou Park path. Follow this paved path through a collection of mature trees of various species.

You'll pass a Devou Park Bike Trailhead. In and around the year 2005, a few residents of Covington, Kentucky, in conjunction with the Kentucky Mountain Bike Association (KyMBA) and in partnership with the Cincinnati Off Road Alliance (CORA), petitioned the City of Covington and the Devou Park Advisory Committee to allow an all-volunteer effort to install an additional 11–12 miles of trails within Devou Park. The project was approved and ground was broken in February 2009. The first phase was completed in September 2011, and volunteers continue to build and maintain the trails.

Follow the path until you come out on Park Lane/Bandshell Boulevard. Cross the street to resume the paved path. As you pass the ❷ **Band Shell,** you pass decades of outdoor concerts, sled rides, and memories compiled in the minds of residents near and far. The distinctive Band Shell was completed in the summer of 1939. In August of that year, 40,000 people came to see Dolly Dawn and George Hall, as well as radio personality Harvey Brownfield. Today, some of the most notable concerts are hosted by the Kentucky Symphony Orchestra.

You'll briefly come out on Montague Road and then continue on the path next to Montague.

Exit the path at the intersection of Parkway Avenue. Cross Parkway Avenue and continue up the road toward The Museum/Prisoner's Lake. Check the wayfinding signage in case you get turned around.

Go up Parkway Avenue to the ❸ **Behringer-Crawford Museum.** The museum is open Tuesday–Saturday, 10 a.m.–5 p.m. and Sunday, 1–5 p.m. Admission is $9 for adults, $8 for seniors (60+), and $5 for children (ages 3–17).

The museum opened in Covington in 1950, after West Covington native William Jacob Behringer passed away in 1948 and left his collection of geological specimens, animal relics, and Indian artifacts to the City of Covington. The city manager at the time suggested that the historic Devou family home (c. 1848–1880) become the museum and Ellis Cummins Crawford be curator. Crawford curated until 1970, and at that time the museum became officially known as the Behringer-Crawford Museum. The influence of these two well-traveled, knowledgeable, quirky Covingtonians focused the museum's exhibits on curiosities, oddities, and prehistory.

In the decades following Crawford, the museum grew to display collections in paleontology, archaeology, and natural and cultural history. In 2007, after years of lobbying, the museum underwent a $5.3 million expansion under the leadership of Executive Director Laurie Risch. The 15,000-square-foot expansion held on to many of the old exhibits but expanded with many new exhibits under the theme "Rivers, Roads, Rails, and Runways," showcasing the history of transportation in the region.

In addition to the exhibits, Behringer-Crawford hosts many programs, camps, lectures, concerts, and a great annual event called Fresh Art. This museum is a wonderful regional amenity and still expresses some of the quirkiness from which it originated.

Just beyond the museum is a children's park called NaturePlay. It's best if you walk up to the museum and then follow the path to the park. This park combines elements of nature with some amenities of a children's park to create an environment for kids to learn and play in nature. The slide, for example, requires a little rock climbing to reach the top.

Continue up Parkway Avenue to **Prisoner's Lake.** Once a stone quarry, this man-made lake gets its name from its unique history. In an attempt to save money on crushed stones, in 1916 the Covington City Commission proposed that prisoners from the Covington Jail be put to work crushing rocks in this quarry. Over the years, the level of the quarry lowered. Also, over the years, many prisoners escaped. The city eventually ended the practice, and in 1924 the quarry was transformed into a lake, appropriately named Prisoner's Lake.

One of the most famous activities that still happens here is the Annual Fishing Derby. Every year since the 1980s, children ages 5–15 bring their own poles and bait to compete in catching some of the city-supplied catfish from the lake.

Turn right on Wayne Road and continue to enter the Kenton Hills neighborhood. For the next few blocks, enjoy your walk through one of Covington's smallest neighborhoods. In 1965, the city added 72 acres near Devou Park, which was then—and is still—known as Kenton Hills. These beautiful homes have stunning views and access to all of the park's great amenities.

Turn right on Edgehill Road.

Turn right on Jerome Street.

Turn left on Park Lane and cross over by the Volpenheim Shelter and around Park Road to the John Voltz Nature Trail. Take a walk around the trail, if you like, or return to your starting point.

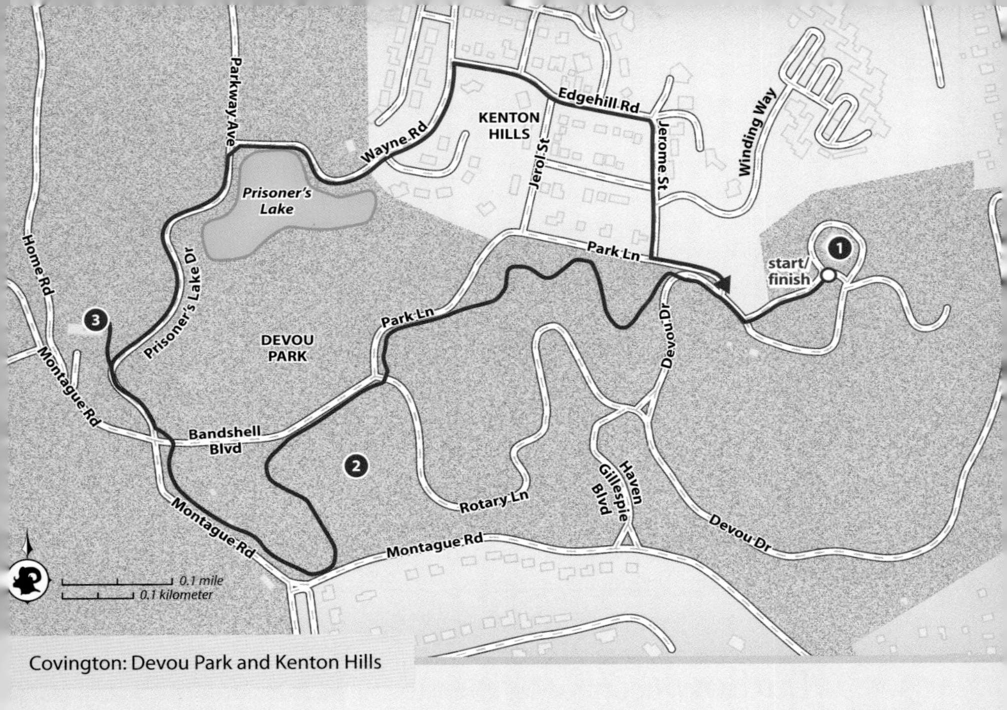

Covington: Devou Park and Kenton Hills

Points of Interest

1. Drees Pavilion 790 Park Ln., 859-431-2577, dreespavilion.com
2. Band Shell Rotary Ln., 859-292-2151, exploredevoupark.org
3. Behringer-Crawford Museum 1600 Montague Rd., 859-491-4003, bcmuseum.org

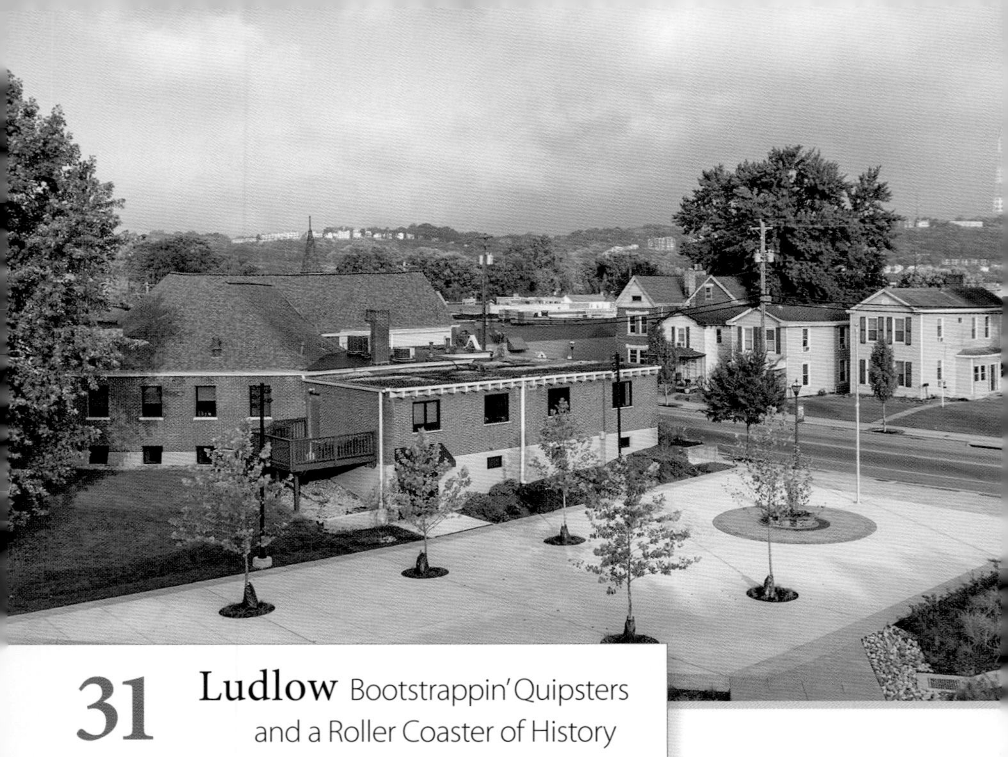

31 Ludlow Bootstrappin' Quipsters and a Roller Coaster of History

Above: View from Ludlow's train-viewing platform at the edge of town

BOUNDARIES: Elm St., Deverill St., Adela Ave., Kenner St.
DISTANCE: 2.2 miles
DIFFICULTY: Easy
PARKING: On-street
PUBLIC TRANSIT: TANK #3 to Elm at Kenner

Ludlow, Kentucky, is one of five river cities on the south bank of the Ohio. With a population of 4,500, this small city is home to charming neighborhoods, quirky local businesses, and open riverfront views. The city itself is about 2 square miles and is nestled between Bromley to the west, Covington to the east, Devou Park to the south, and the river on the north. Ludlow is an evolving community with approachable, affordable single-family homes, a walkable environment, and good schools. It is emerging as a new frontier for creatives and young families wanting a combination of small-city and big-city lifestyles.

The history of Ludlow is unexpected, full of stories, vision, imagination, and, at times, tragedy. "Scenic Railroad" was the name of one of the earliest roller coasters built in the United States, and it was stationed at the Ludlow Lagoon starting at the turn of the 20th century. The Ludlow Lagoon was a major recreational destination from 1894–1917, attracting as many as 30,000 visitors in a day and, interestingly, the destination was a strategic development spearheaded by the streetcar company to bookend the expansion of The Green Line. It worked, and at one point, streetcars left Fountain Square every other minute with a full train headed for the Ludlow Lagoon.

This walk will take you along Ludlow's main commercial district and then south to the former site of the lagoon, where a few remnants remain. You'll explore the adjacent neighborhoods full of American Foursquares, historic cottages, and some Victorian and Italianate homes, as well as the earliest platted blocks of the city, which was incorporated in 1864 and named after the landowner Isreal Ludlow. Before Isreal bought the land in 1830, there was an effort at developing a utopian community on the land, called Hygeia, that was never realized.

Walk Description

This walk starts and ends at ❶ **The Ludlow Heritage Museum** (227 Elm St.), which opened in 2011 with a mission to preserve and protect the historic and cultural artifacts of the city of Ludlow. The museum has limited hours, open only on Saturdays 11 a.m.–4 p.m. from March through December. If it works to align your walk with a visit to the museum, we recommend it.

From the Ludlow Heritage Museum, walk west along Elm Street toward Davies Street. You'll continue on Elm for about two-thirds of a mile; some of the highlights are below.

At 301 Elm is one of Ludlow's first gems, ❷ **Second Sight Spirits.** This microdistillery is the product of ingenuity and passion for small batch rum, moonshines, and bourbons. Co-owner Carus Waggoner (whose former career was in the circus) hosts tours on Thursdays, Fridays, and Saturdays at 12:30, 2, and 4 p.m., and on Fridays and Saturdays at 6 p.m. This tour is a combination storytelling journey and lesson in distilling, entrepreneurship, and problem-solving. Free tastings are available at the end of the tour.

Just a skip away at 326 Elm Street, you'll find an old theater–turned–circus venue, ❸ **Circus Mojo,** and a microbrewery called ❹ **Bircus Brewing Co.** Circus Mojo is a combination school and venue where performances range from juggling to aerial silks, trapeze to fire breathing. And what better way to diversify the circus experience than with the act next door; "beer" plus "circus" equals Bircus. The tasting room at Bircus is open every evening (except Monday) and noon–10 p.m. on Saturday.

Continuing down Elm, ❺ **Folk School Parlor House** is another showstopper in this funky little district. This is much more than a neighborhood coffee shop (as lovely as those are); Folk School Parlor House is a school, a music destination, and a reflection of the local folk music and "beardo culture." (The term *beardo* is derived from the Whispering Beard Folk Festival, which takes place every August in Friendship, Indiana.) Also, famous Cincinnatian Jerry Springer records *The Jerry Springer Podcast: Tales, Tunes, and Tomfoolery* in front of a live audience here at the Folk School Parlor House. Unexpected, right?

Next door is ❻ **Gaither's Gallery,** the studio and shop of renowned Kentucky watercolorist Tom Gaither.

At 525 Elm Street you'll come upon **Ludlow High School.** Constructed in 1932, the school opened as George Washington Memorial High School. Today, Ludlow High School serves about 450 students in grades 7–12 and has received a Bronze Medal Ranking by *US News and World Report* in its list of America's Best High Schools for two of the past three years.

Following the school, you'll pass the ball fields at City Park on the right and, depending on the time of year, the fresh fruit and vegetable stands of Reeves Produce on the left at Elm and Helen Streets. If you need a little break, take a tour of their shop full of locally sourced foods.

Turn left onto Deverill Street, where you'll enter the residential blocks of Ludlow. As you walk north for three blocks toward Adela Avenue, you're traveling the routes that so many followed to reach the Ludlow Lagoon more than 100 years before. You'll also notice the hills and trails of Devou Park ahead of you. If you're in the mood for a little nature hike, you can continue past Adela and trek into the park where you'll find the Ludlow Connector Trail, which connects with the Devou Park backcountry trails.

Turn left on Adela for one block to Stokesay, where you're traversing a portion of the former site of the Ludlow Lagoon. The Ludlow Lagoon's last manager was named J. J. Weaver, who also owned Ideal Supply Company, which still operates today. After the park closed in 1917, Weaver lived in the Ludlow Lagoon clubhouse and built a neighborhood on top of a portion of the former park, including parts of Deverill and Stokesay Streets.

The story of the Ludlow Lagoon is one of a fast-to-rise and quick-to-fall, the fall often summarized in the culmination of four events. In 1913 there was a flood that damaged much of the equipment. Shortly after that, also in 1913, a motorcyclist flew off the track and into the stage where a fire started, killing nine people, injuring hundreds more. In 1915, a tornado hit. And finally, as the First World War started, grains were no longer available for beer, and beer sales were a critical revenue source for the Ludlow Lagoon, and so it closed in 1917.

Turn left on Stokesay Street back toward the river and enjoy a stroll along another quaint Ludlow neighborhood street. Turn right on Oak Street, and then left on Adela, where you'll pass Ludlow High School again. As you pass Elm Street and continue north, you're entering the original plats of the city, where the architecture is more ornate.

Turn right on Victoria Street, then make a left on Ringold Street.

Turn right on Somerset, where you'll notice a grand Greek Revival home on your right. **Somerset Hall** dates back to 1845, when it was constructed by slaves as a summer home for Louisiana plantation owner William Butler Kenner. Kenner made a number of bad business decisions and had to sell the house in 1852; since then it has been owned by the Clossons, the Masons, and, since 1997, the Chapmans.

Turn right on Kenner Street and walk back to Elm to finish the walk.

Today, Somerset Hall is fully restored and a private residence for a family of five.

Ludlow

Points of Interest

1. The Ludlow Heritage Museum 227 Elm St., ludlowheritagemuseum.weebly.com
2. Second Sight Spirits 301 Elm St., 702-510-6075, secondsightspirits.com
3. Circus Mojo 326 Elm St., 800-381-8232, circusmojo.com
4. Bircus Brewing Co. 322 Elm St., 859-360-7757, bircus.com
5. Folk School Parlor House 332 Elm St., 859-206-1269, folkschoolcoffeeparlor.com
6. Gaither's Gallery 333 Elm St., 859-261-3113, tomgaither.com

32 Covington: Latonia

Above: Twin Oaks Golf & Plantation Club is a beautiful spot for a break on this walk.

BOUNDARIES: 36th St., Church St., 44th St., Twin Oaks
DISTANCE: 2.5 miles
DIFFICULTY: Easy
PARKING: On-street or at Holy Cross Church
PUBLIC TRANSIT: TANK Decoursey at 36th or Ritte's Corner

Latonia is a tight-knit residential community with a rich and interesting history. Before 1909, Latonia was an independent city. The area first became a destination for its natural springs and spas in the 1820s. Latonia grew as Covington did, and then in the 1880s, The Latonia Race Track was built. This premier racetrack represented one of the three best in Kentucky: Louisville, Lexington, and Latonia. Latonia also prospered from the railroad companies that began laying tracks in the 1850s. Many residents of Latonia worked for the L&N, which was later bought by CSX. The active tracks still cut through Latonia.

Backstory: Latonia Race Track

The Latonia Race Track existed from 1883 until 1939 and at its peak drew more than 100,000 visitors annually. It was beautifully landscaped with a lake at the center. The track greatly contributed to the businesses and prosperity of Latonia. It also attracted the drinkers, gamblers, and prostitutes.

There were two large meets each year. The first was the Latonia Derby, which paid a higher purse than the Kentucky Derby at the time. During those meets, in the 1920s, were some of the earliest traffic jams in Covington. Cars would be lined up for miles, not unlike the Kentucky Derby today. In 1938 President Roosevelt visited the Latonia Race Track, but that was near the end. The track lost many jockeys and horses to age and more competitive tracks and in 1939 was closed. In 1942, the land was purchased by Sohio Oil and turned into a refinery. In the 1960s, the area began to look more like a shopping center, which is how it still operates today.

Today, Latonia is known as an affordable, family-friendly community, with several neighborhood associations and a business association: Ritte's East, Latonia-Rosedale, West Latonia, and the Latonia Business Association. The community is currently working on developing Ritte's Corner. This walk takes you from the original commercial center through some residential areas to visit the beautiful Twin Oaks golf course, then past Latonia Elementary School and back to the start.

Walk Description

This tour begins at **Holy Cross High School** (3617 Church St.), one of two Catholic high schools still located within Covington. The campus straddles Church Street with the sanctuary and rectory on the east side and elementary school, high school, and convent on the west. There are 385 students in this high school that represent 29 different elementary schools. The school has been open and operating in the same building since 1919.

❶ **Holy Cross Catholic Church** was founded in 1889 as the German Catholic population outgrew St. Augustine's farther north in Covington and parishioners wanted a place closer to home. At this time, Latonia was known as the city of Millville, and the population continued to grow rapidly at the turn of the century. Under Father Reiter, this structure that you see today was completed in 1908. Today, Holy Cross hosts daily masses and three Sunday masses, as well as many other programs.

Follow E. 36th Street west past the school until you reach Decoursey Avenue. On the right is ❷ **Legends Bar & Grill.** This neighborhood watering hole is a popular hangout for the locals.

Turn left onto Decoursey Avenue and continue past Emerson's Bakery, Goodtimers II, and Bard's Burgers. ❸ **Bard's Burgers** is known for their Bardzilla Challenge, in which guests try to eat a 4.6-pound burger. Their burgers are their claim to fame, and in 2016, The Food Network featured the dive burger joint on *Ginormous Food.*

When you get to the intersection of E. Southern, Decoursey, and Winston Avenues, you've arrived at Ritte's Corner. Ritte's Corner is historically the commercial heart of Latonia and has seen ups and downs over the past 100 years, just like the region. During the height of the racetrack, this area was home to several taverns and is named after Henry Ritte's Saloon, which was at the northeast corner. At one time, after World War I, a fountain was built in the center of the intersection by a local doctor in honor of the first Latonia boy who went to the war. It did not last long, though, as another prominent doctor who liked to drink (and drive) "accidentally" hit it three different times in his Reo Flying Cloud, and finally the fountain was done for.

Veer left to stay on Decoursey Avenue, then turn right onto Church Street. At 3800 Church Street, ❹ **Latonia Baptist Church** was built in 1896 after the mission of the Immanuel Baptist in Covington had been meeting in houses for several years. In 1900, Latonia Baptist became independent of Immanuel Baptist and later became known as The Mother of Baptist Churches in Latonia, as Decoursey Baptist, Calvary Baptist, Ashland Avenue Baptist, and Rosedale Baptist were

Holy Cross Catholic Church has undergone numerous expansions and renovations in its 100-plus-year history.

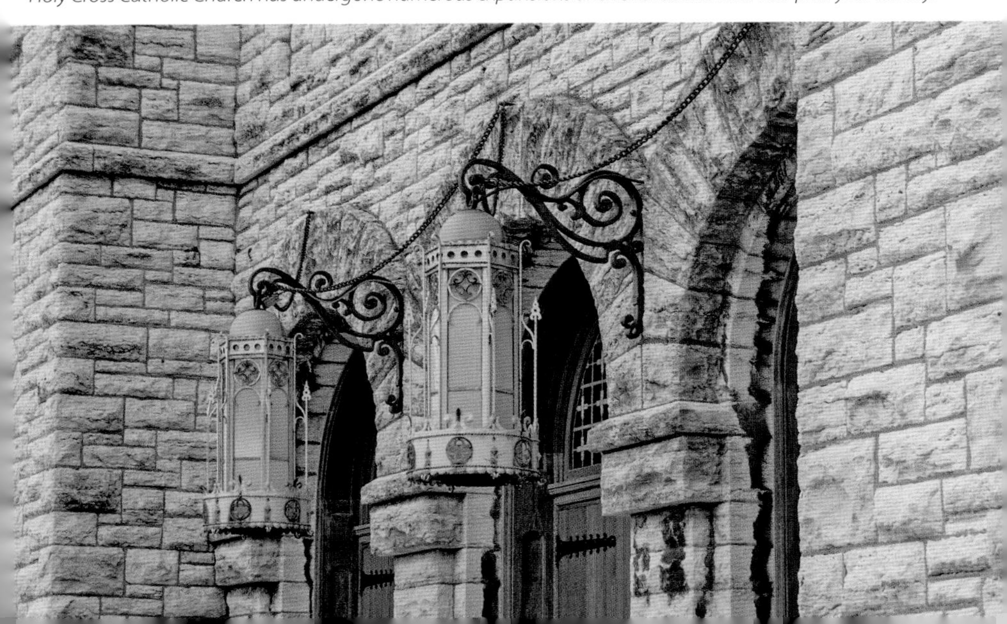

all formed from Latonia Baptist. Latonia Baptist Pastor Dan Francis is an active member of the Latonia community and, in addition to their services and programs, you can catch a free concert here the first Friday of every month at noon.

Continue along Church Street for five blocks and enjoy a peek at the house-lined streets and residential lifestyle of Latonia.

Turn left onto E. 43rd Street. As you continue along E. 43rd, you'll pass by ❺ **Bill Cappel Sports Complex** to the south and an entry point if you want a side trek to explore. Bill Cappel Sports Complex is home field for many local soccer and softball teams. At one time this area was a giant landfill, but since the 1980s it has operated as public recreation space. In the 2000s, the City of Covington built a public zero-depth waterpark addition to the complex. Covington residents can get a free pool pass at City Hall at 20 W. Pike Street.

Turn right to return to Decoursey Avenue for a block, then turn left onto E. 44th Street and continue across the CSX rail line, and make another left onto Glenn Avenue.

Turn right onto E. 43rd Street to visit ❻ **Twin Oaks Golf & Plantation Club.** If you like, follow the road to the left to circle the grounds. This public golf course was built in 1927 and has a full 18-hole course and hosts many weddings and receptions. The clubhouse has a full bar and restaurant. This may be the perfect opportunity for a break on the veranda, overlooking the beautiful grounds.

Return to the main entry of the club and back to Glenn Avenue. Turn right onto Glenn Avenue, where you'll pass the 11-acre campus of Rosedale Green, a nonprofit long-term and short-term care facility. This location was formerly the last stop on the Rosedale-Covington Street Car line.

Turn left onto E. 40th Street.

Turn right onto Huntington Avenue, where you'll walk by **Latonia Elementary School,** one of the five elementary schools that make up the Covington Independent Public School system. You can see here their outdoor classroom and urban garden on the side, called Herbmania. The students learn about biology, gardening, and entrepreneurship through the Herbmania program.

Turn left onto E. 39th Street, and once you pass over Park Avenue, you'll find ❼ **Latonia Christian Church,** a nondenominational church that was founded in 1898. This building was later built in 1923 to meet the rapidly growing congregation. They hold services on Wednesdays at 6 p.m. and Sundays at 10:30 a.m.

Turn right onto Lincoln Avenue and continue until you reach the Latonia Station Post Office at Southern Avenue.

Turn left onto E. Southern Avenue and pass **Trinity United Methodist Church** (101 E. Southern Ave.) as you return to Church Street.

Turn right onto Church Street to return to your starting point at Holy Cross High School.

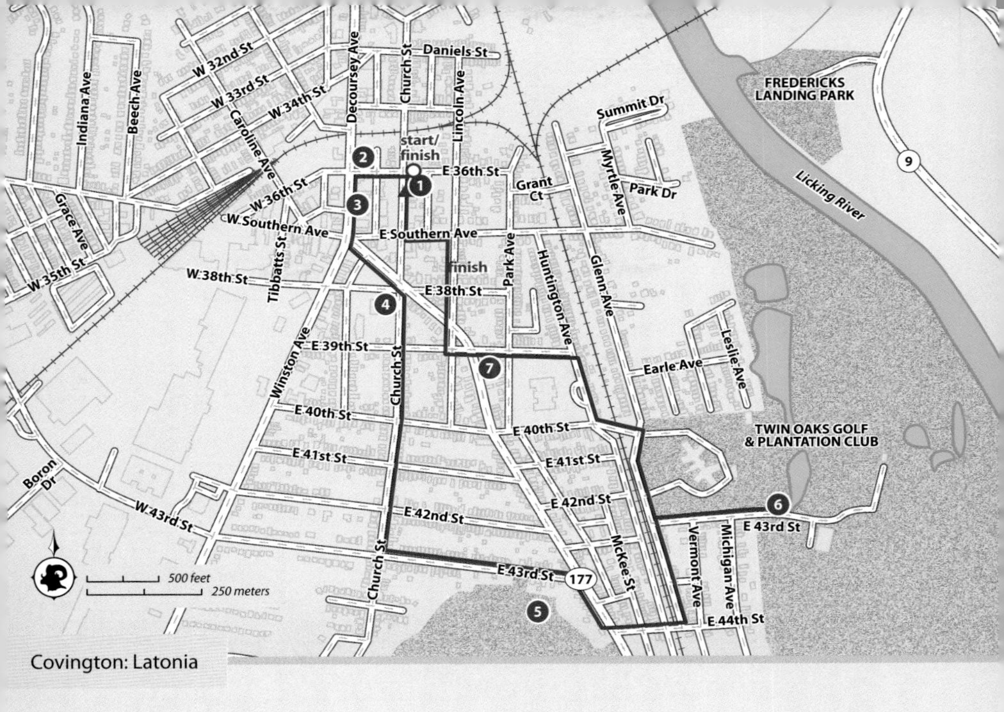

Covington: Latonia

Points of Interest

1. **Holy Cross Catholic Church** 3612 Church St., 859-431-0636, holycrosscov.org
2. **Legends Bar & Grill** 3530 Decoursey Ave., 859-581-4140
3. **Bard's Burgers** 3620 Decoursey Ave., 859-866-6017, bardsburgersandchili.com
4. **Latonia Baptist Church** 3800 Church St., 859-431-8004, latoniabaptist.org
5. **Bill Cappel Sports Complex** 4305 Decoursey Ave., 859-292-2151, covingtonky.gov/visitors/parks/bill-cappel-youth-sports-complex
6. **Twin Oaks Golf & Plantation Club** 450 E. 43rd St., 859-581-2410, golfattwinoaks.com
7. **Latonia Christian Church** 3900 Decoursey Ave., 859-261-8693

33 Newport East Row Historic District

Preservation Success Story

Above: More than 1,100 protected historic buildings compose the east side of Newport.

BOUNDARIES: York St., Third St., Ninth St., Linden Ave.
DISTANCE: 3.1 miles
DIFFICULTY: Easy
PARKING: Newport is composed primarily of one-way streets designed to reduce cut-through traffic, making navigation tough in a car but wonderful on foot. From downtown Cincinnati, take Taylor-Southgate Bridge across the Ohio River to Eighth Street. Metered parking on streets. Walk or bike on Purple People Bridge across the Ohio River to Eighth and York Streets.
PUBLIC TRANSIT: Southbank Shuttle Trolley (tankbus.org/routes/ss) and TANK bus routes 11 (Ft. Thomas–NKU) and 12 (Dayton) serve this part of Newport. Cincinnati Red Bike (cincyredbike.org) has bicycle rental stations at 707 Monmouth St., 317 E. Sixth St., and Newport on the Levee.

Considered one of the most well-preserved historic neighborhoods in Greater Cincinnati, East Row Historic District in Newport contains excellent examples of late-19th- and early-20th-century architecture, while playing a leading role in the development of Northern Kentucky. In 1795, General James Taylor inherited about 1,500 acres along the Ohio River from his father and decided to pioneer the site with his wife, Keturah Moss Leitch. It was during the 1870s and 1880s when Newport's east side flourished and wealthy business owners built impressive Italianate, Queen Anne, and Colonial Revival houses. Newport eventually became a thriving streetcar suburb of downtown Cincinnati and remains a vital neighbor today.

While this walk covers other parts of Newport, the East Row Historic District is the primary focus. The neighborhood is divided into two sections: Gateway and Mansion Hill. The larger of the two, Gateway started in the 1870s south of Sixth Street primarily along Washington Avenue (formerly East Row) and expanded eastward. Each successive block from west to east was built with prevailing architectural styles of the day. Mansion Hill comprises the smaller section north of Sixth Street. Newport is one of 16 communities participating in Go Vibrant (govibrant.org), the largest network of urban walking routes in the country. Look for the Newport map on the website and incorporate the suggested routes into your walk.

Walk Description

Start your walk with lunch at ❶ **York Street Café,** a former drugstore that sits at the heart of the York Street Historic District, which contains mostly mid- and late-Victorian-era buildings. Before crossing Eighth Street and walking east toward Monmouth Street, admire ❷ **Salem United Methodist Church/Stained Glass Theatre,** which is the longtime home of Footlighters. Established in 1963, the theater company hosted is first performance here in 1988 and has remained a community institution since. Cincinnati architect Samuel Hannaford designed the church, which was finished in 1882. The church lost its steeple to a tornado in 1986.

Turn left on **Monmouth Street,** the city's primary historic commercial district. Listed on the National Register of Historic Places in 1996, the district includes about 90 commercial buildings. Along here you can make a bank deposit, place a catering order, and sharpen your knife collection. Three restaurants on Monmouth—❸ **Dixie Chili,** ❹ **Pepper Pod Restaurant,** and ❺ **La Mexicana**—feature good food, a lot of community support, and lively histories. Dixie Chili started here in 1929 and has a surprising number of vegetarian menu items. Pepper Pod offers standard American diner fare (including fried pickles) 24 hours a day. La Mexicana, with Spanish-speaking servers, is authentic Mexican. Next to La Mexicana is ❻ **Reser Bicycle Outfitters,** a regional draw that offers bikes for all sorts of travel and is very active in advancing accommodations for people on bikes around the region. Inside Reser is wonderful **Trailhead**

Coffee, a simple coffee counter with a walk-up window and stools for seating that serves Wood Burl Coffee from Dayton, Ohio.

Continue walking north past the other shops, restaurants, and bars that occupy a variety of buildings dating from 1850 to 1949. Before crossing Sixth Street, look right to ❼ **The Southgate House Revival,** a bar and music venue in a former church that attracts a variety of acts. Cross Fifth Street and look for **Carnegie Hall** on the right, just past Monmouth Row apartments (415 Monmouth St.). Built in 1902, the Beaux Arts building functioned as the main library for 112 years before the library was moved to a new building at 901 E. Sixth Street in 2004. Carnegie Hall is now an events venue and a strong historic anchor on a corner where most everything else around it is from the recent past.

One block west of Monmouth Street, at Fourth and York Streets, is Newport's historic civic square. ❽ **Campbell County Courthouse,** designed by A. C. Nash and completed in 1884, is the most prominent building. It stands on the site of the original log courthouse. Just north of the courthouse is the stone ❾ **St. Paul's Episcopal Church,** built in 1871 with fine stained glass windows. Opposite civic square is the World Peace Bell (425 York St.), one of more than 20 Peace Bells around the world. From 2000 until 2006, it was the largest swinging bell in the world. Dedicated on December 31, 1999, it rang in the new millennium with its first swing.

Continue north on Monmouth Street. On the right is one of three regional locations for ❿ **The Running Spot.** Before turning right on Third Street, look left to the ⓫ **Thompson House,** a performing arts space housed in the historic Southgate-Parker-Maddux House. It was the birthplace of General John Thompson, inventor of the semi-automatic rifle. Look ahead at ⓬ **Newport on the Levee,** which is impossible to miss. Finished in 2001, the entertainment complex is situated between the Taylor Southgate Bridge and Purple People Bridge along the Ohio River and boasts some of the best views of downtown Cincinnati. Planning is underway for Skywheel, a 240-foot-tall Ferris wheel that will jut out approximately 80 feet into the Ohio River near the Levee.

The historic Thompson House, across from Newport on the Levee, features multiple stages and bars.

Turn right on Third Street. Just past the Purple People Bridge across the street and just before Washington Avenue is the first outpost of ⓭ **Hofbräuhaus** outside Munich, Germany. Grab a beer or soft pretzel inside, and then make your way to the one surviving building (behind Hofbräuhaus) on Southgate Street. Built in 1873 and expanded in 1893, Southgate School was the only public school in Campbell County for African American students until integration in 1955. It was designated a local landmark in 2010 and opened as ⓮ **Newport History Museum** in November 2017.

Return to Washington Avenue and enter **East Row Historic District** at Third Street. This lovely historic neighborhood includes nearly 1,100 buildings that look much like they did 100 years ago. It ranks up there with Over-the-Rhine, Clifton, and other iconic Cincinnati neighborhoods for its architectural integrity. Fewer than 40 buildings were built after 1930. The area is protected as a local historic district and listed on the National Register of Historic Places. It continues to improve with age, as residents take great care with their houses, apartments, and gardens, while trees mature along streetscapes and in pocket parks.

The **Davidson House** (315 E. Third St.) is a fine example of the Queen Anne/Shingle style. Walk to the corner of Third and Overton Streets. The **General James Taylor Mansion** (335 E. Third St.) on the left is where General Taylor and his family lived. Completed in 1840 and altered extensively in 1890, it has a great view of the Ohio River and surrounding neighborhood with its hilltop perch.

Turn right on Overton Street, where Italianate houses from the 1880s and 1890s predominate. One exception is the Queen Anne house at 301 Overton, which dates from 1889. An earlier house from 1870 at 311 Overton has a Newport-Plan side porch common throughout the neighborhood. Overton has good versions of adaptive reuse where outdated properties were converted to something different from their original purpose. One example is 616 Overton, which was originally worker housing and later converted to apartments. Another example is the **First Presbyterian Church** (625 Overton), which was converted to condos in the mid-1990s as part of the city's long-running Rehab-A-Rama housing revitalization effort.

Cross Sixth Street into the 700 block, where Italianate houses date from the 1870s. The Wiedemann family of the influential Wiedemann Brewing Company originally lived at 709 Overton. 715 Overton is a rare Queen Anne example with artistically complex Eastlake details. 734 Overton, which once had a corner store, is a tastefully converted single-family home. Corner stores, once common in the East Row, are all gone today. 825 Overton is another adaptive reuse that started as a "spiritual house."

Turn left on Ninth Street and then left again on Monroe Street. Most homes in the next two blocks date from the 1870s and 1880s. ⓯ **St. Mark Lutheran Church/Movement Church** is the first of two churches on Monroe Street. The second (built in 1895) is the former **Central**

Christian Church (417 E. Sixth St.), which features an apartment upstairs and The Sanctuary Event Center downstairs. B. H. and Mary Kroger (founders of Kroger grocery stores) first owned the house at 624 Monroe. The Craftsman bungalow at 522 Monroe is a rare find with its Japanese-influenced detailing.

Turn right on Fifth Street and cross Park Avenue to enter Nelson Place, Newport's only masonry street. Lucien Plympton designed the Swiss Chalet house (circa 1899) at 608 Nelson Place for Judge John T. Hodge around 1899. The residence at 610 Nelson Place is a fine example of the Colonial Revival style. Next door are **Flora Apartments** (624 Nelson Place), built circa 1915. At Linden Avenue, to the right, are the impressive **Hannaford Apartments,** another masterpiece designed by Cincinnati architect Samuel Hannaford. Completed in 1902, the former Catholic girls' school was converted into apartments in 1985.

Turn left on Linden Avenue and walk through **East Row Dog Park,** a popular place for dogs to release energy in a tight urban neighborhood while their human companions bond with one another on the sidelines. Turn left on Fourth Street. This block (referred to as Queen Anne Row) was home to many of Newport's most wealthy citizens in the late 1890s. At the end of the block, George Wiedemann Jr. (son of the famous brewer) built the Colonial Revival **George Wiedemann Jr. Mansion** (401 Park Ave.) in 1899. It's now home to the Northern Kentucky District Health Department.

Turn left on Park Avenue, right on Fifth Street, and then right on Washington Avenue. Row houses at 413–421 Washington Avenue date from the late 1880s. The **Saunders Mansion** (337 Washington Ave.) on the left was built in 1872 for a granddaughter of General James Taylor. It's now apartments.

This almost ends your tour of Newport. To return to the starting point, backtrack to Fifth Street and continue west to Monmouth Street. Turn left and follow Monmouth to Eighth Street. Before heading out, grab a traditional English, Irish, or Scottish beer at ⓰ **Wooden Cask Brewing Company** behind La Mexicana.

Points of Interest

❶ **York Street Café** 738 York St., 859-261-9675, yorkstonline.com

❷ **Salem United Methodist Church/Stained Glass Theatre** 802 York St., 859-291-7464, footlighters.org

❸ **Pepper Pod Restaurant** 703 Monmouth St., 859-431-7455

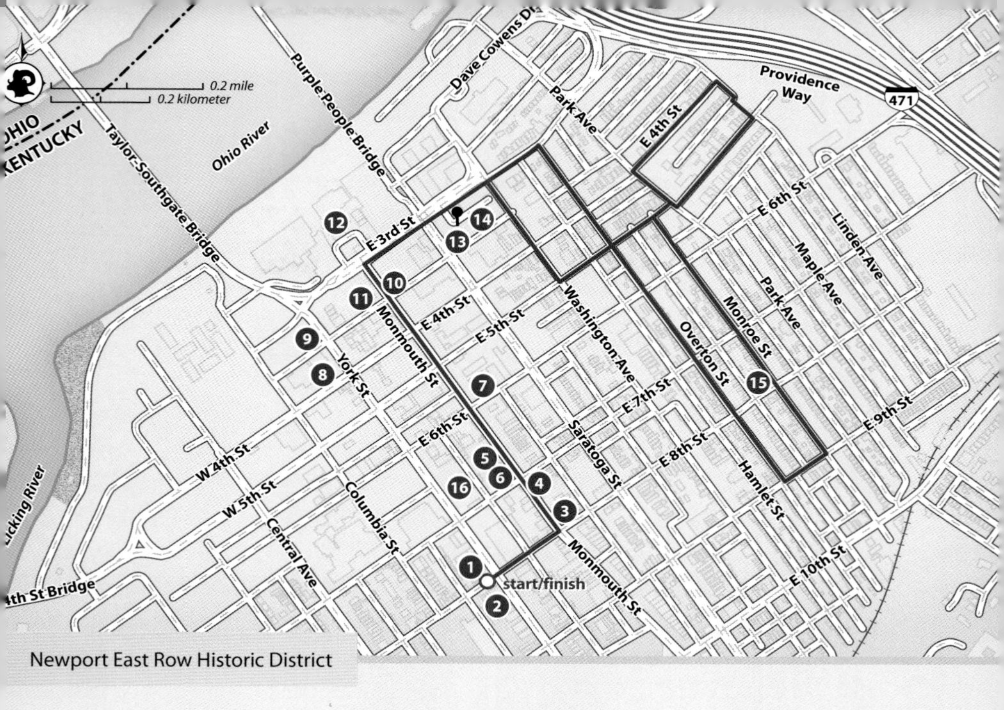

Newport East Row Historic District

- ❹ Dixie Chili 733 Monmouth St., 859-291-5337, dixiechili.com
- ❺ La Mexicana 642 Monmouth St., 859-261-6112
- ❻ Reser Bicycle Outfitters/Trailhead Coffee 648 Monmouth St., 859-261-6187, reserbicycle.com
- ❼ The Southgate House Revival 111 E. Sixth St., 859-431-2201, southgatehouse.com
- ❽ Campbell County Courthouse 330 York St., 859-292-6314, courts.ky.gov
- ❾ St. Paul's Episcopal Church 7 Court Pl., 859-581-7640, stpaulsnewport.org
- ❿ The Running Spot 317 Monmouth St., 859-491-9500, jackrabbit.com
- ⓫ Thompson House 24 E Third St., 859-261-7469, thompsonhousenewport.com
- ⓬ Newport on the Levee 1 Levee Way, 859-291-0550, newportonthelevee.com
- ⓭ Hofbräuhaus 200 E Third St., 859-491-7200, hofbrauhausnewport.com
- ⓮ Newport History Museum 215 E Southgate St., 859-655-6347
- ⓯ St. Mark Lutheran Church/Movement Church 415 E. Eighth St., 859-472-4020, movementnky.com
- ⓰ Wooden Cask Brewing Company 629 York St., 859-261-2172, woodencask.com

34 Bellevue Charming Commercial District bounded by Bourbon, Breweries, and a Beachfront

Above: The Washington Apartments now occupy the former Center Street School.

BOUNDARIES: Distillery Way, Bellevue Beach Park, Van Voast Ave., Center St.
DISTANCE: 3 miles
DIFFICULTY: Easy
PARKING: Parking Lot at New Riff Distillery
PUBLIC TRANSIT: TANK #12 to Riviera at Fairfield, Southbank Shuttle to Party Source, Red Bike at 401 Riverboat Row

Bellevue is a quaint Ohio River city at the most northern tip of Kentucky. About 1 square mile and home to just under 6,000 residents, Bellevue's small-town charm, Fairfield Avenue commercial district, historic neighborhoods, and Beach Park are perfect for a walking tour. Bellevue is situated along KY 8, which is a very popular route for long-distance cyclists wanting to travel the scenic riverfront towns along The Ohio.

The name Bellevue translates from French as "beautiful view." While you might expect this to be a reference to the great views of Cincinnati, it was historically named in reference to a plantation in Virginia owned by General James Taylor. General Taylor originally was granted the land that is now Bellevue after serving as a general in the War of 1812. Most of the streets in Bellevue are named by Taylor, including Foote, Ward, Van Voast, and O'Fallon, which were named for each of the men whom his four daughters married.

Walk Description

This walk starts and ends at ❶ **New Riff Distillery** (24 Distillery Way, Newport, KY). While technically in Newport, New Riff shares a large open parking lot with ❷ **The Party Source,** which carries a Bellevue address, as well as one of the best regional selections of spirits, wines, and beer. The Party Source is also home to a taproom and craft brewery, Braxton Labs, an offshoot of the Braxton Brewing Co. brewery and taproom in Covington (see Walk 28). This taproom is smaller and dedicated to experimental brewing, offering creative and rare brews in limited runs.

New Riff opened in May 2014 as an event center and distillery. In July 2018, they released their first bourbon. If you're feeling like a distillery tour at the beginning or end of your walk, New Riff offers tours Tuesday–Sunday, 12–4 p.m. You can book a tour by calling 859-261-7433 or visiting newriffdistilling.com/experience/tour.

From New Riff, turn left on Riviera Drive and follow it to KY 8/Fairfield Avenue and turn right. Walk northeast on Fairfield Avenue, on the south side of the street. Once you cross Lafayette Street, you've entered the Fairfield Avenue Historic District. Across the street, 201 Fairfield Avenue was constructed in the 1880s, with retail on the first floor and chambers for Bellevue's fraternal organizations on the upper stories. In the early 1900s, a lending library was established on the second floor and the building became known as Library Hall. At that time, the first floor housed the Kroger Grocery and Baking Company.

Continue east on Fairfield Avenue and you'll find ❸ **Darkness Brewery** on your right at 224 Fairfield Avenue. Darkness opened its doors in 2016 and is a small family-owned brewery with a laid-back, dog-friendly taproom. The taproom vibe stands out for the local artists' work on the walls and quirky nods to outer space and *Star Wars.* The beer trends toward dark brews such as imperial stouts and dark saisons.

As you continue down Fairfield, you'll pass an ArtWorks mural on the east side of Petri's Flowers at 229 Fairfield Avenue. This tribute brings together masterpieces from the Taft Museum of Art's collection, including *Portrait of a Man Rising from his Chair* by Rembrandt Van Rijn, *A World of Their Own* by Lawrence Alma Tadema, *Mrs. John Weyland and her Son John* by Joshua Reynolds, *The Song of Talking Wire* by Henry F. Farny, and *Edward and William Tomkinson* by Thomas Gainsborough. The mural shows figures from the works enjoying a day on the lawn at the Taft. This mural was created as a part of the Taft's 80th anniversary celebration, Art for All.

A little farther along on Fairfield, you'll pass a family-owned coffee shop, ❹ **Avenue Brew.** This coffee shop is housed in a unique shared-wall commercial building from the 1920s with urns along the roofline and dark-green glazed tiles. Stop in for a coffee, smoothie, CBD-infused water, or homemade pastry.

If you're looking for something a bit more robust, ❺ **Bellevue Bistro** across the street is home to great breakfast and brunch items. This local bistro pays tribute to regional foods and local businesses, such as the B-List. They offer great vegetarian options too.

Maybe you're not hungry, but instead you're in the market for a new watch? Diamond ring? ❻ **Cleves and Lonnemann Jewelers** is at 319 Fairfield and has been since 1932. Current owner Charlie Cleves is a third-generation watchmaker who is distinguished as one of only a few dozen Certified Master Watchmakers and is certified to repair both Cartier and Rolex. They have an extensive inventory of new, vintage, and costume jewelry, watches, and pens.

At 400 Fairfield you'll pass by another mural by local artist Tyler Hildenbrand. The mural is on the Washington side of 400 Fairfield Avenue, which is home to Farmhouse Primitives.

If you're in the mood for one-of-a-kind small local shopping, visit ❼ **Coda Co.** for unique home goods and ❽ **Torn Light Records** for all your musical needs.

A bit farther down Fairfield, on the same side of the street, you'll find a Bellevue classic: ❾ **Schneider's Sweet Shop.** This old-time ice-cream and candy store opened in 1939. They are well known for their Opera Creams—a recipe developed by an old German candy maker for the Cincinnati Opera. They're also famous for ice balls, caramel apples in the fall, and personalized Easter eggs. Jack, son of the founder Robert Schneider, is still using the same equipment, methods, and recipes that his dad used. Yum!

Turn Left on Foote Avenue and continue down Foote until you reach **Bellevue Beach Park.** The Bellevue Beach Park name is derived from the days when Bellevue was known for its sandy white beaches. The Queen City Beach opened in the summer of 1902 and was considered one of the largest inland bathing resorts in the country. The beach vanished after the lock and dam systems raised the level of the Ohio River. Pictures of the beach can be seen in Schneider's Sweet Shop.

Go right and walk through the park and exit at Ward Avenue. Walk south to return to Fairfield Avenue. To your right you'll see another great local eatery, ❿ **The Elusive Cow.** Across the street you'll find a Little Library, another Cincy Red Bike Station, and situated on top of the small hill, ⓫ **St. John's United Church of Christ.** St. John's has over 115 years of history in Bellevue but over the past 20 years has emerged as a beacon of inclusion and acceptance for all.

Turn left and continue to walk on Fairfield Avenue. On your left you will see the **Marianne Theater.** Constructed in 1942, The Marianne is a great example of Art Deco architecture, with a bright polychrome-glazed tile facade and a neon marquee. The Marianne was named after one of the owners' daughters; he also built the Sylvia Theater (318 Fairfield), which is no longer recognizable as a theater.

Turn right on Van Voast Avenue and pass by the Bellevue City Building, formerly a school.

Cross the iron footbridge. This bridge is one of only two iron footbridges remaining in Kentucky. The other is in Pikeville. Head over the CSX rail, and at the base is a firemen's memorial.

Turn right on Center Street. At the corner of Ward Avenue and Center Street, you'll pass a park and community garden, home to a wood-limb sculpture by Kirk Mayhew.

At Washington Avenue and Center Street, pass the former Center Street School, now the **Washington Apartments.**

Turn right on Taylor Avenue. At 337 Taylor you'll come to ⓬ **Sacred Heart Church,** which is on the National Register of Historic Buildings. Built in 1892 in the Gothic style, Sacred Heart was originally brick with a fairly tall octagonal wooden spire. In 1923, the surface was stuccoed in imitation of rough-surfaced Indiana limestone and the spire was replaced.

At 235 Division Street, at the corner of Taylor Avenue, is **Holy Trinity School.** If you look above the entryways at the sides of the school, you can see the separate entrances labeled Boys (south side) and Girls (north side).

Turn right on Division Street. Just before Washington Avenue, on the left, is ⓭ **The B-List,** a great neighborhood come-as-you-are/who-you-are bar. Stop for a drink and a chat with the locals.

Turn left on Washington Avenue, and then left again on Poplar Street. You'll pass the former St. Anthony Church complex. The grade school is now housing for the elderly. The rectory continues to serve as a rectory and event hall (Charity Hall), and the church was converted into five contemporary condominiums. One of the condos still houses the functioning church bell.

Turn right on Taylor Avenue and continue to Fairfield Avenue. Turn left on Fairfield to return to the starting location.

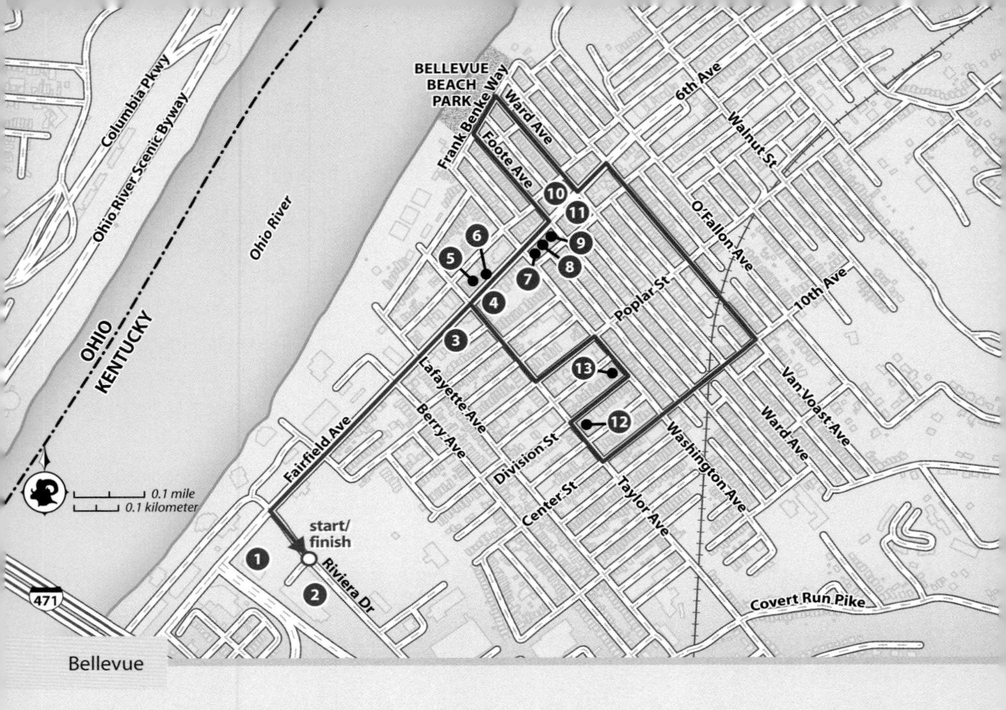

Points of Interest

1. New Riff Distillery 24 Distillery Way, 859-261-7433, newriffdistilling.com
2. The Party Source/Braxton Labs 95 Riviera Dr., 859-291-0036, braxtonbrewing.com/locations/labs
3. Darkness Brewery 224 Fairfield Ave., 859-815-8375, darknessbrewing.beer
4. Avenue Brew 310 Fairfield Ave., 859-261-4381, avenuebrew.com
5. Bellevue Bistro 313 Fairfield Ave., 859-581-5600, bellevuebistro.com
6. Cleves and Lonnemann Jewelers 319 Fairfield Ave., 859-261-3636, clevesandlonnemann.com
7. Coda Co. 400 Fairfield Ave., 859-488-7798, shopcodaco.com
8. Torn Light Records 406 Fairfield Ave., 859-415-2638, tornlightrecords.com
9. Schneider's Sweet Shop 420 Fairfield Ave., 859-431-3545, schneiderscandies.com
10. The Elusive Cow 519 Fairfield Ave., 859-291-0269, theelusivecow.com
11. St. John's United Church of Christ 520 Fairfield Ave., 859-261-2066, stjohnchurch.net
12. Sacred Heart Church 318 Division St., 859-261-6172, dmsbcatholic.com/divine-mercy
13. B-List 343 Division St., 859-261-7033

35 Fort Thomas

1890s Hilltop Army Post

Above: The amphitheater at Tower Park is a popular spot for local performances.

BOUNDARIES: S. Fort Thomas Ave., Douglas Dr., Clitz, Alexander Circle, River Rd.
DISTANCE: 1.5 miles
DIFFICULTY: Easy
PARKING: On-street, Tower Park
PUBLIC TRANSIT: TANK bus 11 or 16 at S. Fort Thomas Ave. and Tower Place

Fort Thomas is full of beautiful homes, lawns, and pristinely restored historic buildings and landmarks. With a population of just over 16,000, Fort Thomas has one of the best public school systems in the country, many well-maintained and accessible public spaces, and great associations of historians and preservationists. Many Northern Kentuckians consider residency here to be a sign of high social status.

There are two commercial districts in Fort Thomas: downtown and the Midway District. This walk takes you through the Midway District and Tower Park. On this tour, you'll see a variety of military fort buildings, from recreational to residential, built in the 1890s. Most of the former military buildings have been fully restored and are managed by the City of Fort Thomas for public recreation or private rental. This gem of Northern Kentucky history tends to be bustling with people playing in the parks, eating at the restaurants, or just enjoying a walk through history.

Walk Description

Start at the tower at S. Fort Thomas Avenue and Douglas Drive. This water tower was built in 1890 to hold water for the surrounding military base. It can hold 100,000 gallons of water, which is pumped from the reservoir just beyond S. Fort Thomas Avenue. The tower is 102 feet high and made of granite and limestone. The Fort Thomas Museum and Fort Thomas Renaissance created a QR-coded walking tour, which will give you additional information about the tower and some other sites along the way, if you have a smart phone. Look for the white placards that say "Fort & Historic Midway Walking Tour."

Turn left on Douglas Drive and walk into Tower Park. Begin walking toward the mess hall. To your right is a public playground, which is active with many families on a nice day. On the left, you'll pass some nice shaded benches—a great spot to relax if you're ready for a break.

Take a slight left and then right on Cochran to approach the mess hall. Built in 1891, it served as a cafeteria and home to a couple of jail cells for AWOL soldiers. During World War I and World War II, the mess hall was an induction site for soldiers. That continued until 1964. After that, the building experienced some neglect until it was restored by the Fort Thomas Heritage Council in the early 1990s. Today, the space is managed by the Fort Thomas Recreation Department as a community center and rental space for special events, such as wedding receptions.

To your right is a public amphitheater. Completed in 2011, many outdoor events and performances take place at this site. Historically, in the 1920s and 1930s, this location hosted boxing tournaments, including World Champion Freddy Miller of Cincinnati. As many as 3,000 people came to watch the boxing matches.

Turn right on Alexander Circle and make a loop. This beautiful yet currently somewhat eerie circle of abandoned buildings is a place of great potential. These 10 gorgeous 1880s Queen Anne homes were being packaged as a single development opportunity by the City of Fort Thomas. After 15 years, they are at last under rehabilitation with the help of historic tax credits. Originally the homes of the United States Army officers, they were built not only as homes but also as places to entertain traveling military personnel.

Turn right on Cochran Avenue and continue straight onto Clitz to walk behind the mess hall.

Continue onto Cochran Avenue and stop in at the ❶ **Fort Thomas Military and Community Museum,** to your left. It's open Thursday–Saturday, noon–4 p.m. and Sunday, 1-5 p.m.

Take a slight right onto Greene Street. This Historic National Community was established in 1894. These beautifully restored and maintained homes were originally built for military field officers. All of the homes are on the National Historic Register and are privately owned.

Turn left on S. Fort Thomas Avenue. As you walk up Fort Thomas Avenue, you're approaching the Midway Commercial District. But before you get there, you'll walk by the old drill hall with a sign that reads FT. THOMAS RECREATION DEPARTMENT. Today, this building is commonly known as the Armory. Built in 1896, the building was used as a drill hall and a gym, early on, and then later for social events, basketball games, Bridge tournaments, Highlands High School graduation ceremonies, and more. In other words, it's a multipurpose space.

Look to your left to see the ❷ **Fort Thomas VA.** On a nice day, residents may be enjoying the outdoor picnic areas or the well-kept urban garden.

The Historic Midway District has long been the commercial support of the military post. Today, there are some great shops, services, restaurants, and bars on this stretch. Enjoy a mix of tavern and Mexican-inspired food at the ❸ **Midway Cafe** or stop into ❹ **New Garden** for Chinese food. ❺ **The Olde Fort Pub** is a great venue for live music, and ❻ **Fort Thomas Pizza and Tavern,** open daily 7 a.m.–2:30 a.m., is a great Northern Kentucky destination for pizza and a beer.

Turn left on River Road.

Turn left on Carmel Manor Road and then left again on Cochran Avenue. Follow Cochran Avenue to walk behind the VA and the Armory.

Turn left on Greene Street, which is so nice it gets a second visit as you near the end of your walk through local military history.

Turn right on S. Fort Thomas Avenue to return to your starting point at Tower Park.

(continued on next page)

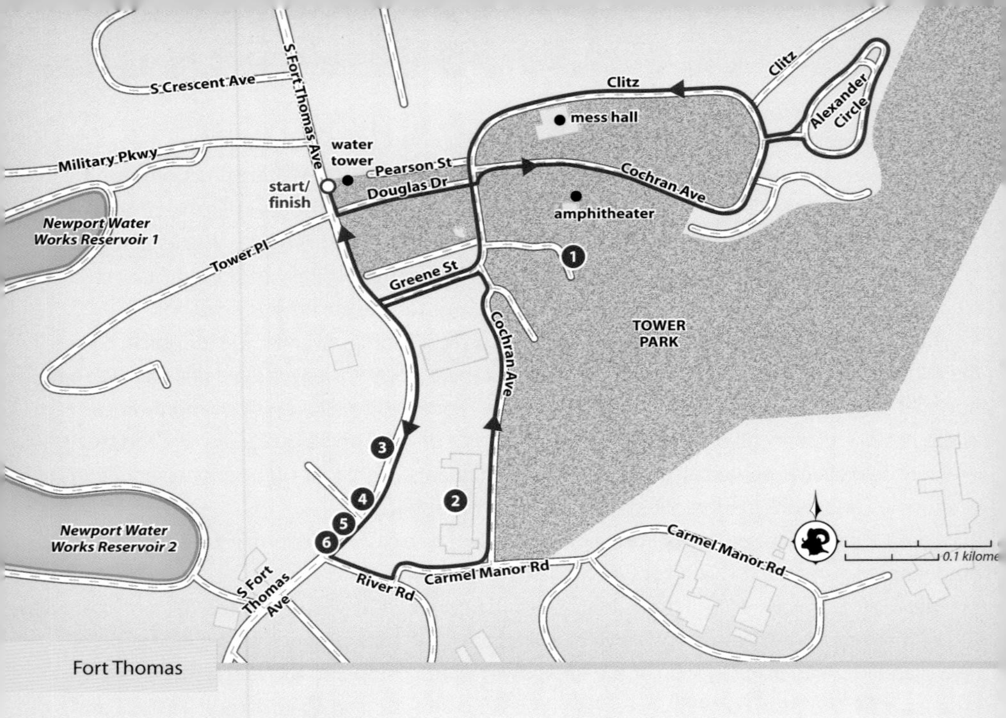

Points of Interest

1. **Fort Thomas Military and Community Museum** 940 Cochran Ave., 859-572-1225, ftthomas.org/renaissance/military-museum
2. **Fort Thomas Division Cincinnati VA Medical Center** 1000 S. Fort Thomas Ave., 859-572-6202, www.cincinnati.va.gov/services /ft_thomas2.asp
3. **Midway Cafe** 1017 S. Fort Thomas Ave., 859-781-7666
4. **New Garden** 1031 S. Fort Thomas Ave., 859-781-7888, newgardenfortthomas.com
5. **The Olde Fort Pub** 1041 S. Fort Thomas Ave., 859-441-1927
6. **Fort Thomas Pizza and Tavern** 1109 S. Fort Thomas Ave., 859-441-5030, fortthomaspizza.com

Appendix: Walks by Theme

Architecture

Downtown Cincinnati (Walk 2)
Over-the-Rhine (Walk 3)
Mount Auburn (Walk 4)
Walnut Hills (Walk 6)
Clifton Gaslight District (Walk 8)
Northside (Walk 9)
College Hill (Walk 10)
Norwood (Walk 12)
Hyde Park (Walk 15)
Mariemont (Walk 19)
Old Milford and Terrace Park (Walk 20)
Wyoming (Walk 21)
Glendale (Walk 23)
Westwood (Walk 25)
Sayler Park (Walk 26)
Newport East Row Historic District (Walk 33)

Eden Park offers numerous overlooks of the Ohio River Valley (see Walks 5 and 6).

Art and Culture

Ohio Riverfront (Walk 1)
Downtown Cincinnati (Walk 2)
Over-the-Rhine (Walk 3)
Northside (Walk 9)
Oakley (Walk 14)
East Price Hill (Walk 24)
Covington: Historic Licking Riverside, Eastside, and Roebling Point (Walk 27)
Newport East Row Historic District (Walk 33)

Food and Breweries

Downtown Cincinnati (Walk 2)
Over-the-Rhine (Walk 3)
Walnut Hills (Walk 6)
Pleasant Ridge (Walk 13)
Oakley (Walk 14)
Old Milford and Terrace Park (Walk 20)
Westwood (Walk 25)
Downtown Covington (Walk 28)
Ludlow (Walk 31)
Newport East Row Historic District (Walk 33)

History

Ohio Riverfront (Walk 1)
Downtown Cincinnati (Walk 2)
Over-the-Rhine (Walk 3)
Mount Auburn (Walk 4)
Walnut Hills (Walk 6)
Clifton Gaslight District (Walk 8)
College Hill (Walk 10)
Norwood (Walk 12)
Hyde Park (Walk 15)
Mariemont (Walk 19)
Old Milford and Terrace Park (Walk 20)
Wyoming (Walk 21)
Reading (Walk 22)
Glendale (Walk 23)
East Price Hill (Walk 24)
Westwood (Walk 25)
Sayler Park (Walk 26)

Covington: Historic Licking Riverside, Eastside, and Roebling Point (Walk 27)
Ludlow (Walk 31)
Covington: Latonia (Walk 32)
Newport East Row Historic District (Walk 33)

Parks

Ohio Riverfront (Walk 1)
Over-the-Rhine (Walk 3)
Clifton Heights, University Heights, and Fairview (Walk 7)
Clifton Gaslight District (Walk 8)
Northside (Walk 9)
Mount Lookout (Walk 17)
Mariemont (Walk 19)
East Price Hill (Walk 24)
Covington: Devou Park and Kenton Hills (Walk 30)
Fort Thomas (Walk 35)

Retail

Over-the-Rhine (Walk 3)
Pleasant Ridge (Walk 13)
Oakley (Walk 14)
Hyde Park (Walk 15)
Old Milford and Terrace Park (Walk 20)
Reading (Walk 22)
Downtown Covington (Walk 28)

Views

Ohio Riverfront (Walk 1)
Mount Auburn (Walk 4)
Clifton Heights, University Heights, and Fairview (Walk 7)
Mariemont (Walk 19)
East Price Hill (Walk 24)
Covington: Historic Licking Riverside, Eastside, and Roebling Point (Walk 27)
Covington: Devou Park and Kenton Hills (Walk 30)
Newport East Row Historic District (Walk 33)

Index

About the Authors

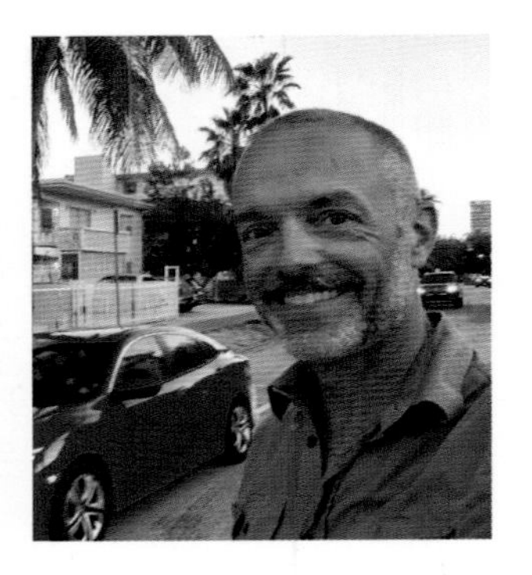

DANNY KORMAN wrote the first edition of *Walking Cincinnati* with Katie Meyer and now lives in Colorado after closing his store, Park + Vine, in early 2017. Prior to this, Danny received a bachelor degree in urban planning from the University of Cincinnati and worked a series of rewarding jobs in program management for nonprofit organizations and government bodies. Danny is a big architecture buff, urban explorer, nature lover, believer in supporting local economies, and steward of the environment and animals. He likes to prioritize activities that are within walking or biking distance.

KATIE MEYER has a deep interest in how cities work and what makes them thrive. After nine years as the executive director of Renaissance Covington, Inc., Katie now has a new job as the smart city policy advisor for Cincinnati Bell. Raised in a rehabbed 19th-century Italianate in downtown Covington, she has an ingrained passion for the art of historic rehabilitation and the value of walkable neighborhoods. Katie has a bachelor of arts degree in political science and journalism from the University of Kentucky and a master's of science degree in urban policy analysis and management from The New School in New York City. She currently lives in the Austinburg neighborhood of Covington with her wife, two stepkids, and two dogs.